fundamentals of human learning and cognition

fundamentals
of
human learning
and
cognition

Henry C. Ellis, 1927-
University of New Mexico

WM. C. BROWN COMPANY PUBLISHERS
Dubuque, Iowa

FUNDAMENTALS OF PSYCHOLOGY SERIES

Frank A. Logan
  General Editor
  University of New Mexico

Copyright ©1972 by Wm. C. Brown Company Publishers

Library of Congress Catalog Card Number: 70–185301

ISBN 0–697–06612–6 (Cloth)
ISBN 0–697–06613–4 (Paper)

Printed in the United States of America

This book is dedicated to my wife, Florence, and to
our children, Joan, Diane, and John.

Contents

Foreword, xv

Preface, xvii

Acknowledgments, xxi

1   Introduction to Human Learning and Cognition, 1
    Objectives, 2
    Scope of Human Learning and Cognition, 3
    A Definition of Learning, 4
    Summary, 5

2   Elements of Conditioning, 6
    Conditioning and Human Learning, 6
    Basic Conditioning Procedures, 8
        Classical Conditioning, 8
        Operant Conditioning, 10
        Operant and Instrumental Conditioning, Distinguished, 11
        Variations in Instrumental Conditioning, 12
        Verbal Operant Conditioning, 12
        Classical and Instrumental Conditioning Compared, 13
    The Concept of Reinforcement, 15
        Positive and Negative Reinforcers, 15
        Why Do Reinforcers Work? 16
        Secondary Reinforcing Events, 17
        Responses as Reinforcers, 17
    Basic Principles of Conditioning, 18
        Acquisition of Responses, 18
        Extinction of Responses, 20
        Partial Reinforcement and Extinction, 21
        Effects of Stimulus and Response Variability on Extinction, 21
        Spontaneous Recovery of Responses, 22

Generalization, 22
Discrimination, 23
Conditions Which Affect Discrimination, 24
Differentiation, 25
Application of Conditioning Principles, 26
Conditioning Principles and Therapy, 26
Conditioning Principles and Programmed Instruction, 28
Summary, 30
To the Student, 30
True-False Items: Elements of Conditioning, 31

3   **Characteristics of Verbal Learning, 33**
Definition of Verbal Learning, 34
Ebbinghaus and Associationism, 35
Procedures and Materials in Verbal Learning, 36
Serial Learning, 37
Paired Associate Learning, 38
Components of Paired Associate Learning, 42
Free Learning, 43
Recognition Learning, 44
Verbal Discrimination Learning, 47
Comparison of Procedures, 48
Factors Which Affect Verbal Learning, 48
Meaningfulness, 49
How Meaningfulness Affects Learning, 51
Familiarity, Frequency, and Pronunciability, 54
Mental Imagery, 54
Intralist Similarity, 56
Additional Factors in Learning, 59
Summary, 59
True-False Items: Characteristics of Verbal Learning, 60

4   **Processes in Verbal Learning, 62**
Some Basic Processes in Verbal Learning, 63
Response and Associative Learning, 63
Stimulus Discrimination, 63
Stimulus Selection, 64
Stimulus Selection, Perception, and Attention, 65
Stimulus Coding, 66
Final Comments on Stimulus Mechanisms, 67
How are Associations Formed? 68
Are Associations Formed Gradually? 69
Directionality of Associations, 69
Organizational Processes in Verbal Learning, 70

Changes in the Order of Presentation, 71
Changes in Specific Items, 72
Mediation, 73
The Learning of Connected Materials, 73
Motivation and Verbal Learning, 74
Intentional versus Incidental Learning, 74
Anxiety and Learning, 75
Handling Anxiety, 75
Summary, 76
True-False Items: Processes in Verbal Learning, 77

5   Transfer of Training, 80
The Concept of Transfer, 81
The Study of Transfer, 82
Design of Transfer Experiments, 83
Basic Transfer Paradigms, 85
Expansion of Paradigms: Similarity Factor, 87
General and Specific Transfer, 89
General (Nonspecific) Transfer, 89
Specific Transfer, 91
Transfer of Stimulus Discrimination, 91
Transfer of Response Learning, 92
Transfer of Forward Associations, 93
Transfer of Backward Associations, 93
Transfer and Task Similarity, 94
The Concept of Similarity, 95
Stimulus Similarity and Transfer, 96
Response Similarity and Transfer, 99
Mechanisms of Transfer, 100
Generalization, 100
Mediation, 101
Some Practical Applications of Transfer, 102
Task (Stimulus) Variation, 102
Transfer from Easy to Difficult Discriminations, 103
Degree of Original Learning, 103
Task Similarity, 104
Summary, 104
True-False Items: Transfer of Training, 105

6   Memory, 108
Learning, Transfer, and Memory, 109
Encoding, Storage, and Retrieval, 110
Approaches to Memory: Associationism and Information
Processing, 110

The Study of Memory, 112
    Recall, 112
    Recognition, 113
    Motivational Factors and Biases in Recognition Memory, 114
    Recall and Recognition Compared, 115
    Savings, 116
Basic Stages of Memory Storage, 117
    Sensory Memory, 117
    Short-Term Memory, 118
    Long-Term Memory, 119
Organizational and Retrieval Processes, 120
    Practice in Retrieval, 120
    Retrieval Depends Upon Organized Storage, 121
    Retrieval Cues, 121
    Reconstruction of Events, 122
Interference in Long-Term Memory, 123
    Retroactive Inhibition, 124
    Proactive Inhibition, 126
    Factors Influencing Retroactive and Proactive Inhibition, 126
    Interference Theory, 128
Study Habits and Memory, 130
    Understand the Objectives of What You are Studying, 130
    Focus Attention on the Study Materials, 131
    Arrange Contingencies of Reinforcement, 131
    Organizing the Materials, 132
    Practice Retrieval, 132
Summary, 133
True-False Items: Memory, 134

7   Concept Learning, 136
    Nature of Concept Learning, 137
    Concept Learning, Generalization, and Discrimination, 140
The Study of Concept Learning, 141
    Features of Concept Learning Tasks, 141
    Basic Paradigms in Concept Learning, 141
    Attributes and Rules, 142
Factors Which Affect Concept Learning, 143
    Positive and Negative Instances, 143
    Relevant and Irrelevant Attributes, 144
    Stimulus Salience and Abstractness-Concreteness, 145
    Feedback and Temporal Factors, 145
    Conceptual Rules, 146
    Memory and Intelligence, 147

Theories of Concept Learning, 147
    S-R Association Theory, 148
    S-R Mediational Theories, 149
    Hypothesis-testing Theories, 150
Some Practical Principles of Concept Learning, 151
    Think of New Examples of Concepts, 151
    Use Both Positive and Negative Instances, 151
    The Importance of a Variety of Examples, 152
    Highlighting Relevant Features, 153
Summary, 153
True-False Items: Concept Learning, 154

8   Perceptual Learning, 156
    Nature of Perceptual Learning, 157
Categories of Perceptual Tasks, 159
    Detection, 160
    Discrimination, 160
    Recognition, 160
    Identification, 160
    Judgment, 161
Categories of Perceptual Learning, 161
    Effects of Practice on Perceptual Skills, 161
    Reward and Punishment Factors, 163
    Adaptation to Transformed Stimulation, 163
    Cross-modal Transfer, 164
    Verbal Labels and Perceptual Learning, 164
    Schema Learning, 166
What is Learned in Perceptual Learning? 167
    Increase in Specificity of Responding, 167
    Detection of Distinctive Features, 167
    Detection of Properties and Patterns, 167
Some Practical Implications, 167
Summary, 168
True-False Items: Perceptual Learning, 168

9   Language, Thinking, and Problem Solving, 171
    Language, 172
    Functions of Language, 173
    Basic Units of Language: Phonemes and Morphemes, 173
    Phrase Structure in Sentences, 174
    Surface Structure and Deep Structure, 175

Language Development, 175
Language and Thought, 177
Thinking and Problem Solving, 178
Nature of Thinking and Problem Solving, 178
General Features of Problem-solving Tasks, 179
Persistence of Set in Problem Solving, 180
Functional Fixedness in Problem Solving, 181
Set in Verbal Anagram Problems, 182
Motivational Factors, 183
Theories of Thinking and Problem Solving, 184
Stimulus-response Theory, 184
Gestalt Theory, 185
Information-processing Approaches, 186
Some Practical Suggestions, 187
Understand the Problem, 187
Remember the Problem, 188
Identify Alternative Hypothesis, 188
Acquire Coping Strategies, 188
Evaluate Your Final Hypothesis, 189
Summary, 189
True-False Items: Language, Thinking and Problem Solving, 189

10   Motor Skills Learning, 191
Definition of Motor Skills Learning, 192
The Study of Motor Skills Learning, 192
Characteristics of Motor Skills, 193
Response Chains, 193
Perceptual-motor Coordination, 193
Response Organization, 193
Feedback, 194
Phases of Motor Skill Learning, 195
Cognitive Phase, 195
Associative Phase, 196
Autonomous Phase, 196
Factors Which Affect Motor Skills Learning, 197
Feedback, 197
Importance of Feedback, 198
Withdrawal of Feedback and Subjective Reinforcement, 199
Delay of Feedback, 200
Distribution of Practice, 200
Stress and Fatigue, 201
Theories of Motor Learning, 201
Some Practical Principles, 204

Understand the Task, 204
Practice on Specific Components, 204
Obtain Feedback, 204
Practice Under Varied Conditions, 204
Finally, Practice, 205
Summary, 205
True-False Items: Motor Skills Learning, 206

11   Concluding Remarks, 208

Glossary, 211

Suggested Readings for Further Study, 215

References, 217

Index, 233

Foreword

There is no single, best way to introduce students to as diverse and complex a subject matter as psychology. The special needs and interests of both student and teacher help determine the course content and organization. The Fundamentals of Psychology Series is designed better to enable the approach that I have found to be most effective.

That approach is to restrict the course content to a relatively small number of topics so as to cover them in greater depth than customary. Of course, this implies that other topics are omitted or mentioned in a very cursory manner. But my conviction is that the student is richer for having explored a few topics sufficiently to begin to comprehend the concepts and to appreciate their roles in understanding behavior.

Accordingly, at the same time this series is intended for the beginning student, its goal is to lead him further into each topic than is typical of introductory texts. This very feature may make the series also valuable in more advanced courses where the teacher wants to begin with a review of the fundamentals before proceeding to more specialized content. In either event, we hope the student will find the series interesting and challenging.

Frank A. Logan

Preface

The purpose of this book is to portray the fundamental principles of human learning and cognition. It is written with the belief that the student can be introduced to the psychology of human learning and cognition through a coherent oversimplification so that the fundamental principles are revealed in bold relief. Emphasis, however, on the fundamentals means that many subleties, details, and important qualifications are left untouched. General principles are described and are portrayed as truths even though they may be inaccurate in certain details or require considerable qualification.

In some sense this process characterizes much teaching. The student is first presented with major generalizations and principles and subsequently begins to learn about their exceptions, qualifications, and limitations. On occasion the complexities of a principle are at least partially described; however, in the main the fundamental principles are presented without discussion of all their potential ramifications. The principal justification of this approach is that the student can more readily acquire a coherent picture of an area and will have an organizational framework for integrating new facts, concepts and principles in human learning and cognition in his subsequent education.

The book is written with the conviction that the principles of human learning and cognition should be introduced in such a way that the student sees their direct pertinence to and potential impact upon human affairs. Illustrations of practical applications are liberally provided with the hope that the student will gain a fuller and richer understanding of the principles when he can relate them to his personal experiences. These illustrations cannot, of course, perfectly reflect principles derived from laboratory settings but they can approximate them and thus hopefully lead the student to think of other illustrations as well as potential exceptions.

This book is one of a series of "Fundamentals of" books produced by the same publisher. It is, therefore, intended to be compatible with others in the series but an understanding of this book does not depend upon reading any of the others. This book shares with the others in the series that assumption that fundamental principles and concepts of psychology can be more readily grasped by the student when these principles and concepts are related to familiar everyday experiences.

This book attempts to bridge the gap between the old and new topics in human learning and cognition. The traditional and more well-developed topics must be related to the newly developing areas. The psychology of human learning and cognition is rapidly changing and an effort is made to convey this portrait of a rapidly expanding area of knowledge. Theoretical developments are in a rapid growth period and stimulus-response, cognitive, and information-processing views of behavior are described where they seem most appropriate. Where possible the continuity among theoretical approaches is emphasized as well as their distinctive characteristics. Finally, in no sense can this book be regarded as some final description; rather, it must be viewed as a momentary state-of-the-science report.

This book deals with the wide range of topics encompassed by human learning and cognition whose scope ranges from simple learning (conditioning) to the complex processes of concept learning, thinking, and problem solving. The first chapter describes the objectives and scope of the book. Chapter 2 provides an introductory statement of the elements of conditioning. Many features and details of conditioning processes are excluded with a description of only the most fundamental features. The justification of including a chapter on conditioning is that some conditioning concepts, especially those of discrimination and generalization, are still used in accounts of more complex behaviors found say, in concept learning. Thus it is in some sense desirable that the student have the opportunity to see how these concepts were initially developed in the context of conditioning. If students have already been exposed to conditioning then this chapter may be easily bypassed.

Chapters 3 and 4 deal with verbal learning. Chapter 3 describes the basic procedures employed in the study of verbal learning and the major variables influencing verbal learning. The basic procedures are carefully outlined since these procedures or variations of them receive widespread use throughout much of human learning. Chapters 5 and 6 deal with transfer and memory, topics which follow from the treatment of verbal learning. Chapters 7 and 8 cover concept learning and perceptual learning, giving increasing consideration to cognitive factors in learning and to the manner in which perception becomes modified by learning. Chapter 9 handles language, thinking, and problem solving and their interrelationships. The final content chapter, 10, deals with motor skills learning and is appropriately placed last because it enables the student to see how both associative and cognitive processes operate in a particular class of learning tasks.

The material in each chapter is not described in isolation from others, but each chapter reflects in some way upon principles and concepts described in earlier chapters and on occasion anticipates subsequent issues. At an elementary level the student is presented comparisons of S-R associative and cognitive conceptions of behavior and indications of advantages and limitations of each are discussed.

As with other books in this series, each major chapter ends with a set of True-False items and explanatory answers. These items provide for review and for feedback for the student in gauging his own comprehension of the material. This, however, is not their only purpose for it is hoped that they will stimulate the student to raise new questions and to engage in additional thinking about the issues. Some of the questions are relatively straightforward whereas others present issues from a somewhat different perspective, hopefully to encourage the student to stretch his imagination.

At the end of the book is a glossary containing a description of the major technical terms defined in this book. The definitions are brief and do not, of course, provide all of the potential meaning of the terms. They provide a convenient refresher for the student but should not be relied upon exclusively. The understanding of technical terms and concepts comes when the student can *use* them in their appropriate context. A list of suggested readings is provided which will enable the student to explore more deeply particular areas. Finally, a list of references by chapter is given. No formal references are cited in the book, and few experiments are presented. The references, however, provide representative materials which will allow the student to explore particular topics in the original literature should the need or wish arise.

Henry C. Ellis

Acknowledgments

I am indebted to several people for their assistance in the preparation of this book. I am especially indebted to Professor Frank A. Logan for his critical comments, helpful suggestions, and warm encouragement during the writing of the book. His generous support and skillful evaluation are gratefully acknowledged. I also wish to thank Profs. Terry C. Daniel and Ronald W. Shaffer, who read the entire manuscript and provided many valuable comments and suggestions, and Profs. Peder Johnson and Samuel Roll, who provided useful reactions to several of the chapters. I also wish to acknowledge the constructive criticism of the late Prof. Kilby Long.

This book was completed while the author was Visiting Professor of Psychology at the University of California, Berkeley. The support of Prof. Leo Postman and the Institute of Human Learning staff is gratefully acknowledged.

For their assistance in typing the manuscript, I am grateful to Elna Parks, Alice Steensgaard, Barbara Hostetler, and especially to Eleanor Orth for her supervisory skill.

Introduction to Human Learning and Cognition

Humans learn, remember, and think. They also plan, solve problems, and use language. Probably the most interesting feature of man's behavior is that he *learns* to modify his behavior when confronted with new situations. Of equal importance is man's learned proficiency to generalize in new situations on the basis of prior learning and to acquire concepts and strategies in coping with both current and forthcoming events. This flexible, adaptive character of human behavior thus emphasizes the fundamental significance of *learning* in the understanding of man.

Learning plays a central role in contemporary psychology. Most human behavior can be said to be influenced by learning, particularly by the time one reaches adulthood. At birth the infant possesses a few basic unlearned responses such as crying, eating, and elimination. Yet even these responses come to be modified by the learning process. The child learns, for example, to expect food at particular times and not at others; he subsequently learns that a crying response may or may not receive attention by the parent, depending upon particular circumstances; and he ultimately becomes toilet trained.

The most significant learning for man is language. Language is a basic tool for thinking, problem solving, and other more complex symbolic activities. The acquisition of knowledge and skills is heavily dependent upon the use of language. Indeed, the possession of language enables man to plan for the future, facilitates his learning of concepts and principles, and enables effective communication.

The importance of learning is reflected in its scope and generality as seen in its influence on other topics in psychology. For instance, your personal feelings and attitudes are the products of an extensive learning history. Thus, the social psychologist studying attitudes is, in fact, studying one outcome of the learning process. Similarly, you learn to interpret events in the world in uniquely individual ways or, alternatively, in ways typical of your particular culture as the result of certain experiences. Your likes and dislikes, prejudices, opinions, values, all of which reflect your particular life style, are the result of a long history of learning experiences. Moreover, your skill in organizing and remembering events, in problem solving and thinking, and in generalizing to new situations are in large part the result of the way in which you have learned to respond in tasks requiring memory, problem solving, thinking, and transfer.

More complex problems such as mental illness and crime can, in part, be understood as the result of individual learning histories. It is widely agreed that many disorders of behavior can be understood as the result of learning where neurological or biochemical influences are known not to be present. Just as many of us learn to be effective in coping with environmental and interpersonal problems, others learn to function in maladaptive, less effective ways in coping with daily events. Indeed, some current forms of therapy employ procedures derived from principles of learning on the assumption that therapy is a form of learning itself.

Finally, many efforts at improving the quality of education are based upon our current knowledge of principles of learning. To the extent that the *conditions* which affect learning and the *principles* of learning are understood, teachers are better able to bring about changes in educational practices directed toward more effective learning of knowledges and skills. In the past decade a rapidly growing technology of learning has emerged which has developed largely from the extension and application of fundamental principles of learning. This technology — reflected, for example, in developments such as programmed — learning, computer-assisted instruction, and individualized instruction — represents a systematic effort to apply knowledge about the psychology of learning to pressing problems of education. Thus the study of human learning is not an isolated or restricted activity, but involves a serious attempt to cope with some of the important practical problems of everyday life.

Objectives

The objective of this book is to examine the fundamental principles of human learning and cognition and to explore some of their practical implications. This book examines the range of processes going from simple learning (conditioning), verbal learning, transfer, and memory, to concept learning, perceptual learning, problem solving, thinking, language, and motor skills learning. The focus of this book will be on the most basic, *fundamental principles* of human learning and cognition. These principles have been developed largely from laboratory studies of human performance in highly controlled experimental situations. Topics such as instrumental learning, conditioning and motivation receive less attention, except insofar as principles derived from their study appear useful in accounting for more complex human activities. Thus no attempt is made to cover the full range of the psychology of learning. The emphasis is on those topics that are central to the understanding of human learning and cognition.

This book is written with the belief that the principles of human learning and cognition should be introduced in such a way that the student sees their pertinence to human affairs. Thus, although the principles are initially described somewhat formally, their applicability to human affairs is given considerable attention. Illustrations of practical applications and implications of the basic principles are liberally provided, with the expectation that the student will gain a clearer understanding of these principles when he can relate them to personal experience.

Scope of Human Learning and Cognition

As a topic in the psychology of learning, human learning may refer simply to any class of learning situations that involves humans. Thus in a larger sense the study of human learning involves the broad range of topics from simple human conditioning to complex processes involving concept learning and problem solving. Sometimes the meaning of the term is restricted principally to those processes involving the acquisition of skills and knowledge, transfer, and memory. Thus, for example, the acquisition of verbal skills such as language would be an instance of human learning. Similarly, learning to drive, to read, or to become proficient in some athletic skill would also represent instances of human learning. At a somewhat more restricted level, the term human learning sometimes refers to those learning situations and principles that are *characteristically* human, providing one basis for distinguishing between principles of human learning and principles of learning derived from the study of lower animals. This book emphasizes, however, the integrated character of learning and the generality of its principles.

The distinction between learning and cognition is to some extent arbitrary. *The term cognition emphasizes the symbolic, mental, and inferred* (not directly seen) *processes of humans.* Thus the sharpening and refining of abstract concepts such as "freedom" and "justice," the search for a solution to a problem, and the use of strategies in games are said to be instances of cognitive processes because they presumably involve mental or symbolic processes on the part of the learner.

Cognition thus typically refers to the class of processes involving such activities as thinking, reasoning, problem solving, and conceptual learning. More generally, reference to cognitive processes implies an active role of the human in learning situations, the use of strategies, and ways in which the learner might organize materials in order to learn and retain them more efficiently. Since it is difficult to think of any human learning situation in which the human is not in some way actively responding, organizing, and reorganizing the material, human learning will almost always involve some kind of cognitive activity. Even in conditioning and in verbal association formation, processes that are relatively less complex in the range of processes to be described, the learner may play an active role. Therefore, this book will make no attempt to distinguish sharply between human learning and cognition. Cognitive processes are intertwined in human learning, and thus the topics are jointly treated in this book.

A Definition of Learning

Although you will develop a definition of learning in reading this book, it is useful to define learning in a general way now so that you may have a working definition of the concept. Learning is a process that is not directly seen but is something inferred from behavioral changes of the individual. Not all behavioral changes, however, allow the inference of learning. Only those changes in behavior which can be attributed to practice variables represent "learning." Performance changes due to drugs, maturation, fatigue, or motivation are not changes attributable to learning.

LEARNING IS A RELATIVELY PERMANENT PROCESS THAT IS INFERRED FROM PERFORMANCE CHANGES DUE TO PRACTICE. Thus skill in reading, which obviously results from practice, is an instance of learning. Similarly, improvement in athletic skills such as golf or tennis are instances of learning because these are changes which can be attributed to practice conditions. In contrast, performance changes due to drugs or fatigue are not changes attributable to learning because the resulting behavioral changes are temporary in nature and do not depend directly upon practice. Extended practice may, of course, produce fatigue; changes in performance due to fatigue do not, however, represent learning.

Fatigue produces a temporary decrement in your performance and hence these performance changes are distinguished from those due to learning. Drugs such as alcohol or marijuana can produce a temporary "high" but the behavioral changes are short-lived rather than permanent. This does not deny, however, the fact that one can learn to behave in somewhat characteristic ways when under the influence of drugs, or while one "thinks" he is under the influence of a drug. Such behavior is likely to depend upon the setting or context in which drugs are used. For instance, it is known that some individuals can experience a "high" while sitting in a darkened room full of incense listening to exotic music, so long as they *believe* they are smoking marijuana. In such experiences, individuals have been given control (placebo) cigarettes without the knowledge that they contain no marijuana. Such findings point out the role of contextual stimuli and suggestion in influencing the manner in which we react to events. In a similar vein, behavioral changes that result from maturation are not attributable to the process of learning since maturational changes will occur despite special practice conditions.

Summary

In this book we will be concerned with the broad range of events encompassed by the topics of human learning and cognition. These topics play a significant role in psychology today and are basic to your understanding of a wide range of human behavior. The focus will be on the fundamental principles of human learning and cognition, with considerable emphasis on the practical application of these concepts to daily affairs.

Learning was defined as a relatively permanent change in performance which is the result of practice. Such a definition distinguishes between performance changes due to practice and changes due to maturation, fatigue, or drugs. Human learning and cognition were not sharply distinguished since the processes were viewed as highly interrelated. The term *cognition* was seen to emphasize the symbolic, mental activity of man.

Before you can apply concepts and principles of learning for your own benefit, you must first have some understanding of the basic principles. The emphasis in this book, therefore, is first on an examination of the basic principles and generalizations in each topic area, and then on discussion of how these principles are applicable. Emphasis is placed both on how these concepts may assist in your personal effectiveness as a learner, thinker, and problem solver, and also how you might assist others in the teaching-learning process.

2

Elements of Conditioning

Psychologists generally agree that the simplest form of learning is conditioning. This by no means implies that conditioning is an uncomplicated process or that all of its aspects are thoroughly understood. What is meant is that conditioning, as one form of learning, is readily observed in lower organisms and thus appears to be phylogenetically a more elementary form of learning than processes involving concept learning, thinking, or problem solving. Sometimes it is implied that an understanding of conditioning requires fewer assumptions and principles than does the presumably more complex phenomena of memory, concept learning, or thinking. Conversely, the implication is that an understanding of more complex human learning requires *additional* principles beyond those developed in the study of conditioning.

Related to this second meaning is the assumption held by some psychologists that principles of learning are hierarchically organized, beginning with conditioning as the simplest and going to concept learning and problem solving as the most complex. These more complex forms of learning are thought by some to depend upon simpler types of learning that involve associative principles. The basic idea is that a classification of types of learning produces a hierarchy of types going from the simplest to the most complex, and that more complex types of learning "build upon" or are composed of simpler elements of learning. Not all psychologists adopt this assumption of a hierarchical classification of types of learning, however, despite the fact that virtually all accept the assumption that conditioning is the most elementary form of learning.

Conditioning and Human Learning

Any discussion of conditioning in a volume devoted to human learning and cognition should describe its relationship to other areas of learning. The usefulness of beginning with an elementary chapter dealing with principles and concepts of conditioning is twofold: First, there is a considerable body of knowledge about conditioning with human subjects. Thus human conditioning is properly one aspect of any study of human learning. This statement does *not* mean, however, that conditioning is "representative" of the broad domain of human learning activities that are considered in this book. All that is meant is that it is one class of learning processes, among several kinds, characteristically observed in humans.

A second reason for briefly examining conditioning concepts and principles is that they have been extended to many aspects of more complex human learning, especially in the areas of verbal learning, transfer, memory, and concept learning. Despite their extension, it must be emphasized that an increasing number of psychologists have questioned what they regard as an uncritical extrapolation of concepts and principles of conditioning to "explain" more complex forms of learning. Some believe that dependence upon conditioning principles for explanatory concepts, while valuable in some instances, has prevented psychologists from focusing on important features of human learning not readily handled by conditioning principles. Others have emphasized what they regard to be the essential dichotomy between principles of animal and human learning and have taken the view that an understanding of human learning will emerge only when principles are developed at this level of analysis.

This book adopts neither the extreme of ignoring conditioning principles, nor of adopting the unrealistic position that all forms of learning are reducible to conditioning principles. Throughout this book we will have occasion to examine explanations of complex human learning derived from conditioning principles. We shall indicate where such principles appear useful and reasonable, while at the same time we shall indicate where additional principles, developed within the context of characteristically human research, appear necessary for a full understanding of human learning.

It is reasonable to assume that a comprehensive understanding of human learning will require the development of some concepts *specific* to human learning situations. This belief is shared by a growing number of psychologists who emphasize the cognitive, purposeful, and organizational character of human learning. Nevertheless, this belief need not carry with it the assumption that we can or should disregard what has been gained from studies of simpler learning. One objective of this book is thus to introduce the student to developments in human learning that appear to require distinctly cognitive conceptions, while retaining those concepts that derive from studies of simple associative learning when they have integrative usefulness. The focus will be on the generality of principles and the still integrative and unifying character of the concept of learning across the broad range of topics included under this process.

Basic Conditioning Procedures

Three basic procedures are employed in the study of conditioning processes. One of these is *classical* conditioning, which refers to procedures developed by the Russian physiologist Pavlov. The second refers to *instrumental* conditioning, sometimes referred to as instrumental learning. We shall use instrumental conditioning and instrumental learning interchangeably, although the student should recognize that some psychologists distinguish these two on the basis of criteria more complex than is necessary for the level of this book. The third is *operant* conditioning, which is similar to many features of instrumental conditioning. This chapter provides only a very brief introduction to the topic of conditioning and the interested reader should refer to any of a number of texts which are almost entirely devoted to the topic. (For a systematic introduction to conditioning principles, the reader should examine Frank Logan's *Fundamentals of Learning and Motivation*, a companion volume in this series.) Since many of the procedures were first developed with animals, these procedures in their original context will first be described followed by human conditioning illustrations.

Classical Conditioning

Classical conditioning refers to a set of training procedures in which one stimulus comes to substitute for another in evoking a response. These procedures are called classical because of their historical priority as developed by Pavlov.

The procedures characteristically employed by Pavlov involved placing a laboratory animal, such as a dog, in a restraining harness before training. A small opening was made in the dog's cheek so that saliva could be collected and measured during the training session. The experimenter, not visible to the animal, sounded a tuning fork and then presented food powder to the animal. The food powder would, of course, automatically elicit the response of salivation, whereas the sound had no initial effect on the animal's behavior. After a number of pairing trials of food powder and sound, the sound was presented by itself and the animal was observed to salivate. Thus an initially neutral event, the sound, acquired the capacity to elicit a response by virtue of being paired with the food powder.

Pavlov called the food powder an *unconditioned stimulus* (UCS), which means simply that a given stimulus has the capacity to produce a response at the beginning of an experiment. The UCS may possess some innate biological capacity to produce a response, in the sense of being unlearned, or it may have acquired this capacity as a result of learning that occurred before the animal was brought to the laboratory. The response elicited by the UCS, which in this instance is salivation, is called the *unconditioned response* (UCR). Pavlov referred

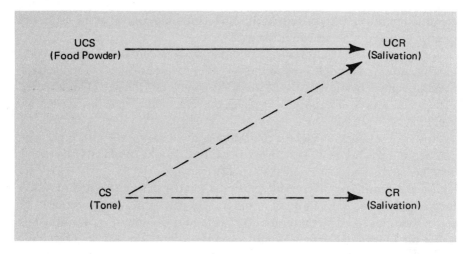

Figure 1. Schematic diagram of classical conditioning.

to the sounds of the tuning fork as a *conditioned stimulus* (CS), which is any initially "neutral" stimulus that acquires the capacity to elicit a response as a result of CS-USC pairing. The salivary reponse produced by the tuning fork is called a *conditioned response* (CR) to emphasize that it is a learned response dependent upon the presentation of the CS.

The basic procedure of classical conditioning is schematized in figure 1. The procedure begins with an UCS-UCR connection as shown. The solid line emphasizes that the UCS-UCR connection is present at the beginning of the experiment. The CS is presented shortly before the presentation of the UCS for optimal conditioning. Eventually the CS gains the capacity to elicit the salivary response by itself, which defines the conditioning operation. The dashed line between the CS and CR denotes that this is a learned association. Several procedural variations relating the presentation of the CS and UCS are possible; this procedure describes only one of several options.

Are the UCR and the CR the same response? In a qualitative sense they can be regarded the same, since in our example they were both salivary responses. Otherwise, they are different responses, especially because their *quantitative* features usually differ. For example, the magnitude of the CR is usually less than the UCR.

Other classical conditioning procedures have been developed. Pavlov's procedures are referred to as classical *appetitive* conditioning because the UCS (food) is an emotionally positive stimulus. Procedures that are called classical *defense* conditioning are widely used and involve presentation of an emotionally negative or aversive stimulus such as an electric shock. The conditioned galvanic skin response (a change in the electrical resistance of the skin) and conditioned finger withdrawal, both of which employ shock as an UCS, are examples of this class of conditioning.

A typical example of classical conditioning with humans is eyelid conditioning. A puff of air delivered to the eye will automatically elicit an eyeblink response; here, obviously, is the UCS-UCR sequence. If the puff of air is paired with a tone over a series of presentations, the tone alone will come to elicit the eyeblink.

Instances of human classical conditioning are numerous. For instance, you can become conditioned to pictures of food in that advertisements portraying delicious steak dinners may elicit a salivary response even though you may not be hungry. Similarly, we become somewhat temporally conditioned to expect food at particular times and not at others. Human salivary responses can be easily conditioned in the laboratory by pairing the presentations of candy and tones; the tones alone will eventually elicit salivation after a series of training trials.

Words and symbols also serve as conditioned stimuli for humans. The phenomenon of *semantic* conditioning has been well-explored and indicates that word stimuli, when paired with UCS, can come to elicit a wide range of responses. Such findings help to explain why particular words and symbols can become such strong emotional stimuli for humans. Merely thinking as well as saying a word can come to function as a conditioned stimulus. Many people react immediately when labeled in a derogatory fashion; the label has come to serve as a conditioned stimulus. Similarly, certain political concepts such as "socialism," "communism," or "fascism" may elicit strong emotional responses from individuals who may favor the concept or who alternatively look at it with abhorrence. Indeed, the generality and applicability of conditioning principles has been widely recognized in literature, as seen for example, in Aldous Huxley's *Brave New World*.

Operant Conditioning

In the Pavlovian conditioning situation, the organism [*in classical*] is *relatively* passive. The experimenter decides when to administer the stimuli and awaits the virtually inevitable response of the organism. The organism, of course, has no control over when these events occur. In contrast, *operant conditioning* is a situation in which the organism has greater control over events. The response that the organism comes to make is necessary in order to obtain reward.

Consider the following situation. A very young child is placed in front of a device which has a small lever. The device is so arranged that when the child presses the lever he receives a piece of candy. The task of the child is thus to discover what response will lead to the reward of obtaining candy. Initially the child will make a variety of responses, including looking at the device, exploring the device with his hands, and touching the lever. If the child is very young, the experimenter may employ the procedure of _successive approximations_ and reward responses that approximate pulling the lever, such as approaching or touching it. Eventually, however, the child will pull the lever firmly and be rewarded by receiving the candy. The child quickly "catches on" to this arrangement and learns that he must pull the lever in order to obtain reward.

A similar arrangement is used in studying operant conditioning in lower animals. An animal is placed in a square chamber that is sound-deadened. The chamber itself is sometimes called a Skinner-box after the psychologist B. F. Skinner. The interior of the chamber contains a small bar or lever which the animal must learn to press and a food mechanism for delivering reward in the form of food pellets to the animal. When the animal is initially placed in the chamber he will most likely explore the walls, corners, and other features of the chamber. The vigor of his exploration is dependent, in part, on how long he has been deprived of food. As in the previous example, the experimenter may employ successive approximations by first rewarding the animal as it approaches the bar, subsequently as the animal places his paw on the bar, and finally as the animal presses the bar. As the animal acquires the bar-pressing response, he will approach a fairly steady rate of bar pressing, at which time it is concluded that acquisition of the response has been established.

Operant and Instrumental Conditioning Distinguished

Sometimes psychologists make a distinction between operant and instrumental conditioning. The distinction is essentially a procedural one and lies in the manner in which the trials are administered during training. _Instrumental conditioning_ refers to situations in which there are discrete trials. A trial is completed, the subject is removed from the apparatus, and another trial begins. Thus, the experimenter controls the sequence of trials. For example, consider a simple discrimination-learning task in which a subject must learn in which arm of a Y-shaped maze he will obtain reward. At the end of each trial the experimenter removes the subject from the apparatus and returns him to the start box for some specified period and then begins the next trial.

In contrast to discrete trial procedures, the subject may be allowed to respond freely, controlling or regulating his own rate of responding. For example, in the Skinner box the animal may be allowed to respond freely, thus defining a class of operations known as _operant_ conditioning. The distinction between operant and instrumental conditioning is of no great importance for our purposes and the two terms may be used interchangeably at an elementary level. At a more complex level, psychologists may choose to make this distinction on additional grounds, depending upon particular assumptions they may wish to make about these procedures.

Variations in Instrumental Conditioning

Just as there are procedural variations in classical conditioning, there are several variations in procedures used in instrumental and operant conditioning. So far we have described only one procedure, that of simple *reward* training.

We can modify the task described above by placing a light on the wall of the chamber so the animal can easily see it. Then we can arrange the situation so that when the light is on and the animal presses the bar he obtains food. When the light is off, however, a bar-pressing response does not lead to food reward. By consistently rewarding the animal in the presence of the light and not rewarding him when the light is off, the animal will come to discriminate when to *respond*. This procedure describes the basic procedure of *discrimination* training, which is essentially an extension of reward training, but with a discriminative stimulus or cue present.

In general, instrumental or operant conditioning situations can be arranged so that discriminative cues are either present or not. In addition, the experimental procedures may use either reward or punishment. For instance, we may reward an animal with food when he makes the appropriate response or we may punish an animal by applying electric shock. Finally, the response to-be-learned may be one that is produced or one that is withheld. Variations in any one of these three general conditions (cue present or not, reward or punishment, and response produced or withheld) produce several kinds of instrumental learning paradigms. Let us consider one further example.

Consider the arrangement in which an animal is placed in a compartment or chamber, the floor of which consists of a metal grid through which current may be passed. Periodically, the animal is shocked and his task is to learn to turn a wheel in order to escape the shock. When the grid is first charged, the animal moves about quite vigorously trying to escape the shock. As soon as the animal touches the wheel the experimenter turns off the current. Fairly rapidly the animal will learn that turning the wheel is instrumental in escaping from shock and will come to respond almost instantly when the shock is presented. This procedure describes the basic paradigm of *escape* conditioning in which a response comes to be produced in order to escape the aversive event.

Verbal Operant Conditioning

Operant procedures have also been applied to verbal conditioning. For example, in laboratory settings a human subject may be required to emit words from certain response categories such as nouns, verbs, adjectives, and pronouns, and the experimenter arbitrarily decides to reinforce one class of these responses and not the others. Subjects may simply be asked to say words, or construct sentences, or even tell stories. The basic procedure is to get the subject to make verbalizations of some kind and then to selectively reinforce one class of responses. With such procedures, the response or response class that is selected for reinforcement will strengthen, that is, increase in probability.

A wide variety of reinforcers have been used in these experiments. Sometimes the experimenter may simply say "um-hum" immediately following a word of the correct class. Other verbal responses, such as "good," "fine," or "all right," can serve as reinforcers. In addition, lights and buzzers have also been used; however, the effectiveness of such stimuli depends upon how much information they convey to the subject.

A theoretical issue with such procedures is whether the human subject must be aware of the response-reinforcement contingency in order for verbal conditioning to occur. Conscious awareness of the relationship or contingency is usually defined as the ability of the subject to verbalize the contingency, that is, to state that the experimenter reinforced a particular class of responses. The evidence indicates that subjects who are "aware," as defined by some set of operations, do verbally condition faster than unaware subjects. Nevertheless, awareness does not appear to be necessary for verbal operant conditioning to occur.

The fact that verbal responses can be controlled by operant procedures has general implications for the control of human behavior. One implication is that our verbal behavior is, at least to some extent, under control of external reinforcing events. Another implication is that such procedures are applicable to speech and behavior disorders in that it is possible to change the type and frequency of verbal responses emitted by humans by careful control of reinforcement contingencies. We will discuss applications of conditioning principles at the end of this chapter.

Classical and Instrumental Conditioning Compared

A comparison of classical and instrumental conditioning is presented in Table 2.1. These comparisons emphasize that the distinctions between the two forms are principally procedural.

The response-reward sequence clearly differs with the two types of conditioning. In classical conditioning the UCS, which may be regarded as a reinforcing stimulus, produces the particular response of interest. Food powder elicits salivation; electric shock applied to the finger produces finger withdrawal; a puff of air to the eye produces an eyeblink. Regardless of whether the stimuli are emotionally pleasant or aversive events, they precede the response. Thus we prefer to identify the UCS as a reinforcing stimulus, about which we will say more later, rather than the more familiar term reward. In contrast, the response must be produced prior to obtaining reward in instrumental or

TABLE 2.1

Comparison of Classical and Instrumental Conditioning

Comparison	Classical Conditioning	Instrumental Conditioning
1. Response-reward sequence	1. UCS precedes response	1. Response is prior to reward
2. Role of stimuli	2. Response produced by a specific stimulus	2. No specific stimulus produces a response
3. Character of response	3. Response is elicited	3. Response is emitted
4. Observed changes	4. Effectiveness of formerly neutral stimulus on magnitude of a response	4. Change in speed, force, frequency of response
5. Involvement of nervous system	5. Usually involves autonomic nervous system	5. Usually involves somatic nervous system
6. What is learned	6. Emotions such as fears, attitudes, feelings	6. Instrumental (goal-seeking) behavior

operant conditioning. The animal must press the bar to obtain food; the child must say "please" before he obtains the candy; the student must complete his assignment before he is given a reward in the form of a free period.

In classical conditioning the response is produced by a specific discrete stimulus. In instrumental conditioning no specific stimulus is identifiable, so that we cannot conclude that some particular stimulus evokes a response. Many stimuli may be present in instrumental conditioning, but none can be said to elicit the response directly. Thus, sometimes the response in instrumental conditioning is said to be *emitted*, whereas the response in classical conditioning is said to be *elicited* by a specific stimulus. A blast of air to the eye or a tap on the knee will elicit or produce the response directly. But consider learning to dance, which is an instance of instrumental learning. We cannot say that the sound of the music elicits the response of dancing, because music doesn't "force" the response. All we can say is that music as a stimulus may set the occasion for the response of dancing.

The observed change in classical conditioning is essentially that of stimulus substitution. A formerly neutral stimulus, the CS, acquires the capacity to "substitute" for the USC. In instrumental conditioning what is observed is characteristically a change in the frequency of a response emitted, its speed, or its force.

Classical conditioning characteristically involves the autonomic nervous system, whereas instrumental conditioning involves the somatic nervous system. This distinction is not always perfect, since both components of the nervous system may be involved in either conditioning situation.

Finally, classical conditioning typically involves the learning of emotional responses such as fears and hopes, the learning of attitudes, opinions, feelings, and expectations. In contrast, instrumental conditioning involves the acquisition of goal-directed instrumental responses.

Despite the procedural differences, differences associated with nervous system involvement, and type of response learned, there appears to be strong evidence for regarding both types of conditioning as involving fundamentally the same processes. For example, they both obey the same laws or principles, which we shall describe shortly. Moreover, many autonomic responses formerly regarded as subject only to classical conditioning procedures have been shown to be instrumentally conditioned. Thus, we can regard these two types of conditioning as procedurally differing operations that nevertheless appear to reflect some common set of underlying processes.

The Concept of Reinforcement

The view that behavior is dependent upon its consequences has occupied a central position in the psychology of learning since the early experiments of Edward Thorndike. It was Thorndike's belief that learning was fundamentally dependent upon rewards and or punishments that closely followed the response that was produced. Indeed, our description of instrumental learning emphasized that the rewarded responses become learned, whereas nonrewarded responses fail to become learned.

Psychologists frequently employ the term *reinforcement* rather than reward. Reinforcement is theoretically a more neutral term and refers, in general, to the process by which some response tendency comes to be strengthened. Moreover, it is somewhat more convenient to discuss classical and instrumental conditioning jointly with this concept, particularly because it is a bit awkward to use the ordinary concept of reward in classical conditioning.

Positive and Negative Reinforcers

A REINFORCER IS ANY EVENT WHICH, WHEN OCCURRING IN CLOSE TEMPORAL RELATIONSHIP TO A RESPONSE, INCREASES THE LIKELIHOOD THAT THE RESPONSE WILL BE REPEATED IN THE FUTURE. We know that many events can serve as reinforcers. Obviously, food to a hungry organism can serve as a reinforcer. For some individuals praise may serve as a reinforcer; however, not all individuals are affected by praise in this fashion. Teachers frequently discover that praise may "work" for middle-class children, whereas it may not function for young boys who may, in fact, lose status among their peers if they receive teacher praise. Praise from the teacher may cause such children to "lose face" among their friends and thus inadvertently produce undesirable behavioral by-products in the classroom.

A vast number of events can serve as reinforcers. We cannot, however, always identify a particular reinforcing event in advance of a learning situation. At a functional level, however, we can identify any event as a reinforcer if it acts like one, namely, that it serves to increase the strength of a particular response.

In instrumental conditioning we can distinguish between positive and negative reinforcers. POSITIVE REINFORCERS ARE ANY EVENTS WHICH STRENGTHEN A RESPONSE WHEN THEY ARE PRESENTED. Thus food, candy, praise, and money are said to be positive reinforcers if their presentation following a response tends to strengthen that response.

In contrast, NEGATIVE REINFORCERS ARE ANY EVENTS WHICH STRENGTHEN A RESPONSE WHEN THEY ARE TERMINATED OR REMOVED. Negative reinforcers are emotionally aversive events which we are desirous of removing or avoiding. For example, electric shock is a negative reinforcer in instrumental learning if we learn a response in order to escape or avoid the shock. In our description of escape learning, shock served as a negative reinforcer because the animal learned a response in order to terminate the shock. Similarly, if a student works hard in order to avoid possible sarcasm or ridicule from the teacher, he can be said to learn as a result of negative reinforcement.

Our learning is under control of both positive and negative reinforcers and both factors may be present on a given occasion. A high school student may, for example, try to obtain high grades so he will be admitted to a university, receive notice from his friends, or even receive an increase in his allowance from his parents. He may also study diligently in order to avoid parental nagging, teacher disapproval, or fear of the long-term consequences of not being admitted to a university. It is not always easy to disentangle both elements in everyday learning.

Why Do Reinforcers Work?

It is clear, of course, that the principle of reinforcement is empirically valid. Responses that are followed closely by reinforcing events tend to be strengthened. Indeed, this statement is roughly comparable to Thorndike's classical law of effect. At a descriptive level the principle simply states that reinforcers work. This, of course, does not tell you why they function as they do.

Several theories have been advanced to explain the operation of reinforcers upon behavior. A long-standing theory first formalized by Clark Hull was that of the *drive-reduction hypothesis.* This notion stated that reinforcers work as they do because they reduce some prevailing drive of the organism. A hungry organism has his hunger drive reduced by food; a thirsty organism reduces his thirst drive by water. The basic idea is that a reinforcing agent modified some metabolic state of the organism.

Although this theory had considerable appeal at the time of its formulation, its generality was subsequently shown to be limited. For instance, animals will learn responses when they are given a nonnutritive substance such as saccharine. Saccharine cannot be regarded as drive-reducing, despite its sweet taste, indicating that the drive reduction theory cannot readily handle this kind of result. Other experiments have indicated that the drive reduction interpretation simply cannot handle all the facts. We do not, as yet, have an all-inclusive theory of reinforcement. The best we can conclude is that several theories appear to be necessary in order to account for the facts. Nevertheless, despite the fact that we do not have a complete theoretical account of reinforcement, the empirical law of reinforcement still holds.

Secondary Reinforcing Events

Psychologists distinguish between primary and secondary reinforcing events. Primary reinforcers refer to events such as food and water and are closely tied to biological needs of the organism such as hunger, thirst and pain-avoidance. Secondary reinforcers refer to events that function so because of learning. Money and praise may function as secondary reinforcers but do so because humans learn to regard them in this fashion. STIMULUS EVENTS WHICH ARE INITIALLY NEUTRAL TO THE ORGANISM MAY ACQUIRE SECONDARY REINFORCING PROPERTIES AS A RESULT OF BEING ASSOCIATED WITH PRIMARY REINFORCING EVENTS. Regardless of whether we are dealing with primary or secondary reinforcers, they both act the same way in the principle of reinforcement. As we saw in the section on verbal operant conditioning, verbal responses can act as secondary reinforcers.

Responses as Reinforcers

So far we have described reinforcers largely as if they are *stimulus* events or objects. Food, water, money, candy are all stimulus events that may reinforce behavior. Reinforcing events may also be *responses,* a point emphasized by David Premack. His view is that organisms are reinforced by being allowed to engage in behaviors which they prefer. More formally, Premack contends THAT HIGH-PROBABILITY RESPONSES, WHICH ARE RESPONSES WE MOST FREQUENTLY EMIT (AND HENCE, PRESUMABLY PREFER), MAY SERVE TO REINFORCE LOW-PROBABILITY RESPONSES. The appropriate contingency is to arrange high-probability responses so that they *follow* low-probability responses. The sequence is critical if a low-probability response is to be strengthened.

This principle can be easily illustrated. Suppose, for example, that a child wishes to eat dessert and is uninterested in his meat or vegetables. You may say to him "eat your meat and vegetables and then you may have dessert." Eating dessert is a high-probability response; eating meat and vegetables is the lower-probability response. The sequence is arranged so that the high-probability response can occur *only after* the low-probability response has occurred. Similarly, the child may be told that he can play outside after he has picked up his toys. Thus playing outside is made contingent upon picking up the toys. Similarly, you arrange such a contingency when you insist on doing your homework before you watch television or attend a film.

The principle is most effective when the low-probability behavior required represents a reasonable amount of activity for the child as distinct from some endless task. Thus you can require too much behavior, making the principle far less effective. The low-probability behavior should represent some reasonable task not too difficult for the child, ideally one that can be completed without much frustration. Systematic use of the principle will allow you to make greater behavioral demands on an organism as learning progresses.

The principle is a very practical one in that it allows you to identify a reinforcer for a particular individual. Knowing what is reinforcing for an individual allows you to plan learning sequences far more efficiently than if you simply assumed that some activity was reinforcing. This principle is receiving considerable application in kindergartens and schools, where the child may "contract" to do a certain amount of work which, when completed, is followed by reinforcement in the form of some activity of his own choosing. What is sometimes arranged is a *reinforcement menu* in which the child, following completion of some task, goes to a particular room where he may choose from a variety of games and activities including, for example, pinball machines, chess, and interaction with his peer group.

Basic Principles of Conditioning

The study of classical, instrumental and operant conditioning has yielded several basic principles which are observable in the various forms of conditioning. In this section we shall outline the salient aspects of each of these principles and indicate in a limited fashion how these principles are applicable beyond the immediate context in which they emerged. These principles can best be regarded as basic empirical generalizations about conditioning phenomena.

Acquisition of Responses

We have already described the process by which responses are acquired in classical, instrumental, and operant conditioning. In classical conditioning we

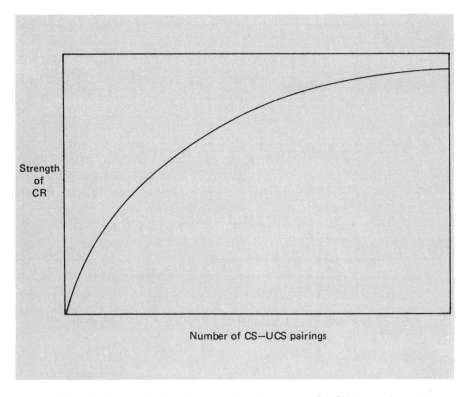

Figure 2. Hypothetical function showing strength of CR as a function of CS-UCS pairings.

noted that the CS *acquires* the capacity to elicit the CR. In instrumental and operant conditioning, the response that receives reinforcement is gradually strengthened, while other responses fail to gain strength. In classical conditioning the strength of the CR is a function of the number of CS-UCS pairings as shown by the curve in figure 2. This curve is a hypothetical function showing that the strength of the CR gradually increases with the number of CS-UCS pairings. If the particular response was salivation, then this curve reflects the fact that the *amount* of salivation increases on test trials (when the CS is presented alone) as a result of the number of tone-food powder pairings.

Similarly, in instrumental conditioning the strength of the response, as measured, say, by the speed of responding, increases as a function of the number of reinforced trials.

Finally, the acquisition of CRs is dependent upon several variables in addition to number of CS-UCS pairings and number of reinforced trials. Classical conditioning is dependent upon both CS and UCS intensity, with more rapid conditioning occurring with increased stimulus intensity. (The

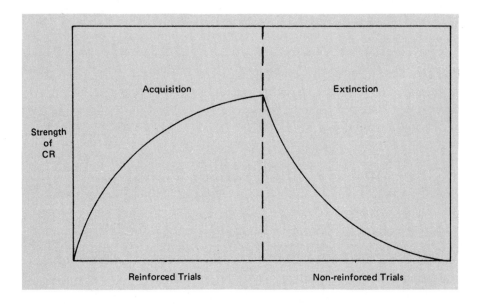

Figure 3. Graphic portrayal of acquisition and extinction of a conditioned response.

interested reader should consult entire volumes devoted to conditioning for detailed discussion of variables influencing classical conditioning.)

Extinction of Responses

Once an instrumental response has been acquired, such as bar pressing at a fairly steady rate, we may then remove the reinforcement. When we do, the organism will continue to respond briefly, followed by a gradually diminished rate of responding, a process called *extinction* of the responses. EXTINCTION IS THUS THE REDUCTION IN RESPONSE STRENGTH FOLLOWING REMOVAL OF THE REINFORCEMENT. Similarly, in classical conditioning repeated presentation of the CS alone will lead to a reduction in response strength.

Figure 3 illustrates both acquisition and extinction of a CR. The left portion of the figure portrays acquisition of a CR as a function of number of reinforced trials and the right portion of the figure portrays extinction of that same response. The figure portrays extinction going to zero responding. In actual practice, the extinction of a CR is defined usually in terms of no responding for some conventionally agreed time interval.

Resistance to extinction, that is, the tendency to continue responding during the extinction period is dependent upon both factors that were present during acquisition and factors present during the extinction session. One important factor is the variability in the training conditions; another is punishment.

Partial Reinforcement and Extinction

The manner in which reinforcements are presented during acquisition affects performance in subsequent extinction. In operant conditioning, reinforcement variability can be introduced by reinforcing some but not all of the responses. Similarly, in instrumental conditioning we may administer *partial* reinforcement, which is to give the reinforcement only on some of the trials. A general principle is that PARTIAL REINFORCEMENT INCREASES RESISTANCE TO EXTINCTION, a principle so general that it is known as the *partial reinforcement effect.*

Consider a hypothetical gambling situation. Suppose that in one situation a slot machine is rigged so that every time you play the machine you are rewarded. This, of course, is an instance of continuous reinforcement. In another, however, the arrangement is that you are reinforced irregularly for only 25 percent of your responses. Now let us imagine that following extended training in these two settings an extinction session is introduced; in neither case are you rewarded for playing the machine, although you are unaware that the rules of the game have changed. What happens? You are likely to persist playing the machine for a much longer period of time following partial than continuous reinforcement.

Human instances of the partial reinforcement effect abound. If, for example, you are denied a date from a girl after going with her regularly, this can be a frustrating experience; if she continues to deny you dates, you will rather rapidly extinguish your requests. On the other hand, if your experience is one of occasionally being told "yes" between periods in which you are told "no," then you learn to persist in your request for dates. In effect, since you never know when you will be reinforced, you are more likely to persist in making responses.

Effects of Stimulus and Response Variability on Extinction

Partial reinforcement in instrumental conditioning represents the general case of reinforcement variability. In general, the more variable the conditions of reinforcement during acquisition, the greater the resistance to extinction. In a similar vein, organisms that are trained in situations IN WHICH THE STIMULUS CONTEXT IS MORE VARIABLE SHOW GREATER RESPONSE PERSISTENCE DURING EXTINCTION. The principle of stimulus variability helps to explain why certain habits are extremely difficult to extinguish. Consider, for example, the difficulty reported by many individuals who attempt to quit smoking. The smoking response is one that is likely to have developed in a great variety of stimulus situations. The various conditions in which a person might smoke a cigarette include when he awakes, after breakfast with coffee, on his way to work, when he arrives at work, during the coffee break, at lunch, when he arrives at home, at a party, and so forth. The occasions for smoking are almost infinite. Thus the response of smoking can become tied to a large number of environmental (as well as internal) stimuli, providing a large number of habits to be extinguished.

Likewise, response variability leads to greater resistance to extinction. This principle can be understood if it is assumed that with greater response variability, a greater number of *different* habits are being strengthened during acquisition. Thus, during extinction as one response is extinguished, other responses remain available, allowing for prolonged response persistence.

Spontaneous Recovery of Responses

A third conditioning principle is that a response that has undergone extinction is subject to spontaneous recovery. For example, if we remove an animal from an operant chamber for some period of time, after having extinguished a bar-pressing response, and then return the animal to the chamber, we will observe the temporary resumption of bar pressing at a rate above that of the extinction criterion. THIS TEMPORARY RESUMPTION OF RESPONDING AFTER EXTINCTION IS DESIGNATED *SPONTANEOUS RECOVERY OF RESPONSES* AND INDICATES THAT THE HABIT TENDENCY IS STILL PRESENT EVEN THOUGH THE RESPONSE WAS PREVIOUSLY EXTINGUISHED.

Generalization

So far our discussion of conditioning has emphasized that learning is fairly specific to the particular events that occur during training. Nevertheless, learning in one situation or context can *generalize* to another. Your learned dislike of sixth-grade arithmetic may "generalize" to a fear of mathematics in subsequent grades. Similarly, your fear of a particular teacher of mathematics may "generalize" to a fear of other teachers or to mathematics in general. Likewise, your liking of one person may generalize to other individuals who possess similar traits.

The basic principle of generalization notes that WHENEVER A RESPONSE IS LEARNED IN ONE STIMULUS SITUATION, OTHER STIMULI SIMILAR TO THOSE IN THE TRAINING SITUATION ACQUIRE SOME TENDENCY TO PRODUCE THAT RESPONSE. For example, in a classical conditioning paradigm in which an animal learns to salivate to a CS of a particular tone, say 1000 cycles second, he also acquires some tendency to respond to other tones. Moreover, the greater the similarity of these tones to the CS, the greater the likelihood that the animal will respond.

This tendency to respond to similar stimuli is called *stimulus generalization*. Its basic importance is that it emphasizes that learning is *not* entirely *specific* to the situation in which responses are acquired. The principle is important in that it provides for flexibility and generality in learning, emphasizing that our learning is not always bound to specific stimulus events. Indeed, the principle of stimulus generalization underlies our learning of many simple concepts and provides the basis for much of what is called *transfer of training*. These issues will be described in subsequent chapters.

There are actually two principles involved in the concept of generalization. One is the principle of *stimulus generalization* just described and the other is the principle of *response generalization*. This second principle refers to the fact that responses *similar* to the learned response also have some tendency to occur, especially during the early stages of conditioning. If the learned response is momentarily unavailable, another similar response may be emitted. For example, in learning to pronounce a new word you may be unable to produce the correct pronunciation but can still produce some approximate pronunciation of the word, one that is highly similar to the correct pronunciation.

We have already noted that the amount of generalization depends upon the degree of similarity between two stimulus events. The greater the stimulus similarity, the greater the probability of generalization. The factors that affect resistance to extinction also effect the degree of generalization. In general, the greater number of different stimuli present during acquisition, the greater the likelihood of generalization. Similarly, the larger the number of different responses practiced during acquisition, the greater the likelihood of generalization. Finally, the more variable the conditions of reinforcement during acquisition, the greater the likelihood of generalization.

Discrimination

Although generalization can be adaptive in the sense that it provides for flexibility in behavior, for transfer, and for your ability to form simple concepts, unlimited generalization can also lead to inappropriate behavior. Two people may look alike, hold the same occupation, live in the same neighborhood and yet can hold quite different beliefs about important features of life. Inappropriate generalization to similar stimuli can thus form the basis of much human error. Fortunately, however, humans also come to discriminate among environmental stimuli, which is to say that we can learn to respond differently to highly similar stimuli.

THE PROCESS OF LEARNING TO RESPOND DIFFERENTLY TO SOMEWHAT SIMILAR STIMULI IS CALLED STIMULUS DISCRIMINATION. This process occurs when responses in the presence of one stimulus are reinforced, while responses produced in the presence of another are not reinforced. The differential reinforcement of responses made to different stimuli is the basis by which discrimination learning occurs.

Consider, for example, our illustration of classical conditioning in which a salivary response becomes conditioned to a CS of 1000 cycles/second. Other tones, we noted, also acquire some capacity to elicit the CR through the process of stimulus generalization. This generalization tendency can be weakened, however, by training that employs differential reinforcement of the response tendency in the presence of different stimuli. If we continue to pair the CS and UCS, the CS will continue to elicit the response. By presenting similar stimuli, such as tones of 600 and 1400 cycles/second, *without* the UCS (food powder), the organism will gradually come to respond principally to the CS and with much less magnitude to stimuli similar to the CS.

In a similar vein, we can arrange for a discrimination to be acquired in the instrumental or operant conditioning paradigm, a procedure which was described earlier in this chapter. Recall that an animal could be trained to press a bar in the presence of light and not to press when the light was off. In this example, reinforcement of bar pressing was made contingent upon the presence or absence of the light.

Stimulus discrimination is a basic feature of virtually all learning and is evident in many everyday experiences. We learn, for example, that it is generally more reinforcing to stop in the presence of a red light and go in the presence of a green light. Similarly, the young child learns to discriminate between letters of the alphabet that are perceptually similar. In school, he learns that $3 + 3$ is a stimulus for the response "6" but that 3×3 is not. The discrimination of speech sounds, of letters and words, of symbols, of numerals, of people, are instances of a whole range of events for which we must acquire discriminations. As adults we acquire more complex and sophisticated discriminations. The skilled wine taster, for example, learns to discriminate among ordinary red table wines, a good California burgundy, and a 1964 vintage Chateau Lafitte Rothschild as he acquires a taste for French wines.

The concepts of generalization and discrimination have received extensive use in accounting for more complex human learning phenomena, particularly in the areas of verbal learning, transfer, and concept learning. The learning of simple concepts can be regarded as involving the processes of generalization and discrimination. For instance, learning color and shape concepts involves "generalizing" among the class of instances that belong to the concept while "discriminating" among the conceptual categories. We can only allude to the applicability of generalization and discrimination at present and we will discuss these issues in subsequent chapters.

Conditions Which Affect Discrimination

We noted earlier that stimulus discrimination was the process by which you learned to respond differentially to somewhat similar stimuli. An obvious factor, therefore, that influences stimulus discrimination is the *similarity* of the stimulus events. In general, THE GREATER THE SIMILARITY OF STIMULI, THE MORE DIFFICULT IT IS TO LEARN TO DISCRIMINATE THE STIMULI.

The failure to learn discriminations with reasonable ease is frequently the result of inconsistent reinforcement of responses made to similar stimuli. Consider a simple example. Many children enjoy a snack after a day at school upon arrival at home. The mother may allow a snack if the child asks for it shortly after arrival at home. If the child waits too long so that the dinner hour is approaching, the mother may veto the snack. Thus, the mother's basic task is that of teaching the child a temporal discrimination of asking for a snack within, say, a half-hour after arriving at home. If the mother, however, allows the child to have the snack on some occasions even when dinner will shortly be served, the child will have difficulty in learning this discrimination. Thus the *consistency* of differential reinforcement of responses made in the presence of different stimuli is fundamental for discrimination learning.

Another essential feature in developing discriminations is getting the learner to attend to or focus on the essential or *relevant* dimensions of the stimulus. Many stimuli in our environment are quite similar and yet call for different responses. The letters *b* and *d* are physically similar; thus effective discrimination of these events can occur only when the relevant features of these stimuli are attended to by the child. Two individuals may be very similar in many of their attitudes and personality traits and yet be different in other critically important ways. If you have learned to respond to their similar characteristics, you may stereotype the individuals by placing them in the same category, thus making it much more difficult to detect their distinctive characteristics. This is simply to say that a learned tendency to respond to similar stimuli in the same way makes it more difficult to establish a discrimination.

Differentiation

The fact that humans can discriminate among stimuli was seen as a process that can work against unlimited generalization tendencies. Generalization is, of course, adaptive when the behavior is appropriate. As we saw, discrimination is important in a variety of situations if you are to function most effectively. We learn, however, not only to *discriminate* among stimulus events but we also learn to *differentiate* among responses.

RESPONSE DIFFERENTIATION REFERS TO THE PROCESS WHEREBY SOMEWHAT SIMILAR RESPONSES ARE DIFFERENTIALLY REINFORCED. In this fashion one response becomes strengthened and the other is gradually weakened. The process of response differentiation emphasizes that responses can become shaped or more precise in the course of learning.

Let us first consider a laboratory illustration of response differentiation. In this illustration an animal has learned to bar press in order to receive a food award. We now arrange the task so that we reward the animal *only* when he makes a bar press of a specific force. Responses with less force are never reinforced and responses equal to or greater than the criterion force always receive reinforcement. With this arrangement the animal will come to bar press at or above some specific force, which means that he has *differentiated* this response (actually response class) from others.

Response differentiation is such a frequent part of learning that you may fail to notice its regular occurrence. Parents shape the speech behavior of children when they encourage a child to pronounce a word in one way rather than another. Thus proper pronunciation and articulate speech is the outcome of a long history of response differentiation. Similarly, many athletic skills require that a response be executed with a particular force or a particular speed. Again, the development of these response properties is a matter of response differentiation. Learning skills such as swimming, diving, tennis and golf all involve the differentiation of responses, that is, the acquisition of a particular response or response class most likely to achieve satisfaction and the corresponding elimination of irrelevant, nonreinforced responses. As we will subsequently see, the process of response differentiation is relevant to processes in motor skills learning. Let us now turn our attention to two areas in which conditioning principles have been applied: therapy and education.

Application of Conditioning Principles

Psychologists have not been content just to describe the fundamental principles of conditioning but have also attempted to extend or apply these principles to the understanding of much more complex events. In recent years, conditioning principles have been employed in accounts of social learning and developmental processes, in personality theory and therapy, and in applications to individual and classroom learning situations. The past decade has witnessed new developments in educational technology, such as programmed instruction and computer-aided instruction, which are based upon assumptions about the learning process derived largely from studies of operant conditioning. In a similar vein, behavior modification approaches to therapy have conceptualized the therapeutic process as one that can be understood in terms of conditioning principles. In this section we shall briefly outline certain features of the way in which principles of conditioning have been applied to problems of therapy and education.

Conditioning Principles and Therapy

There are many approaches to therapy. One approach, however, is directly based upon the principles of conditioning which are applied to the treatment of behavior disorders. This approach has been most extensively applied to the less severe behavior disturbances (neurotic behavior), but in some instances it has been applied to more severe disturbances, such as the psychoses.

The basic assumption underlying conditioning therapy is that maladaptive behaviors are learned behaviors, and that such learning occurs in accordance with the same principles under which other learning occurs. This is simply to say that if adaptive behavior is acquired in accordance with principles of learning, then it is reasonable to assume that many maladaptive behaviors may also be learned. In other words, given that behaviors become strengthened through differential reinforcement, the principles should be applicable regardless of the adaptive or adjustive character of the behavior.

Given these assumptions, behavior disorders are thus viewed as *learned events*. In effect, we can learn to become "sick." Therefore, one of the principal tasks of the therapist becomes one of attempting to reduce or eliminate the undesirable behaviors by extinguishing such behavior. The basic idea is to ensure that the maladaptive behaviors are no longer reinforced. For example, a hospital patient who hallucinates is no longer allowed to have the hallucinatory behavior reinforced. Such reinforcement may occur when attendants or others ask the patient about his hallucinations. Therapists employ *extinction* of the responses as one aspect of therapy, but also emphasize a second way of weakening responses which is through *counter-conditioning*. Here maladaptive behaviors are weakened by strengthening incompatible or competing responses. If anxiety is the characteristic response to a particular situation, the therapist attempts to strengthen responses incompatible with anxiety, such as, for example, relaxation responses. Relaxation is nevertheless just one possible response that may be strengthened. THE BASIC PRINCIPLE OF COUNTER-CONDITIONING IS THAT AN INCOMPATIBLE RESPONSE OR CLASS OF RESPONSES IS TO BE STRENGTHENED.

Behavior modification approaches to therapy have been applied to a wide variety of disorders such as phobias, alcoholism, overeating, sexual disorders, and speech disturbances. Mental hospital patients long hospitalized have responded to therapy using these general procedures when other approaches have failed.

Behavior therapists have sometimes been criticized by more traditional therapists who contend that behavior modification is essentially a superficial approach to behavior disorders because it deals only with surface behavior rather than root causes of the disorders. Presumably, whatever is producing the conflict may still remain unresolved. Behavior therapists counter by contending that it is necessary to eliminate the maladaptive behaviors if successful therapy is to occur. Moreover, success in eliminating some maladaptive behavior, such as fear of crowds, may lead to additional changes such as growth in self-confidence.

While the arguments over the merits of behavior modification approaches to therapy still continue, their resolution is not possible within the scope of this book. The important point to note is that principles of conditioning are receiving extensive application in the treatment of behavior disorders.

Conditioning Principles and Programmed Instruction

The teaching process can be regarded, at least in part, as the task of arranging instructional experiences so as to maximize learning outcomes. It therefore follows that principles of conditioning, as well as human learning and cognition, have relevance to practical problems of education. Principles of conditioning and learning carry no special implications about what topics should be taught, but they do not have implications about *how* teaching should be conducted for the purpose of maximizing learning.

The potential application of principles of instrumental and operant conditioning to educational practices was most clearly recognized by B. F. Skinner in the mid-fifties. This recognition led Skinner to embark upon a program for the expansion and use of these principles to problems of individual instruction, which led to the instructional technology of *programmed instruction.*

Programmed instruction is a way of presenting educational materials to students in a step-by-step fashion. The student is presented a small amount of information and asked to respond to a question or problem. Each step is called a *frame,* and a frame has a *stimulus* component, which presents the information, a *response* component in a place in which the learner responds and a *confirmation* component in which the student is given feedback or knowledge of results. Figure 4 is an example of two frames from a sequence designed to teach the concept of "learning."

The learner proceeds through a series of frames until he acquires a full understanding of the concept of "learning." At each step enough information is presented so the learner's response is likely to be correct. The objective of the frame is to guide the student toward making the correct response.

Programmed instruction makes use of certain basic principles of instrumental and operant conditioning. First, from our earlier discussion, it is clear that the learner must be *active* if learning is to occur. The important point is that the learner must respond in some manner; learning is not a passive process. The sequence of frames keeps the learner actively responding at each step.

The second principle is that responses must be reinforced if behavior is to be changed. In this instance, the confirmation of the learner's response to each frame can be regarded as somewhat analogous to reinforcement. While there is current doubt about simply equating reinforcement with confirmation, the desirability of producing some form of immediate feedback for the learner is clearly recognized. Thus, the learner is given immediate knowledge of results regarding the adequacy of each response he makes.

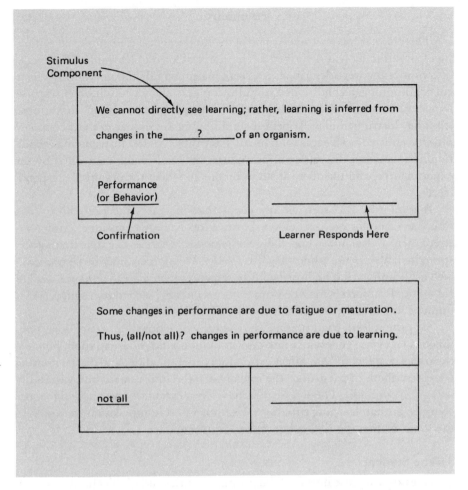

Figure 4. Example of two frames in a programmed learning
sequence designed to teach the concept of "learning."

The learner is led through a series of frames in which his concept is
gradually sharpened and refined. The learner is not simply emitting responses,
but is responding to carefully written items that are designed to lead the
student to learn a concept.

Each student sets his own pace, so in this sense working through the
program is analogous to a free operant situation, since the learner is responding at his own rate. It is this feature which is characteristic of much
individualized instruction.

We can only briefly refer to these features of programmed instruction.
Their general significance is that they represent the emergence of an instructional technology which is derived from studies of simple learning.

Summary

This chapter has portrayed some of the fundamental elements of conditioning. Conditioning was described as the simplest form of learning. Three types of conditioning were described: classical, instrumental, and operant. In classical conditioning, a conditioned stimulus comes to elicit a conditioned response as a result of repeated presentations of an unconditioned and conditioned stimulus. Instrumental and operant conditioning are similar in that a response must be emitted before it is reinforced. They differ in that instrumental conditioning involves a discrete trial procedure, the trials being controlled by the experimenter, and the operant situation one in which the organisms responds freely.

A reinforcer was seen as any event that increases the probability of a response. Reinforcers are either positive or negative; positive reinforcers strengthen a response when they are *presented*, whereas negative reinforcers strengthen a response when they are *removed*. Reinforcers may be responses as well as stimuli in that high-probability responses may serve to reinforce weaker responses. Reinforcers may be primary or secondary; secondary reinforcers for humans are usually verbal or symbolic in nature.

Six principles of conditioning were described: acquisition, extinction, spontaneous recovery, generalization, discrimination, and differentiation. Some of the important factors that affect extinction, generalization, and discrimination were described. In particular, the role of partial reinforcement and variability was given emphasis. These principles have been extended and applied to more complex human learning situations. Examples of this application were seen in the areas of therapy and programmed instruction.

To the Student

A list of true-false items will be presented at the end of this chapter and the remaining chapters. The answer to each item is given following a brief discussion of the item. These items sample the content of the chapter and thus provide you with some index of your comprehension of the material. Since the answer follows the item, *it is to your advantage to cover up the answer until you have carefully thought about the question.* This will prevent you from inadvertently looking at the answer, and will provide you with maximum benefits. The questions are not exhaustive of the content of the chapter and hence should not be relied upon exclusively for study and review. A good practice would be for you also to make up several items and answer them.

True-False Items: Elements of Conditioning

1. Conditioning principles can be extrapolated to "explain" all forms of more complex human learning.

(Although conditioning principles appear useful in explaining some forms of more complex learning, it appears that additional principles are needed to account for the more complex phenomena of memory, concept learning, and problem solving. False.)

2. Classical conditioning involves the process of stimulus substitution.

(In classical conditioning a formerly "neutral" stimulus, the CS, comes to elicit a response that initially was produced only by the UCS. True.)

3. In instrumental conditioning the response occurs after the reinforcement.

(The contingency is just the reverse. The reinforcement must follow the response if learning is to occur. False.)

4. The basic difference between operant and instrumental conditioning is that the response is freely available in operant conditioning.

(In operant conditioning no constraints are placed on the organism's responding within the time limit allowed for responding. True.)

5. Looking in your refrigerator for a snack is an instance of an operant response.

(As long as you are free to look in the refrigerator whenever you chose, looking is an operant response. It is no longer a free operant, however, if you are permitted, say, to look only once a day. True.)

6. Negative reinforcers lead you to cease making a response.

(Negative reinforcers actually strengthen a response when the negative reinforcer is removed or terminated. For example, you may work hard around the house in order to avoid nagging from your parents. In this case the response of working is strengthened because it prevents the occurrence of nagging. False.)

7. If you assume that nursery school children like to run and scream but rarely clean up the play area, then allowing them to run and scream *after* they clean up the play area will tend to strengthen "cleaning-up" responses.

(This is the case because you are arranging for high-probability behavior [running and screaming] to follow low-probability behavior [cleaning-up], a contingency which strengthens low-probability behavior. True.)

8. The basic procedure for extinguishing a response is to make sure that no reinforcement follows emission of the response.

(This statement is simply the principle of extinction. True.)

9. The extinction of responses learned in various environmental settings is relatively easy.

(Responses learned in various settings are much more resistant to extinction because the learned habit is tied to many stimuli. False.)

10. When a young child erroneously calls the milkman "daddy," this is an instance of discrimination.

Teachers who control classroom behaviors by the tech described in item — are using "contingency management."

(This example illustrates generalization, in which the child responds to another adult male as if he were "daddy." False.)

11. The loudness with which you characteristically talk and the skill with which you characteristically write are learned response properties. Such learning represents instances of response differentiation.

(Properties of responses such as loudness, speed, force, etc, are learned as result of differential reinforcement. True.)

12. The application of conditioning principles to therapeutic procedures assumes typically that the behavior disorder being treated developed as a result of learning.

(Conditioning therapy assumes that the maladaptive behavior is learned in accordance with the same principles in which adaptive behavior is learned. True.)

3

Characteristics
of Verbal Learning

Most human learning involves verbal processes. It is verbal in the sense that such learning involves language, a significant feature of the human organism. Learning a foreign language, solving a problem in mathematics, associating names and dates, are all situations that involve what is known as verbal learning. Learning to understand the meaning of an abstract document such as the Bill of Rights or learning to understand the meaning of an unfamiliar word also constitute everyday tasks that involve verbal learning.

The fact that one uses language in so much of everyday learning may make this activity seem commonplace or even unimportant. Nevertheless, the fact that a human can engage in verbal learning activities provides him with powerful ways of dealing with his environment. Language can serve to reward or punish behaviors and thus can have motivational effects. The effects of saying "good" or "bad," or even saying very little, are obvious examples. Similarly, language is used for communication purposes and operates in the development of concepts from the most elementary to the most complex. Language, or verbal behavior, is clearly tied up with thinking and symbolic activities, and serves to mediate a variety of events. For example, by saying to yourself that "I should study tonight and tomorrow night for the test, and then see the film," you are able to mediate behavior verbally in order to secure a successful outcome.

The systematic study of human learning began with verbal learning, and the principle issue was the formation of verbal associations. Consider the question: How is it that the majority of humans, when asked to think of an association to the word "table," think of the word "chair" as the most dominant associate? In turn, why are words such as "door" and "dog" less frequently given as associates? A longstanding view is that events and things tend to become associated because they are experienced together frequently. The basic idea is that if events A and B occur together – that is, contiguously – then

33

A will on some future date tend to evoke B, and if they occur together frequently, then they will become strongly associated. Thus, according to this classic view, "table" and "chair" are likely to be strong associates because of the frequency with which they have occurred together in the past. In turn, "table" and "door" will be weaker associates because they have occurred together less frequently. Although this account involving frequency and contiguity is a classic one, and is partly true, we will subsequently see that it does not represent a completely satisfactory explanation.

In the above discussion two important concepts have been introduced: *contiguity* and *frequency*. By contiguity is meant that events are overlapping or close together in space or in time. If a book and a coffee cup are next to each other on your desk, they are spatially contiguous. If your eye blinks following a blast of air, the two events are temporally contiguous. Frequency, of course, refers to how often two events occur contiguously. The concepts are important because they are the longstanding principles that presumably governed the development of associations. Moreover, it was an interest in the *laws of association* that provided the background for the early study of verbal learning.

Definition of Verbal Learning

Verbal learning is any learning situation in which the task requires the learner to respond to verbal material, such as words, or to respond with verbal responses. It includes a wide variety of learning situations ranging from the association of nonsense verbal materials to the solution of complex verbal problems. For example, a learner might be required to associate a list of unfamiliar verbal materials, such as XUJ and BAL, as an instance of a relatively simple task. In contrast, the human learner might be presented with a verbal analogy such as *Toulouse* is to *Lautrec* as *Rimsky* is to _?_ , the answer being *Korsakov*. In this case the solution to the analogy would be aided if the person recognized that Toulouse-Lautrec is the name of a famous French painter. Therefore, he might anticipate that Rimsky would be the first part of a double-name of another well-known artist, in this case a composer. The analogy might be solved, however, if you recognized that Toulouse-Lautrec was someone's name even though you could not identify him as a painter, an artist, or even as French. Recognition of the name as a name could lead you to search your memory for the class of events that include double names beginning with Rimsky.

From the example above it is clear that verbal learning involves complex processes such as problem solving, thinking, and concept formation. For the sake of convenience, however, these topics will be discussed in subsequent chapters. This chapter will focus on relatively simple kinds of verbal learning, principally those that involve the memorization of serial lists and lists of pairs of verbal materials. Keep in mind, however, that even these relatively simple tasks, which may appear to you to be no more than *rote* learning, almost always involve some kind of more complex activity on the part of the learner. This activity usually involves an attempt on the part of the learner to use certain strategies, to organize or group the verbal materials in certain ways, or to code the materials, sometimes through the use of mnemonic or other devices.

Ebbinghaus and Associationism

The study of verbal learning was first systematically begun by Hermann Ebbinghaus, a German psychologist, in 1885. Ebbinghaus was interested in the conditions under which humans learned to form associations, and in the way in which associations were forgotten over time. Prior to this time it was generally believed that such complex processes did not lend themselves to experimental investigation, and that it was not possible to measure such processes. Ebbinghaus was able to demonstrate, however, that it was not only possible to measure human memory in a precise, quantitative way, but that it was possible to examine experimentally the conditions of human learning and memory.

Ebbinghaus was strongly influenced by the thinking of a group of philosophers known as British associationists. This group of philosophers is represented by such men as John Locke, David Hume, George Berkeley, and James and John Stuart Mill, to mention a few. Two features of British associationism are noteworthy: One was the belief that man's knowledge arises directly from *experience*. Man had no innate or inborn ideas and gained knowledge through experience with the world. The beginning of man's knowledge occurred with the acquiring of simple ideas through experience. A second feature of British associationism, as implied by the name, was that simple ideas could become linked together to form more complex ideas by *association*. These philosophers did not, however, study the formation of associations and it remained for Ebbinghaus to initiate the experimental study of association formation.

In order to examine association formation in a way that he felt was largely free of past experiences of the learner, Ebbinghaus developed the nonsense syllable. The nonsense syllable is a verbal unit consisting of a consonant-vowel-consonant combination, such as XOB. The use of familiar words or sentences as learning materials for adult humans would obviously be unsatisfactory *if* the objective of the psychologist was to study the learning process "from scratch," that is, uninfluenced by past learning experiences. We now know, however, that nonsense syllables are not free from the influence of past learning because they are known to possess associative properties and they vary in their meaningfulness. As a result, studies of verbal learning today use a wide variety of materials including words, sentences, and paragraphs, as well as the classical nonsense syllable.

Procedures and Materials in Verbal Learning

Various materials are used in the study of verbal learning. At the simplest level, single letters may be used. Similarly, combinations of two letters, called *bigrams*, may be used. Three-letter nonsense syllables, called *trigrams*, may be used. Trigrams may be either consonant-vowel-consonant (CVC) combinations, or consonant-consonant-consonant (CCC) combinations. The term trigram has come to replace the term nonsense syllable because it is more convenient to refer to the meaningfulness of trigrams.

Trigrams vary in their associative properties such as association value. In order to determine association value, human subjects are shown trigrams one at a time for a brief period and asked if they have an association to it. The percentage of subjects having an association to a verbal item defines its association value. For example, the trigram BAL has an association value of 100 percent, meaning that for all subjects it had an association. In contrast, YIW has an association value of only 7 percent. An extensive scaling of the 2,480 possible CVCs was conducted by the psychologist James Archer, in which he asked each subject whether the item was a word, sounded like a word, reminded them of a word, or could be used in a sentence. He then determined the meaningfulness of the items by calculating the percentage of subjects who regarded each CVC as meaningful.

Other associative properties of verbal materials are known. For example, we can measure the number of associations that subjects give to verbal units, and we can have subjects rate the pronunciability and familiarity of verbal materials. When individual words are used, a useful measure has been the average number of associations given to the word in a fixed time period, a measure that defines meaningfulness. The meaningfulness of two-syllable words, including a small number of artificial words, has been described by Clyde Noble. Examples of artificial words are "gojey" and "neglan," which average only one association in a one-minute period. You might try this with a friend by asking him to write all the associations that come to mind to these artificial words in a one-minute period. Highly meaningful words, such as, for example, "office" and "wagon," average about eight written associations in the same period.

Groups of words and sentences are also used in studies of verbal learning. When we deal with groups of words we become interested in the interitem associative connections among the words. Words such as "summer," "swimming," and "warm" are interrelated and yet do not belong to the same type of class as do "orange," "apple," "banana," and "lemon." Finally, when we deal with sentence learning, we are concerned with specifying grammatical properties of the sentence. For the present we will emphasize that a wide variety of materials are used in studies of verbal learning, and that one important feature of these studies is the *measurement* and *control* of their various properties.

of these studies is the *measurement* and *control* of their various properties.

Let us now examine some ways in which we study verbal learning. There are five basic procedures in the study of verbal learning: (1) serial learning, (2) paired-associate learning, (3) free learning, (4) recognition learning, and (5) verbal discrimination learning.

Serial Learning

In serial learning the verbal units are presented in the same order from trial to trial. A familiar example of serial learning is learning to recite the alphabet. Another obvious example is learning the days of the week as well as the months of the year. The fact that you can recite the days of the week, the months of the year, or the alphabet in perfect order is the final result of learning a serial task. Thus, any task which requires you to learn a series of verbal responses in a particular order represents an instance of serial verbal learning.

While these examples may strike you as relatively simple kinds of learning, many of our everyday tasks require responding in a particular serial order. The grammatical structure of the English language determines, in part, the particular serial order of sentences that you speak and write. Certain word types have a high probability of being followed by other word types; for example, verbs usually follow nouns, thus imposing a particular order. The learning of geological ages in their proper chronological order, such as cenozoic, mesozoic, paleozoic, proterozoic, and archeozoic, is another instance of serial learning; the particular sequence is important because each age implies particular changes and characteristics.

Other tasks, not exclusively verbal in nature, but involving *motor* components, also involve serial learning. A simple example is tying your shoe. Another is starting a car, where a particular sequence of responses must be made. Many tasks involve *both* verbal and motor components. A simple example of serial learning that involves both is learning the combination of a lock. In this instance you must learn the correct sequence of numbers and you must be able to turn the dial (motor component) in a precise and careful fashion.

In laboratory studies of serial learning, verbal units are presented one at a time in a fixed order. The units may be presented to the subject on index cards but are usually presented by means of a memory drum, which is a device for exposing verbal units in some prespecified order. An example of serial verbal learning is described below, in which the learner is required to learn a sequence of eight adjectives in the particular order shown:

Happy	Related
Slowly	Increasing
Cringing	Angry
Pretty	Changing

On the first presentation of the list, the learner is shown each word singly, beginning with "Happy" and ending with "Changing." The list is arbitrarily arranged and no *necessary* associations exist among the words. Nevertheless, the learner may quickly develop some connections on the basis of associations that link one item with another. On the next presentation of the list, the learner is shown the word "Happy," and is required to *anticipate* the next word "Slowly" before it is presented in the window of the memory drum. When the word "Slowly" appears, the learner must next try to anticipate the word "Cringing," and so on. When the learner can anticipate the entire list, learning is completed.

In this description of serial learning it is tempting to say that each item except the first and the last serves both as a "stimulus" and a "response." In the illustration given, "Slowly" is both a response to the word "Happy" and a stimulus for the word "Cringing." This view of serial learning, in which each item is a stimulus for the next response, is a longstanding one. Nevertheless, we now know that the position in the list may also become a cue for the correct response.

A reliable characteristic of serial learning is the bowed serial position curve. Figure 5 presents a typical serial position function showing the percentage of errors made during learning as a function of position in the list. THE FIGURE DESCRIBES THE FACT THAT MORE ERRORS ARE MADE WITH ITEMS IN THE MIDDLE AND JUST BEYOND THE MIDDLE OF THE LIST. FEWER ERRORS ARE MADE AT THE END OF THE LIST, AND FEWEST ARE MADE AT THE BEGINNING. The general shape of this curve holds for both meaningful materials as well as nonsense syllables.

Why is it that items in the middle of a verbal series are more difficult to learn, and that those at the beginning and end are easier to learn? Although we do not have a complete theory which can account for the serial position curve, two kinds of factors are known to be important. First, the items in the first and last positions are more readily discriminated by the learner since he quickly recognizes when the list begins and ends. There is more uncertainty on the part of the learner in locating the last item compared with the first, but both positions are more *discriminable* than items in the middle. Second, the middle items are subject to greater interference, in that confusion among these items is more likely to occur.

Paired Associate Learning

In paired associate learning, the task of the learner is to learn to associate pairs of items, one member of the pair being the stimulus item and the second member being the response term. With this procedure the experimenter designates which item serves as the

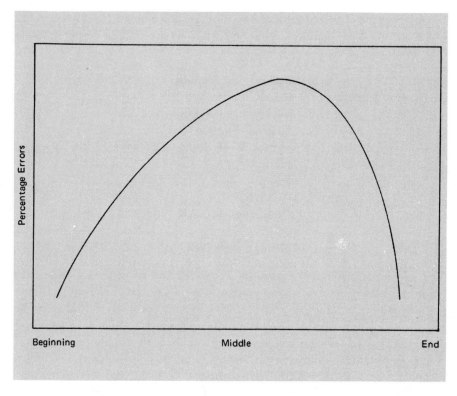

Figure 5. Graphic illustration of the bowed serial-position curve following learning of a serial list of items. Items just beyond the middle of the list show the largest percentage error, whereas items at the beginning and end of the list show fewer errors.

stimulus and which item serves as the response, in contrast to serial learning in which an item can serve both functions.

A familiar example of paired associate learning is the learning of foreign language vocabulary. Each foreign word is paired with its English equivalent and the task of the learner is to learn to produce the foreign word when presented with its English equivalent. The familiar procedure of learning foreign language vocabulary by the use of flash cards represents one instance of paired associate learning. More generally, any procedure that requires you to associate specific verbal responses to specific stimuli constitutes paired associate learning. It must be cautioned that not all aspects of foreign language learning are paired associate in nature; those features of language learning involving grammar and sentence construction involve other aspects, which will be described in a later chapter.

An example of paired associate learning is shown below in which familiar words are used as stimulus terms and trigrams are used as response terms.

Stimuli	*Responses*
Steady	
Steady	→ RUK
Urgent	
Urgent	→ LOZ
Happy	
Happy	→ VIR
Changing	
Changing	→ XAK
Slowly	
Slowly	→ NEQ

The pairings are completely arbitrary in this list and no necessary associative connection exists between the stimulus and response terms. The subject's task is to learn to associate each response with its stimulus word so that when he sees the stimulus word alone he can produce the correct response. This procedure is the paired associate *anticipation* method. Using the list above, the subject is first shown the stimulus term "Steady," and is then shown the stimulus-response pair, "Steady→RUK." He then sees "Urgent," and then "Urgent→ LOZ," followed by the remaining items. The items are presented for a constant duration, usually 2 seconds for the stimulus and 2 seconds for the stimulus-response pair. After seeing the entire list once, it is repeated for successive trials and the learner attempts to anticipate the correct response while each stimulus is present.

The order of the pairs in the list is varied from trial to trial, randomly, in order to prevent the learner from using serial position as a cue. An interesting example of the *failure* to vary the position of the pairs in a list is sometimes seen when a student, learning foreign language vocabulary by the use of flash cards, fails to change the order of the cards. In so doing, the student may deceive himself into thinking he has actually learned the pairs when, in fact, he may correctly recall some of the foreign words simply by inadvertently remembering the position of the pair in the series. This same problem can arise in memorizing foreign language vocabulary directly from the items printed in the text. Since the order of the printed items is fixed, failure to vary your test sequence may lead you to learn some of the items *only* on the basis of their printed position. Thus, whenever a task requires paired associate learning, it is critical that the order of presentation is varied on successive study trials to ensure that specific associations are being acquired.

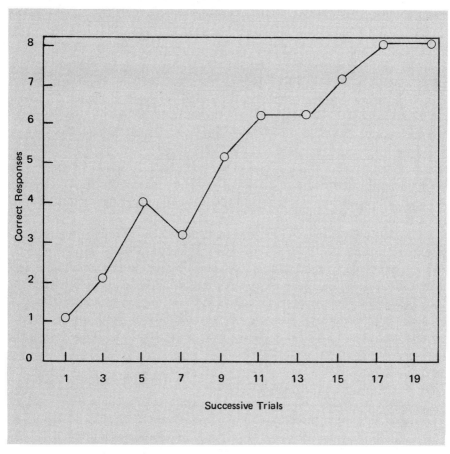

Figure 6. Paired associate learning curve for single subject. Graph shows gradual course of improvement with practice trials.

Subjects are required to learn the list of pairs to some performance criterion determined by the experimenter. Conventionally, the learner is required to learn to a complete mastery criterion of one or two perfect successive anticipations of all the response items in the list. The number of correct responses produced on each trial is recorded and a graph of this record portrays a learning curve for paired associates. Figure 6 shows such a record for a single subject whose task is to learn a list of eight paired associates.

The figure shows a plot of the number of correct anticipations for each trial. The first exposure trial is not counted since the subject does not anticipate; thus, the second exposure trial is the first anticipation trial. The figure shows a gradual although somewhat irregular course of improvement.

Components of Paired Associate Learning

What are the *components* of paired associate learning? This is simply to ask what are the processes or subprocesses that operate in paired associate learning. At least ten different processes have been identified; however, for the present only six of these will be briefly described. It is important to note that paired associate learning is a *multi-process* affair. Indeed, although the paired associate procedure was originally developed to study what was regarded as the formation of simple "rote" associations, it is now known that paired associate learning is far more complex than originally recognized, involving complex coding and organization of the materials. Important processes include those of: (1) stimulus discrimination, (2) response integration, (3) stimulus selection and coding, (4) association formation, (5) mediation, and (6) organizational processes.

The first process refers to the fact that subjects must learn to discriminate among or distinguish the stimulus terms in the list. *Stimulus discrimination* becomes a particularly significant process when the similarity among the stimuli is high. Obviously, the more difficult it is to distinguish among a set of stimuli, the greater the effect this process plays in retarding the rate of learning.

Response integration refers to the ability to produce or recall the response in the absence of the response term. If the response is difficult to pronounce or low in meaningfulness, then response learning plays a greater role than in the case where the response is highly familiar or available. For example, if the response terms are low-meaning trigrams such as WUH, XAV, and XEQ, then considerable effort must be made in learning to pronounce them reliably; in contrast, if familiar three-letter responses such as COW, ICE, and BOY are used as responses, then the role of response integration is minimal.

Stimulus selection refers to the fact that human subjects tend to use only a portion of an experimenter-presented stimulus. For example, if the stimuli consist of the trigrams HAV, BAZ, WUH, and XEQ, the learner need only *use* the first letter in each item in order to cue his response correctly. Rather than attend to the entire stimulus, humans tend to select certain portions of stimuli whenever this is possible. Subjects also *encode* stimuli, which means that they may transform them into some new state or representation. This process will be described in the next chapter.

After stimulus discrimination, selection, and encoding has occurred on the stimulus "side," and response integration and learning has occurred on the response "side," *association formation* can take place, which is the hookup of specific stimuli and specific responses. Subjects may also engage in *mediation*, which is the production and use of verbal linkages in helping to associate stimuli and responses. For instance, learning to associate the words "stem" and "smell" may be facilitated by a mediating link such as "flower." Finally, various *organizational* processes can take place. For example, the learner may group the pairs according to some rule that appears to make the task easier to learn.

These processes will be only briefly described at present. The principal point to note is that paired associate learning is far more than simple "rote" learning and involves a number of processes. Of particular importance is that the human is not passively acquiring stimulus-response associations as such, but is actively engaged in organizational, coding, and mediational processes in his effort to learn the task. This brief discussion alerts you to some of the complexities of a standard verbal learning task. In the following chapter we will explore these processes in greater detail.

Free Learning

In free learning the subject is presented a series of verbal items, one at a time, and required to recall the items without regard to order. The order of presentation of the units on each trial is varied and the learner is free to recall in any order he chooses. Hence the term *free learning,* or *free recall learning,* as it is sometimes called.

The units can be presented singly in several ways. The experimenter presents the materials at a steady rate. Frequently a memory drum is used and the exposure time is fixed for each item, such as 2 seconds. An alternative procedure is to present the subject with the complete list, give him a study interval, and then test for recall. An apparent limitation of this last procedure is that it does not permit control of the study time for each unit.

Methodologically, the free learning procedure is the simplest procedure to study verbal learning in that it is less "structured" by the experimenter. As an example, you would be presented a set of words, singly, such as the ones listed below, and asked to recall as many as you can. You would be given successive presentations of the list until you could recall all items, or until you reached some arbitrary criterion. With repeated trials, this is known as multitrial free recall learning. Imagine that you are presented these sixteen items:

Apple	Tea	Elephant	Soda
Lion	Potato	Spinach	Pear
Coffee	Orange	Milk	Cow
Cabbage	Seal	Lemon	Carrot

After the first few presentations, perhaps even on the first, you would probably notice that the verbal materials can be classified into four categories: vegetables, fruits, beverages, and animals. In turn, this could affect the *order* of recall of the items, in that during recall you would tend to report one category first, then another, and so on. THIS CLUSTERING IN THE ORDER OF RE-CALL IS TAKEN AS EVIDENCE THAT HUMANS ORGANIZE

EVENTS IN MEMORY. Indeed, one of the basic reasons for using the free recall procedure is to study organizational processes.

The above example is a simple one in that the categories are fairly obvious. We can, however, increase the difficulty of detecting the categories and study the ways in which humans try to organize materials when the cues for organization become extremely subtle or are not actually present in the list. In general, human subjects are sensitive to the cues present in "preorganized" lists and reorganize the list, as presented by the experimenter, in accordance with the cues, rules, or categories that are present in the list.

What about lists that have no evident structure or preorganization? Even where the experimenter makes no effort to preorganize the list, the learner attempts to organize the material in some fashion. This finding has been demonstrated by Endel Tulving, who found that there were significant consistencies in the order in which subjects recalled items from trial to trial, even though the order of presenting the items varied randomly. Tulving calls this *subjective organization,* emphasizing that humans impose their own organization in order to recall the items.

The results of free learning studies lend powerful support to the importance of the learner as a decision maker. The learner is clearly not passive, but is actively involved in seeking and trying strategies, looking for grouping rules, and imposing structure or organization in learning tasks, even those that involve relatively meaningless material. As a result, the free learning procedure has become increasingly popular in recent years in an attempt to discover what the subject does in learning activities. The free learning procedure is important because it permits an investigation of: (1) how the learner organizes the material, (2) the cues (for example, conceptual categories) that he detects during learning and uses during recall, and (3) what strategies the learner uses in retrieving items from memory.

Recognition Learning

The procedure of recognition learning has received increased use in recent years. *In recognition learning, the learner is shown the items in a study phase and then is tested for recognition on subsequent trials.* Recognition learning is similar to free learning during the study phase but is different during the testing phase. During testing the learner is presented with a series of items and asked to recognize them saying "yes" or "no," or "old" or "new," when he looks at each item. The series of test items consists of both "old" items that the subject has seen and "new," distractor items that are similar to the old items, in the sense of being from the same class.

Recognition learning does *not,* therefore, require the learner to recall or produce the items but only to recognize them in the sense of identifying them as "old" (previously seen in the set of items) and "new" (not previously seen).

Instances of recognition learning are quite common in our everyday experience. Learning to recognize the faces of people is an obvious instance. Becoming familiar with particular landmarks along a highway, or along a route that you frequently drive or walk, is another instance. *In essence, recognition learning is the process by which we become able to distinguish familiar from unfamiliar events in our environment.* It is very similar to the process of *discrimination learning*, the critical difference being that discrimination learning involves making specific responses in the presence of the stimuli. Recognition learning, in contrast, does not require the learner to make specific responses of any kind but merely requires him to indicate whether an item is "old" or "new." Paired associate learning can therefore be regarded as a special case of discrimination learning, in the sense that specific responses must be made to specific stimulus terms.

Recognition learning can be illustrated as follows: A subject is shown a series of items, singly, such as these words:

> Happy
> Slowly
> Cringing
> Pretty
> Related
> Increasing
> Angry
> Changing

Then he is shown a test sheet and asked to indicate which items were ones seen in the list and which items were not in the list. The test sheet contains the items the subject saw plus a set of distractor items as well. The distractor items are frequently synonyms of the words seen, or associates of the words, and new distractor items are used in each test with repeated-trial recognition learning experiments. An example of the test sheet would look like this; half of the items are old and half are new.

> Increasing   Furious
> Unstable   Cringing
> Frightened   Happy
> Pretty   Coupled
> Crawling   Related
> Slowly   Enlarging
> Changing   Angry
> Delighted   Attractive

In general, the more similar the distractor items are to the old items, the more difficult is recognition learning. For example, suppose that you were shown the following trigram pairs, or "doublets," and asked to learn them:

JOBFAD
RUMWIG
GIWYUB
VAWXIS
MITNOD
YEVCOJ
WEBFON
QUJGEC

The list is, of course, harder to learn than the list of familiar words, because the items are less meaningful. But now look at the recognition test, where the distractor items are extremely similar to the study items. It is quite clear that this is not any easy recognition task.

RAMWIG	WEBFON
VAWXIS	GIWYUB
QUJQEC	YEVCOJ
MITNOD	JOBFAD
GOWYUB	RUMWIG
YUVCOJ	QUJGEC
JEBFAD	VEWXIS
WIBFUN	MUTNOD

Indeed, it would require a number of study-recognition trials before you could correctly recognize all items. An important implication of this example is that if one wants to be sure of a "high" level of recognition learning, the distractor items should be made similar to the training items. When they are, you are forced to pay careful attention to the events that you must learn to recognize.

Two kinds of recognition tests are used: (1) In the *single-item* procedure, each item is shown one at a time and the subject is asked to say "old" or "new" to each item. Sometimes the subject is asked to rate his confidence in how old or new the item is so that the experimenter can obtain an estimate of "memory strength" for the items independent of the particular subjective criterion the subject has. The principal point to note is that with a single item procedure no direct control over the subject's criterion or response bias is present. For example, one person might be very conservative and therefore reluctant to say "old" or "yes" in the recognition test. Another person might be willing to say "old" frequently and thus get a higher recognition score just by virtue of his response bias. (2) In the *multiple–item procedure*, the subject is shown each item learned along with one or more distractor items. For instance, you might be shown the following set of items and asked to select the one that you saw in the list:

MUTNOD   MURCAD   MITNOD   MURNOD

Usually the experimenter requires the subject to select one of the items, thus making this a *forced-choice* procedure. The advantage of this approach is that it controls for possible differences in response bias that may be present.

On the basis of the above discussion, you may perhaps have tentatively decided that a multiple-choice exam is like a recognition learning experiment involving, unfortunately, only one trial. This is precisely the case, in that multiple-choice exams usually present you with four or five choices for each question and your task is to recognize the correct item. The student frequently asks the question: "Should I answer (guess?) all questions even though I don't know the answer to all of them?" The answer to this question hinges on whether your instructor uses what he calls a "correction for guessing." If he does not, then your best and only strategy is to answer all questions even if you have to guess on some. With a four-item choice you have a 1/4 chance of getting the answer correct by guessing, and since there is no penalty for guessing you have nothing to lose. Suppose, however, that he imposes a "guessing penalty." If you can narrow your choices by crossing out one or more obviously wrong answers it is still to your advantage to guess. Finally, if your instructor tells you to answer all questions, then it is obviously to your advantage to do so since, presumably, no guessing penalty will be used.

Verbal Discrimination Learning

Verbal discrimination learning procedures have not received the degree of use that have serial, paired associate, and free learning procedures. *With this procedure, subjects are presented verbal items in pairs, one of which has been arbitrarily selected as correct. The subject is required to learn which item of each pair is correct.* The list is repeated for successive trials and the subject has to anticipate the correct item on each trial. Usually the pairs are presented by means of a memory drum. An illustration of this procedure is given below, in which the verbal pairs are shown in the left-hand column and the arbitrarily correct responses in the right-hand column.

Happy Related	Happy
Cringing Increasing	Increasing
Angry Slowly	Slowly
Changing Pretty	Pretty
Rural Flabby	Rural

Drastic	Drastic
Icy	
Exact	Random
Random	
Lovely	Vacant
Vacant	

The verbal discrimination procedure is actually more like recognition learning than discrimination learning, in that the subject has only to recognize as distinct from recalling the responses.

Comparison of Procedures

Our five basic procedures vary not only in the degree of "task structuring" or control by the experimenter, but in the processes that operate. Different processes operate in each of these tasks, so we cannot regard verbal learning as always some homogeneous or general process. The various verbal learning procedures are not equivalent in the sense of tapping the same processes or mechanisms. In paired associate learning we can identify several processes, as noted earlier. There is response learning, associative learning, as well as stimulus discrimination and stimulus selection. Here the subject must learn to associate specific responses to specific stimuli.

In contrast, free learning does not require you to associate specific responses to specific stimuli; indeed, no item serves a specific stimulus function. The learner does have to recall the response terms, so free learning is a process that emphasizes response learning. Organizational processes also operate in the sense that the order of recall may be quite different from the order presented. In the case of category clustering, where the order or recall is correlated with the categories in the list, the category concept acts as a "stimulus." In this case, however, the stimulus is one that is derived from the properties of the list as distinct from being item-specific. In both recognition and verbal discrimination learning, the response learning component is eliminated in the sense that all the learner must do is look at the item and recognize it or select it. No recall of responses is necessary.

Factors Which Affect Verbal Learning

Let us now turn our attention to some of the major factors that affect the ease with which verbal materials are learned. Although a large number of factors are known to influence verbal learning, our discussion will concentrate on the major variables. The effect of a particular factor can vary with the kind of procedure used, so that in some instances we must describe the effects of a given variable on free learning, or paired associate learning, rather than verbal learning in general. We must also distinguish between the learning of discrete or single items, such as letters or trigrams, from the learning of connected materials, such as sentences or paragraphs. Important factors that affect the rate of learning verbal materials are meaningfulness, frequency, pronunciability, intralist similarity, imagery, associative relations, organizational processes, and grammatical structure.

Meaningfulness

Meaningfulness is unquestionably one of the major, if not the major, factors that determines the rate of learning verbal units. We have already noted that meaningfulness refers to the average number of associations elicited by a verbal item in a fixed time period. Meaningfulness is also used to denote, collectively, a number of scaled attributes of verbal materials, such as their association value, rated pronunciability, rated or judged number of associations an item will produce, and judged ease of learning. REGARDLESS OF HOW THE MEANINGFULNESS OF THE VERBAL UNIT IS MEASURED, MEANINGFULNESS IS A MAJOR FACTOR INFLUENCING THE EASE OF LEARNING VERBAL UNITS. This holds for all of the methods of learning described.

A typical relationship between item meaningfulness and ease of learning is portrayed in Figure 7. The figure indicates that the number of trials needed to learn a serial list of items decreases as the meaningfulness of the items increases.

The fact that all of our measures of meaningfulness predict learning extremely well does not, of course, explain the powerful relationship between meaningfulness and learning. In one sense, this relationship is not surprising because what a person is telling us when he rates the meaning of an item is how much he already knows about the item. Thus, the more he already knows the easier it is to learn.

Let us now consider the effects of meaningfulness in paired associate learning. Here our findings are somewhat more complicated. In paired associate learning we can, of course, vary independently the meaningfulness (M) of the stimulus and response terms. In this manner we can determine the relative importance of the two. The typical finding is graphed in figure 8, which shows acquisition curves for paired associates for four conditions involving all combinations of low- and high-stimulus-M and response-M. The figure shows a number of relationships. Clearly obvious is that the most rapid learning occurs when *both* stimulus and response-M are high (H-H), whereas the slowest rate occurs when both are low (L-L). The difficulty in learning increases in the order H-H, L-H, H-L, and L-L. The first letter of the sequence designates stimulus-M; the second letter, response-M.

More important is the fact that the effect of stimulus-M depends on whether response-M is low or high. Specifically, the figure reveals that VARIA-

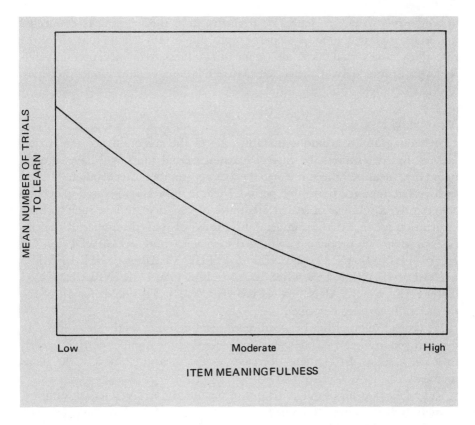

Figure 7. Relation between mean trials to learn a list and item meaningfulness. As the items increase in meaning, fewer trials are required to learn the list.

TIONS IN STIMULUS-M PRODUCE A MUCH GREATER EFFECT ON LEARNING WHEN RESPONSE-M IS LOW THAN WHEN IT IS HIGH. You can confirm this for yourself by noting that the difference between the curves for H-L and L-L conditions is much larger than the difference between the H-H and L-H conditions. When the effect of one or more factors on performance depends upon the values of another factor, we have what is called an *interaction*, in this instance, stimulus and response-M interact in their effect on the learning of paired associates. The figure shows another interaction in that *the effect of response-M on learning is greater when stimulus-M is low than when it is high.* You can see this by noting that the difference between the curves for L-H and L-L is greater than the difference between H-H and H-L. If you ignore, however, the complications of the interactions, *response-M has a larger overall effect on learning than does stimulus-M.*

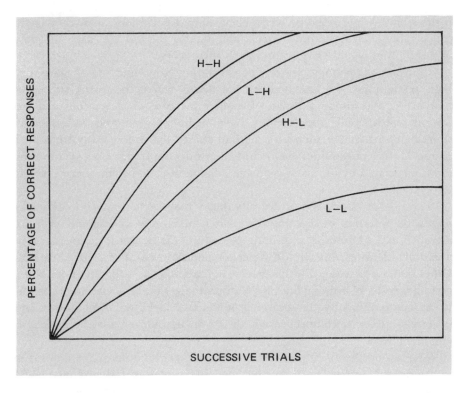

Figure 8. Paired associate acquisition curve for all combinations of low- and high-stimulus meaningfulness and low- and high-response meaningfulness. The first letter designates stimulus meaningfulness and the second letter response meaningfulness. For example, "H-L" means high-stimulus meaningfulness and low-response meaningfulness.

How Meaningfulness Affects Learning

Given that meaningfulness exerts a powerful effect on the learning of verbal materials, how do we account for this fact? What kind of theory is available to handle this finding? Intuitively, you might speculate that more meaningful material is easier to learn because it is more familiar, or because more associations come to mind, or that the material seems easier to integrate into a functional unit, or is perhaps less fragmented. These ideas capture, in part, two kinds of theories that have been proposed: (1) association probability theory, and (2) stimulus and response unitization.

The classical interpretation of the effects of meaningfulness on learning has come from *association probability theory*. The basic idea is that the more associations elicited by members of a pair, the greater the likelihood that an association from a stimulus and a response will link up in some manner. Moreover, if the stimulus and response terms elicit many associations, then they could conceivably elicit a common association, making the linkage easy. A variety of possibilities would exist according to this theory.

Consider, for example, the task of associating "cow" and "dog." Since they both are animals, the link between the two is easy if the learner thinks of animals as a common associate. Consider the case of associating two less obvious words, "bull" and "picnic." Here the linkage might be established by thinking of a sentence such as "The bull chased the couple away from their picnic." Other possibilities may readily occur to you. In this case, we have the terms associated by means of connected discourse rather than discrete, single associations.

Plausible as association probability theory may seem, it runs into difficulty on several accounts. First is that the greater the number of responses that are attached to a stimulus in a training procedure, the poorer is performance in a second task using these stimuli, a phenomenon know as the *interference paradox.* Other difficulties arise with this theory, in particular its difficulty in handling certain transfer of training findings. Suffice it to say that association probability runs into difficulty on several grounds and lacks sufficient power and generality to be a comprehensive theory in accounting for the effects of meaningfulness.

The second theory emphasizes that high-M verbal units are responded to in a more integrated, more unitized, or less fragmented fashion than low-M units, and that it is this feature that determines the ease with which they are learned or associated with each other. This theory stems from two directions, one emphasizing response learning and the other emphasizing stimulus learning.

On the response side, the theory emphasizes that response-M exerts its effect in learning because more meaningful responses can be treated as a *unit* by the learner. More meaningful responses are more integrated, or "unitized," and hence can enter into association formation more readily. This process has received considerable emphasis by George Mandler and subsequently by Benton Underwood and Rudolph Schulz. Words such as "table," "chair," "love," or "psychology" are obviously familiar and highly practiced words. You have already learned how to pronounce them and they function, therefore, as integrated units. On the other hand, verbal units such as REH, ZQ J or GXC are much less familiar and require considerable practice before they become integrated as a unit.

The matter of response integration can be further illustrated by comparing two trigrams, CEN and KYH. CEN has an association value of 100 percent and KYH a value of 0 percent. CEN enters into many words that you have already learned such as "century," "cent," "centimeter," "accent," "accentuate," to mention only a few. In contrast, KYH enters into no immediately obvious word. Thus, CEN is a response that is readily available as an integrated unit and requires little, if any, additional effort in learning. In contrast, KYH is not integrated and will require more trials to bring it to a state where it can enter into association formation.

A quite similar kind of explanation accounts for the effect of stimulus-M in paired associate learning. Here stimulus-M is seen to exert its effect via the stability of perceptual-recognition responses made to stimuli. The basic idea is that for a stimulus term to function reliably in evoking a given response, the stimulus must eventually be perceived in a relatively consistent fashion over successive trials. This theory contends that the learner makes some kind of *identifying* response to a stimulus term, a response that is implicit and serves as some kind of "representation" of the actual stimulus term. It is not so important to know what this representation or implicit response is, so long as one learns to respond to each stimulus term in some consistent or reliable fashion. Unless the learner can respond to each stimulus consistently, he cannot treat the stimulus of the moment as he did when he previously saw it, and hence cannot associate the stimulus and response terms except by chance.

Consider that CEN and KYH, used in our previous example, are stimulus terms in a list of paired associates. The high-M stimulus, CEN, produces its effect on learning because it can readily be treated as an integrated unit. As a high-M stimulus, it will likely be encoded in one way, and if the learner makes a subvocal response to the stimulus, a likely response is "sin." In contrast, the low-M stimulus, KYH, is fragmented, and does not readily produce a stable identifying response. In general, THE EFFECT OF STIMULUS-M IS DEPENDENT UPON THE EASE WITH WHICH STIMULI ARE CAPABLE OF PRODUCING STABLE, CONSISTENT IDENTIFYING RESPONSES.

One practical implication of how meaningfulness affects learning is the importance of integrating verbal stimuli and responses as units. Thus, when learning unfamiliar or relatively meaningless verbal materials, it is important to pronounce carefully and consistently the materials and to practice responses so that they can be readily recalled. Another implication that follows from our discussion applies to the learning of foreign language vocabulary, much of which is a case of response learning. It will be harder to learn a sequence going from English to, say, French items than it will be going from French to English. Since you must be able to recall the French words, your study of vocabulary should emphasize going from English to French, rather than the other direction. Learning a foreign language is not simply a matter of recognizing the English equivalents, but of integrating the foreign language vocabulary so that it is readily available for recall.

Familiarity, Frequency, and Pronunciability

The factors of familiarity, frequency, and pronunciability are all related to meaningfulness and are important factors affecting the rate of verbal learning. The fact that more familiar verbal materials are easier to learn is not too surprising, since ratings of familiarity are a measure of how much a person already knows about the material. Frequency refers to how frequently a word or unit appears in the English language, or to the frequency of actual use of the word. In general, the more frequently spoken or frequently used verbal units are easier to learn. Pronunciability is also an important factor in learning, with more pronunciable materials being easier to learn.

Although all three factors are good-to-excellent predictors of learning, the major concern in studying these factors has been to see if one of these is the *fundamental* factor underlying all the others. The discovery that these variables, including meaningfulness, could be reduced to a single fundamental one would allow a much simpler description of verbal learning. We are unable at present, however, to identify with certainty what the basic or fundamental factor is. Nevertheless, a good candidate for the fundamental factor is the frequency of actual use of the word in our natural language.

An interesting question arises should frequency turn out to be the basic factor underlying these other variables. We must still ask *how* is it that sheer frequency influences verbal learning. It may well be that it is not frequency as such, but that frequency produces its effect by allowing the learner to integrate and organize verbal materials. Regardless of how frequency affects learning, the fact is that some repetition is necessary for response learning. Thus, although what is sometimes called "meaningless drill" is insufficient as a complete approach to learning, some drill or repetition is still necessary if basic response sequences such as letters of the alphabet or multiplications are to be learned.

The point to be emphasized is that there is no escape from drill, practice, or repetition as long as the task involves a response learning component. Whether it be learning to read, to play tennis, or golf, to play the piano, to give well-delivered talks, or to speak a foreign language, the factor of frequency is very important.

Mental Imagery

Our ability to use mental images is a powerful factor in verbal learning. For instance, when learning paired-associate word pairs, the use of mental images or "pictures" greatly facilitates learning. By mental images is meant the kind of pictorial representation or arrangement which humans can construct on the basis of their own self-instructions, as when you "visualize" sitting down to a juicy steak dinner or, on the basis of instructions from someone else, conjure up a mental picture of some event or thing.

Mental imagery has been studied in two general ways. One way has been to instruct humans to construct mental images while learning verbal materials. The typical procedure is to instruct a subject just prior to his learning a list of paired-associates to "try and think of a mental picture that will relate the two words that must be associated." The second procedure is to vary the *imagery-value* of the words or verbal units in a learning experiment. The imagery of verbal materials is measured very much like meaningfulness; subjects are asked to rate the materials in their ease of generating imagery. Even without imagery instructions, HUMANS LEARN HIGH-IMAGERY PAIRS FASTER THAN LOW-IMAGERY PAIRS.

Imagine learning a set of paired associates in which three of the pairs were dog-bicycle, black-butter, and candy-cigar, and that you are instructed to construct a mental image or picture that will group or relate each pair. With the first pair you might visualize a picture of a dog riding a bicycle in a circus, or a dog running beside a boy riding a bicycle, or any of a number of possible images. A plate of black butter might come to mind with the second pair, unpleasant as that might be, and a picture of a candy cigar or a picture of a candy and cigar counter in a local drug store might arise with the third pair. All of these would serve to relate both words in the same picture, and thus would facilitate learning.

An additional fact about imagery is that imagery or mental practice can improve performance in motor skills. For example, mental rehearsal or practice can facilitate basketball shooting. Although we are unclear if the effect is due to mental imagery as such as distinct from covert verbalization about basketball shooting, it is clear that instructions to mentally practice a skill can lead to actual improvement in the skill.

As we noted earlier, the imagery value of verbal materials determines their ease of learning. In paired associate learning we can vary independently the imagery-value of the stimulus and response terms, just as we vary meaningfulness. In this case, imagery value of both stimulus and response terms facilitates learning. In addition, however, STIMULUS IMAGERY IS A MORE IMPORTANT FACTOR THAN IS RESPONSE IMAGERY IN AFFECTING RATE OF LEARNING. This is of interest because it contrasts with the effect of meaningfulness on the rate of verbal learning, where response meaningfulness was seen to be more important than stimulus meaningfulness. We will return to the matter of how imagery and meaningfulness are related shortly.

Why does stimulus imagery exert such a powerful effect on learning? Allan Paivio has proposed a conception in which the stimulus term is viewed as "conceptual peg" to which the subject hangs his response during learning. The response term is recalled during testing by way of the conceptual peg. The more likely a stimulus term arouses an image, then the better able the learner is to recall or retrieve the appropriate response.

Given that imagery is so important in learning, you may then wonder if it is possible for humans to become trained in skillfully producing images. Although we have no experimental evidence on this question, causal thought would indicate that this could be achieved. Certainly you could try to do this yourself by attempting to visualize mental pictures when reading text or other materials. You may already tend to do this when you read novels and you can do this with course materials. For instance, when reading a history text, try to visualize mental images of the significant events involving such things as diplomatic negotiations, important battles, and major cultural achievements. Similarly, in courses such as biology and geology you should try to construct mental images of the important features of the subject. Instances of such features in biology would include cross-sectional drawings of leaf structures and anatomical structures of animals, whereas soil stratification would be one in geology. Even in mathematics, mental imagery is important; here you can visualize graphic pictures of equations so that you "see" how one variable changes as a function of another. *More generally, whenever you can conveniently generate mental images of things or events, you should do so as a powerful aid to both learning and memory.*

The matter of imagery and meaningfulness will now be considered. These two variables, as you might suspect, are highly correlated. Therefore, you might conclude that since they are correlated, one factor can serve to explain the effects of the other. This, however, is not the case. If, in studies of paired associate learning, the imagery-value of words is varied with their meaningfulness kept constant, imagery continues to facilitate learning. On the other hand, if meaningfulness is varied with imagery-value kept constant, the effect of meaningfulness on learning is completely eliminated! This finding is extremely significant because it suggests, first, that the previously described effects of meaningfulness on learning may actually be due to uncontrolled variations in imagery, and second, that the imagery-arousing properties of verbal materials may be the fundamental factor in verbal learning. Whatever the outcome, our results regarding mental imagery make it stand as one of our most powerful variables in verbal learning, one that cannot be neglected by the learner.

Intralist Similarity

Intralist similarity is another factor which exerts considerable influence on verbal learning. Moreover, the effects of similarity depend on the kind of verbal learning task; in some cases, similarity aids learning and in others it hinders learning. Before we examine these effects in detail, we need first to look at what is meant by similarity in verbal learning.

Formal similarity of verbal materials is defined by the number of common or overlapping letters that are used in constructing a list of items. The greater the number of "common elements" the greater the similarity of the items. The two lists of trigrams below represent lists high and low in similarity:

High Similarity	Low Similarity
TRM	RFG
THR	KJC
TRH	DPZ
TMR	VMX
THM	LNS
TMH	HQB

The high-similarity list contains only four different letters, while the low-similarity list is made up of 18 different letters. No letter is repeated in the low-similarity list. In the high-similarity list, T is the first letter in each trigram; R, H, and M are each represented twice in the second-letter position, and are each represented twice in the third-letter position.

In addition to verbal materials, other stimuli, such as shapes, dot patterns and objects, can be varied in formal similarity (number of features in common).

Words can also vary in *meaningful similarity*, in that a list high in similarity would consist of synonyms such as productive, hard-working, efficient, ambitious, driving, etc., whereas a low-similarity list would consist of unrelated words.

Words may also be *conceptually similar* in that they belong to the same category, or represent instances of the same concept. If the list contained the items "Phoenix," "Tucson," "Albuquerque," "El Paso," and "Las Vegas," you would recognize tham as cities in the Southwestern United States.

As we noted above, the effects of similarity depend upon the nature of the learning task. In *free learning*, both meaningful and conceptual similarity facilitate learning. If the items in a free learning experiment can be categorized or classified conceptually, we find that such words are recalled more readily than if the words belong to different categories. Both meaningful and conceptual similarity produce their effect on recall because, when the items are highly similar and thus easily classified into a category, you can recall the various items by recalling the category name. This point was made earlier in the discussion of free recall as a method. Moreover, when the items are conceptually or meaningfully related, the likelihood that one instance of a category will produce recall of another instance is increased. For example, if the category class is American automobiles, then recall of one instance, Chevrolet, can lead to the association of Buick, as well as many others.

In *paired-associate* learning, similarity produces mixed effects on rate of

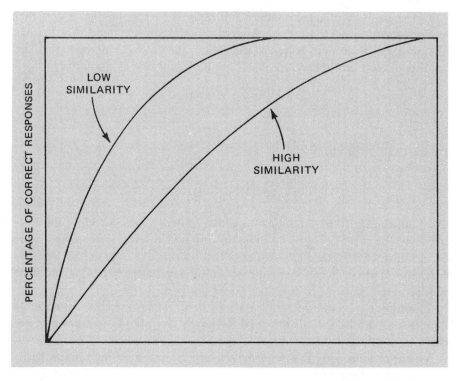

Figure 9. Paired associate acquisition curves for two conditions of intralist stimulus similarity. The graph shows that the rate of acquisition is slower when the stimuli are high in intralist stimulus similarity.

learning. If the response terms are made increasingly similar, along meaningful or conceptual dimensions, the response learning stage is achieved faster even though overall rate of learning is reduced. This is simply to say that response similarity aids response learning but interferes with associative learning.

Increasing the formal similarity of the stimulus terms in a paired associate task greatly increases the difficulty of learning. For example, figure 9 shows paired associate learning curves for lists in which the stimulus terms were those illustrated above, and response terms were meaningful three-letter responses, such as "cow," "ice," and "boy." The figure indicates that the high-similarity list is more difficult to learn, taking almost twice as long to learn as the low-similarity list. That this should happen does not seem too surprising. When the stimuli are highly confusable, or difficult to distinguish, you are unable to be sure on each trial exactly which stimulus term is appropriate. More generally, it is simply more difficult to acquire stable identifying responses to stimuli that are highly similar, and thus learning is retarded.

This discussion further implies that what determines the difficulty of learning is not so much a matter of features or properties of a single stimulus, but rather properties of the entire stimulus set. In other words, it is not simply the characteristics of the individual items, but also the *structure* of the set that determines how we learn.

Additional Factors in Learning

Our discussion has emphasized the factors of meaningfulness, familiarity, frequency, pronunciability, imagery, and similarity as important in human verbal learning. Additional factors that include associative relations, coding and organizational factors, and grammatical structure will be discussed in the following chapter. We have alluded to these factors in our present discussion, but will explore them more fully.

Finally, although we have described how these variables affect learning, and have illustrated their role in a number of everyday situations, we shall delay extensive consideration of practical use of these findings until we have completed our account of verbal learning and memory.

Summary

This chapter has described the major laboratory procedures for studying verbal learning and the fundamental factors that affect verbal learning. The study of verbal learning began with the effort to understand how humans form and retain verbal associations. Verbal learning was seen, however, to be a much more complex process than originally conceived; it is currently viewed as being composed of several processes.

The laboratory study of verbal learning has typically employed five types of procedures: serial learning, paired associate learning, free learning, recognition learning, and verbal discrimination learning. Each procedure "taps" somewhat different processes or components of verbal learning and hence there is no single procedure for studying verbal learning. A detailed account of each procedure was given, since the procedures and variations upon them are widely used throughout human learning research.

The major factors influencing verbal learning were described. Meaningfulness was seen to be a principal factor and its effect on learning was described as being due to the more integrated (or less fragmented) character of meaningful verbal materials. Familiarity, frequency, and pronunciability are also important factors facilitating the ease of verbal learning. These factors were seen as especially important when the task involved a heavy response learning component. The use of mental images was also observed as a potent factor in verbal learning. Imagery appears to be an important factor in learning because it allows humans to relate verbal materials as a functional unit. The similarity of materials (intralist similarity) was seen to have a complex effect on learning, both retarding and facilitating learning, depending upon type of similarity and component of learning involved.

The study of verbal learning employs a wide range of verbal materials from single letters, trigrams, and words to sentences and paragraphs. Many of these materials have been scaled for properties such as meaningfulness and association value, so that these effects upon learning can be examined. The choice of particular materials is largely dependent upon the type of process under investigation.

Everyday learning situations were seen to contain many of the features of typical verbal learning procedures. Illustrations of these were cited with each basic procedure; however, no extensive applications of the principles of verbal learning were given in this chapter since the purpose of this chapter was principally one of describing basic procedures and factors influencing learning. More thorough application of these principles will begin and continue in subsequent chapters.

True-False Items: Characteristics of Verbal Learning

1. Since verbal learning is essentially a matter of rote ("brute-force") learning, it is of little consequence to human behavior.

(Verbal learning is a fairly complex affair consisting of coding and organizational processes, as well as response learning, stimulus selection, etc. These more complex processes are important in many aspects of human behavior. False.)

2. The learning of meaningless nonsense syllables enables psychologists to study verbal association formation "from scratch."

(Even nonsense syllables can be meaningful to adults, in the sense that a nonsense syllable will tend to elicit one or more associations. False.)

3. The memorization of several lines of poetry would be an instance of serial learning.

(You have to learn this material in a particular order, which makes it a case of serial learning. True.)

4. In learning a serial list of verbal items, items near the middle of the list are hardest to learn, with items at the beginning and end of the list being easier.

(This principle holds over a wide range of verbal materials and is known as the serial position effect. True.)

5. In paired associate learning, the verbal pairs are presented in a fixed order and sequence.

(The position of the pairs in the list is varied from trial to trial so that particular pairs rather than positions are learned. False.)

6. Learning the alphabet in the sense of learning to pronounce properly each letter of the alphabet, when shown each letter alone, is an instance of paired associate learning.

(Here the task is that of learning to associate a particular response [pronunciation] in the presence of a particular stimulus [letter symbol]. True.)

7. In free learning situations, humans can organize the material only if there are objective categories present in the list.

(Humans tend to organize the material in some fashion, even if readily available objective categories are not present. This process is called subjective organization. False.)

8. Both free learning and verbal discrimination learning emphasize the response learning process.

(Free learning does demand response learning in that recall of the responses is required; however, verbal discrimination learning requires only that the learner recognize and select the correct response. False.)

9. Meaningful verbal items such as words are more readily learned than, say, low-association-value trigrams, because the meaningful items can be more readily treated as a unit.

(More meaningful verbal materials are more easily treated as an integrated unit. True.)

10. In paired associate learning, being able to construct a mental image of the response term is more important than constructing an image of the stimulus term.

(Just the reverse is the case. The more likely the stimulus arouses an image, the easier it is to retrieve [get to] the response term. False.)

11. The items "San Francisco," "Los Angeles," and "San Diego" are more likely to be recalled together than the items "Seattle," "Kansas City," and "Atlanta," because the former items are conceptually similar, and hence can be easily grouped for purposes of recall.

(The former items are all related in that they belong to the category of California cities; the latter three cities cannot be grouped so easily. True.)

12. Increasing the formal similarity of stimuli in a paired associate task increases the ease of learning the task.

(On the contrary, as the stimulus items are made more confusable [similar], rate of learning is decreased. False.)

4 ——————————————————————————————

Processes in Verbal Learning

In this chapter we shall turn our attention to the examination of fundamental processes in verbal learning. Psychologists are not content simply to describe the factors that govern human learning but seek to discover the basic processes that underlie a variety of learning situations. Learning psychologists try to understand the fundamental features of various learning situations by analyzing them into their simplest processes. For example, learning how to read is a complex event that can be analyzed into various components or processes that make up the total learning situation. Reading involves a variety of processes; obviously, in order to learn to read you must learn to discriminate among the letters of the alphabet, and to make the appropriate "sound" to each letter. You must learn to recognize the letters, to pronounce the letters, and to "blend" the individual letter pronunciations into integrated units, since reading is obviously not simply a matter of "sounding" individual letters.

This process of breaking down learning tasks into their individual components is called *component analysis*. Component analysis seeks to isolate and study the processes or components that contribute to some overall event. The fundamental objective of this approach is to discover the laws under which the various processes operate. The search is thus for general laws of human learning, laws that will enable us to understand a wide variety of particular learning situations.

We have already alluded to the component analysis of verbal learning tasks in the previous chapter when we noted some of the processes in free recall and paired associate learning. We will now examine these processes in greater detail, with an emphasis on the paired associate learning task to illustrate the various processes.

Some Basic Processes in Verbal Learning

In the last chapter we noted that paired associate learning is composed of at least ten identifiable processes, of which several were briefly described. Since the paired associate situation allows for the operation of so many processes, it serves as a good model for study purposes.

Response and Associative Learning

What must you do in order to learn a list of paired associates? Two things appear immediately and intuitively obvious. First, you must learn the responses to the point that you can recall them, and second, you must "hook-up" the responses to the stimuli. This first stage, in which the responses become integrated so that they are available for recall, is the *response learning stage*. The second stage, which requires hooking up particular responses to particular stimuli, is the *associative stage*.

If the responses are low in meaningfulness or are difficult to pronounce, then much of your effort will be devoted to response learning, that is, integrating the responses into available units. This must be achieved to some reasonable level before associative learning can take place. The responses do not have to be fully integrated before some associative learning begins to take place; nevertheless, before association formation can occur, *some* kind of response must be available. The distinction between response and associative phases identifies the two-stage theory of paired associate learning first noted by Carl Hovland and Kenneth Kurtz and later developed by Benton Underwood and Rudolph Schulz.

The term response learning may be troublesome to you if you have learned to think of learning entirely as the establishment of stimulus-response associations. Keep in mind that all that is meant by response learning is that process by which you integrate a verbal response so that it functions as a readily recallable unit; that is, so that it becomes available. If the response items are familiar words from the English language, then in no sense are the responses "learned." Such words are already available and can readily enter into association formation with stimuli. Indeed, the way psychologists bypass the study of response learning is to use highly available responses such as English words or numbers.

Stimulus Discrimination

Now let us turn our attention to processes that operate on the "stimulus side" of paired associate learning. Although the first influential theory of verbal learning emphasized stimulus learning processes, these were subsequently regarded as playing only a minor role in verbal learning. In turn, response and associative learning were regarded as primary because of the wide acceptance of the two-stage theory. In recent years, however, a substantial renewal of interest in stimulus processes has developed. It is now widely recognized that what humans do with stimuli is an important part of the learning process.

Discrimination among stimuli is a basic process in paired associate learning. We have already noted that the learner must reliably distinguish among the stimulus terms if he is to associate specific stimuli with specific responses. Moreover, the greater the similarity of the stimuli, the more important this process becomes. On the other hand, if the stimuli are already highly distinctive, then discrimination plays only a small role.

But what does it mean to say that a person discriminates among stimuli? At a fundamental level this simply means that you can respond differently in the presence of different stimuli, despite the fact that the stimuli may possess many common features. Identical twins appear very much alike, and yet you know of instances where you can reliably distinguish between them. The cockpit of a commercial airliner contains many dials and panels which look quite similar, yet the trained pilot can quickly discriminate them. Burgundy and chianti may taste similar to you when you initially experience these two red wines, yet with experience you can readily tell the difference even if blindfolded.

Stimulus Selection

But we do not always deal with stimuli "just as they come." Humans engage in *stimulus selection*, that is, they will use only a portion of an experimenter-presented stimulus as distinct from the entire stimulus. The experimenter-presented stimulus is the *nominal* stimulus, whereas the *functional* stimulus is that part which the subject uses to cue a response. For example, in a paired associate task the stimuli that are actually presented by the experimenter, such as XOL, KUF, and TAZ, are the nominal stimuli. What the learner chooses to use constitutes the functional stimuli. With these trigrams the learner may select and use only the first letter of each, so that the functional stimuli are X, K, and T.

What functional stimulus selection does is to enable more efficient learning. You do not have to attend to and recognize the entire stimulus unit, but only a portion of the stimulus. In this fashion, redundant information can be ignored so as to facilitate learning.

Stimulus selection is such a frequent and routine process that you may not be aware of its operation. You need not, for example, see an entire person in order to identify him; you need only see his face. Moreover, you can identify some of your close friends even if you saw only a portion of their faces. You might, as an exercise, have someone cover up portions of a photograph of someone you know and see how much "loss" you can take and still identify the person.

The fact that we respond to fewer than all of the cues present, which is to say that we learn to ignore redundant information, is quite evident from the behavior of skilled readers. The fast reader does not look at each individual word and ignores much unnecessary information. Words such as *the, an,* and *of* tend to be ignored by the fast reader because he can pick up the meaning of each sentence from less than the total sentence. He has learned to respond to subtle grammatical cues which will do the job of cueing his reading. Similarly, when we read someone's poor handwriting, we can guess the words on the basis of the likely sequence of letters in the English language.

Stimulus selection experiments involve presenting the learner with a set of *compound stimuli.* Compound stimuli contain two or more elements that can be used to cue a response. For example, in a paired associate task, each stimulus in the list can consist of a word and a color, both elements being relevant cues. By "relevant" is simply meant that the learner can actually use the cue to recall the response term. Following paired associate training, the subject is shown each element alone and in combination and asked to recall the appropriate response. In this manner it can be determined if the subject is using the word cue alone, color alone, or the word-color combination to cue his response. Sometimes subjects respond to elements alone and sometimes they respond to the pattern of stimulation, that is, the combination of elements.

When do subjects select elements and when do they respond to patterns? In general, subjects will tend to select elements if the stimuli are constructed so as to allow this. In other words, we will use some component that differentiates the stimulus from others in the set, which is to say that we tend to minimize stimulus redundancy if possible. On the other hand, if the stimuli have a high degree of overlap, then we will tend to respond to the pattern rather than individual elements. This will occur because the stimuli do not allow the selection of particular elements as valid predictors of the response.

What factors influence stimulus selection? In general, humans select the more *meaningful* elements, the more *familiar* elements, and the more *salient* or attention-getting elements. The use of gaudy roadsigns, bright neon lights, and banner headlines are examples of salient stimuli.

Stimulus Selection, Perception, and Attention

The fact that we engage in stimulus selection does not mean that we fail to perceive the other stimuli present. Some stimuli are perceived by the learner but are not necessarily used, in the sense that they do not become associated with the response terms. In other cases, the "secondary" or less "dominant" element may become associated with the response term, but to a weaker degree. There is evidence that under conditions of extended practice involving overtraining, humans tend to acquire some associative strength between the "secondary" cues and the responses. For instance, in laboratory investigations of cue selection where word-trigram compounds are used as stimuli (such as "Happy XUJ"), humans first learn to associate the word with the response term, but with overtraining the less meaningful element (trigram) will gain some strength in controlling recall of the responses.

The fact that secondary or less dominant cues gain some control with overtraining seems consistent with our everyday experience. For example, in driving on a strange road where you are completely unfamiliar with the landmarks, you first govern your driving by paying attention to the highway signs. These signs function as the dominant stimulus elements. After you have travelled over this road a number of times, other cues along the way can come to control your behavior. Bridges, mountains, farmland, stores, gas stations, etc., can also serve as useful cues enabling you to be sure that you are driving in the correct direction. Indeed, you may be able to reach your destination without using the highway signs at all, being totally cued by other stimuli.

The fact that with overtraining we tend to pick up secondary cues suggests that we tend to *relax* our attention or focus on the dominant cues with over-training. It is as if at the beginning of a learning task we narrow our attention to some dominant or focal stimulus. As we attain mastery of the task and continue to overlearn, we can relax our attention and attend to other cues in our enviroment.

But why would we relax our attention with extended practice? We certain-ly do not need to use the additional cues in a learning situation once we have learned to associate the dominant cue with the correct response. Although we are not entirely clear why we would relax our attention, we most likely do this because it relieves boredom. In our example above, to continue looking at and *using* only the highway signs could become boring if we have to travel this road frequently. Although we do not *need* to use the other cues along the road, they provide for stimulus variation. Thus, there is truth to the old notion that "variety is the spice of life."

Stimulus Coding

In addition to stimulus discrimination and stimulus selection, humans will *code* stimulus input. *Stimulus coding is the process in which you change or transform a nominal stimulus into some new "state" or representation.* For example, if the stimuli in a learning task consisted of the geometric figures △, ○, □, you will readily code these stimuli as "triangle," "circle," and "square." It is not necessary that you say these words aloud; implicit or subvocal verbalization may serve to code the stimuli. Moreover, codes may involve mental images as well as being verbal. Except perhaps for the simplest kind of stimuli, our performance seems not to depend directly upon the physical properties of nominal stimuli, but upon the manner in which we code the stimuli.

Transformations of nominal stimuli into some "representation" may be of the one-to-one variety, involving a particular transformation of each nominal stimulus as in the above example, or they may be of a several-to-one arrangement in which two or more nominal stimuli receive the same transformation. We also distinguish between *substitution coding*, which is the replacement of the stimulus input with a new representation, and *elaboration coding*, which requires the storage of additional information with the unit to be remembered. An example of the latter would be changing the trigram FAV into "favor."

We frequently code stimulus events by giving them shorthand verbal labels. For example, the student union building becomes the SUB; the University of Southern California becomes SC; International Business Machines becomes IBM. We also code unfamiliar visual patterns by giving them verbal labels.

The coding of stimuli does not always improve our ability to learn paired associates. Consider the anagrams RELABV and RELASN which, as stimulus terms in a paired associate list, would require some effort to discriminate. By coding (transforming) them into VERBAL and LEARNS they can be more readily discriminated than in their initial state. If, however, it requires more effort on your part to code the stimuli than it does simply to discriminate them as they exist, then coding will not facilitate learning.

Final Comments on Stimulus Mechanisms

The processes of stimulus discrimination, stimulus selection, and stimulus coding all emphasize a major principle: IT IS ESSENTIAL THAT THE LEARNER COME TO PERCEIVE EACH STIMULUS IN A LEARNING SITUATION IN A RELATIVELY CONSISTENT FASHION IF A GIVEN STIMULUS IS TO BECOME ASSOCIATED WITH A GIVEN OVERT RESPONSE. The stimulus of the moment must, in the course of learning, come to be regarded as it was on previous occasions; otherwise it cannot serve as a valid signal or occasion for a response. Treating a nominal stimulus in a consistent fashion is the process of *stimulus identification*, a process that must occur if association formation is to be achieved.

The process by which humans come to treat a stimulus on one occasion as the same as on another involves at least two distinct but related components. First, the learner must search and scan the nominal stimulus, especially if it involves many dimensions or elements, and then the learner must make some kind of identifying response to the stimulus. Although we are unsure of the exact nature of the identifying response, it is some kind of implicit response that classifies a given nominal stimulus in a consistent manner over the course of training. Intuitively, stimulus identification is the process by which you look at a stimulus and say to yourself, "Yes, that is one that I have seen before in this learning task and it is the stimulus for a specific response."

How Are Associations Formed?

Let us now turn our attention to *how* we form associations. We have described many of the important factors that influence association formation, but we have not yet touched on how associations are formed. The answer to this question is complicated by the fact that the study of association formation in humans typically involves associations that they have already learned. If, for example, you are asked to pair such words as boy-girl and table-chair, your already-existing associations will help you learn the pairs. If there is no direct connection between the items, then we frequently use mediating associations to help us link the terms. Thus, the study of association formation from "scratch" is difficult to achieve with human subjects.

We obviously learn associations by bringing to bear our rich associative networks in linking stimuli and responses. But can association formation take place without these links? Can two things be associated just because they occur contiguously, without any mediation linkages or intent on the part of the learner to learn? The answer appears to be yes.

Let us see how association formation on the basis of *contiguity* of stimuli and responses can occur. In an experiment by Norman Spear and his colleagues, human subjects were required to learn a verbal discrimination task. You will recall that in verbal discrimination learning, the subject has only to recognize which member of each pair of words the experimenter has designated as correct. He is under no instructions, of course, to associate the two words, and is not required or motivated to do so. Under such circumstances, will any association formation develop between the two words, given that they are presented and perceived contiguously?

The test of this was to place the words, after they were first used in a verbal discrimination task, into a paired associate task. The subjects did not know that they would be shifted to a paired associate task, so there is no reason to suspect that they intentionally tried to associate the words. Nevertheless, the results indicated that prior verbal discrimination training substantially facilitated subsequent paired associate learning, compared with control subjects who did not receive practice on these pairs. This finding is strong evidence for the view that *contiguity* itself may be all that is necessary for association formation to occur, a view which harkens back to British associationism. This position emphasizes that we learn something about everything to which we are exposed.

Are Associations Formed Gradually?

Everything that has been said so far implies that associations are formed gradually. Presumably, repeated presentations or trials are necessary for association formation to occur. According to this view, association formation is a gradual and continuous process which takes place over repeated trials.

In contrast to this gradual or *incremental* view is the notion that associations are formed on an *all-or-none* basis. This latter view emphasizes that once an association is formed, it develops full associative strength. In other words, it develops maximum strength or none at all.

Common experience tends to support the incremental view. As we reflect on our everyday learning experiences, they seem to be gradual in nature, taking place over several or many trials. Yet this apparently gradual nature of association formation may hide or cover up the fact that single pairs are learned in an all-or-none fashion. For example, single pairs could be learned on an all-or-none basis despite the fact that an ordinary learning curve for paired associates is gradual in nature.

At present we are unable to give a definitive answer to this question. Indeed, the issue of incremental versus all-or-none conceptions of association formation turns out to be far more complicated than it was originally thought to be. At present it can be said that some results regarding association formation are best viewed as evidence for an incremental view, whereas others seem consistent with an all-or-none view. Like theoretical problems in other areas, such as physics, we will have to be content with two views of a process. For example, in physics we have two theories of light, one regarding light as a wave propogation process and the other regarding light as consisting of units or quanta of energy. Under certain circumstances the wave conception best handles known findings and under other circumstances the quantal conception does a better job.

Directionality of Associations

Are associations learned in both directions? We commonly describe association formation in terms of recalling the responses to the appropriate stimuli. These are called *forward associations* in that the direction is from stimulus to response. In contrast, a *backward association* is assumed when you can recall a stimulus when presented the response as a cue.

It is quite clear that we do form backward associations in the course of learning paired associates. People do learn the reverse relationships, even though the backward association is usually weaker. For instance, in learning the vocabulary of a foreign language, you not only learn the pairs in a forward direction but you also learn the reverse association to some extent.

The fact that the backward association is usually weaker is quite understandable. We have, in the course of learning, only to *recognize* the stimulus terms, whereas we must *recall* the response terms. This means that the responses are much better learned, in the sense of being more available for recall than are the stimuli. Thus, when we test for backward associations we may be unable to recall the stimulus even though we are able to recognize it. This finding stresses that associations are *asymmetrical*, being stronger in the forward than in the backward direction.

There is, however, a contrasting view which emphasizes *associative symmetry*. According to this view, the strength of a forward association between *a* and *b* is equal to the strength of the backward association between *b* and *a*. Although this may seem counter-intuitive, the argument for symmetry is based largely on the typical difference in availability of stimulus and response terms. Since the response terms are more available than the stimulus terms, it is argued that *if* the stimuli were made as available as the responses, then no difference in the strength of two associations would exist. Attempts to make the stimuli as equally available as the responses have not always produced associative symmetry, however, which leaves the issue unresolved. One thing is clear: backward associations are weaker, given the greater availability of responses over stimuli.

Organizational Processes in Verbal Learning

We shall now turn our attention to the role of the *learner* himself. Everything that has been said so far has emphasized the importance of organizational processes in learning. The learning of verbal materials is achieved not simply by the mechanical "stamping in" of associations. Nor can verbal learning be viewed as simply a special case of classical conditioning, in the sense that responses become "elicited" by specific stimuli through a strictly associative process. Analogies between conditioning principles and human verbal learning have not always been useful in helping us to unravel the complexities of human verbal learning or to understand the contributions of the learner himself.

In our analysis of free recall learning in the previous chapter, we saw that humans *react* to learning tasks in that they organize verbal materials in a fashion different from the way they are presented. The fact that materials are recalled in an order different from the input order was seen as one kind of evidence for organizational processes in learning. Another kind of organizational process was the transformation of specific stimulus items, which is known as *stimulus coding*. In both instances, we emphasized the learner as active rather than passive, as one who brings to bear a diverse set of processes to the learning situation in an effort to learn the task.

Organizational processes are those activities engaged in by humans which involve some kind of change or transformation of the materials to-be-learned. You must be careful, however, not to use organizational processes in some glib way and you should note that organizational processes are something that we *infer* from differences between input characteristics of the materials and output features of performance. In general, we distinguish between *three* kinds of organizational efforts engaged in by humans: (1) changes in the order of items presented to the subject, (2) changes in the items themselves, and (3) mediational activities which involve the linking of items that have been changed.

Changes in the Order of Presentation

We have already described the fact that humans will rearrange the order in which materials are presented. When you are presented with a series of verbal items and required to recall them, your recall order or "output" of the items can differ from the "input" order in which they are presented. This change in recall order is called *clustering* and, as we noted earlier, is one kind of evidence for organizational processes in verbal learning.

Sometimes we cluster or organize verbal materials simply by associating one item with another. If the materials presented contain mutual associates, then we tend to recall them as such. This process is called *associative clustering*. For example, the pairs *boy-girl*, *night-day*, *bread-butter*, and *cat-dog* are likely to be recalled together even though the items were presented in a scrambled order.

Another kind of clustering is *category clustering,* in which the recall of items is related to specific conceptual categories in the list. Things that can be classified in some way tend to be recalled together. For instance, in recalling names of people we know, we may tend to recall close friends, then relatives, and then acquaintances. Moreover, we tend to recall more items from conceptually related lists than from lists in which the items are unrelated.

Finally, humans will impose their own organization on verbal lists when no evident organization or structure is present. This, we have noted, is called *subjective organization*.

Let us suppose, for example, that I attempted to recall the names of all my acquaintances and friends. My recall of the list would most likely show evidence of clustering in accordance with the names of personal friends, relatives, professional acquaintances, neighbors, etc. If I then gave you my complete list of names and asked you to learn them, you would organize them, but obviously in a quite different way from my organization. My recall would show category clustering, whereas your recall would show subjective organization.

How would you recall the list if no evident organizational basis was present? You might, perhaps, recall the list in a variety of ways; clusters might appear in accordance with alphabetic groupings of last names, with groupings of names in accordance with national origins, or in accordance with length of names, just to mention a few possibilities.

Why is it that conceptually related materials are better recalled than materials from an "unrelated" list? There are two kinds of explanations and there is evidence for both. One account emphasizes that conceptually related items are recalled better because of what we do *during* learning. Better recall occurs because we *store* conceptually related items more efficiently. How this is the case is somewhat complicated and will be discussed in chapter 6 on memory. For the moment, keep in mind the basic idea that conceptually related items are better recalled because they are better learned. As you can see, this explanation emphasizes what gets *stored* in memory.

Another possibility is that recall for conceptually related items is better because we have a better plan for *retrieving* the items. During recall, when we think of one item this may lead us to think of another item rather than because the items were better learned in the first place.

A simple analogy will help you see the difference between *storage* and *retrieval* of items. Consider memory as a matter, in part, of placing things in a filing cabinet and taking things out when you want them. An item placed in the filing cabinet is an item stored; however, an item can be in storage but we may be unable to locate (retrieve) it. Consider that one person may be able to locate items in the file, whereas another person may not. In this case the material is clearly stored but differences exist in the ability to retrieve the items. For the moment we may say that our first person has developed some kind of retrieval system, whereas the second person has not. As indicated, both storage and retrieval mechanisms may underlie the superiority of recall of conceptually related items. We shall discuss these processes in more detail in chapter 6.

Changes in Specific Items

The process of changing specific items is called *coding*. We have already described stimulus coding and need not discuss this further. Humans code not only stimuli but also code *response* terms as well. *Response coding* refers to the rearranging or alteration of response terms in order to facilitate learning. For example, if the response terms were BYO, CIE, and IPL, you might code these as BOY, ICE, and LIP. Once you code response terms, you are faced with the task of *decoding* the words back into their original form during the recall task. For example, after you have recalled the word LIP, you must decode it to IPL. If the task of decoding is very difficult, you are better off learning the response terms as they are. Therefore, the fewer coding rules you use to transform an item, the easier it is to decode the item. If, however, the decoding rules apply generally to all the items, such as transcribing shorthand, then the system is useful.

You should, therefore, be cautious in attempting to code response terms because the coding rule must be relatively simple if coding is to facilitate learning. The point is that the code may be so complex that you have difficulty in recalling the original response term. Such caution is of less concern in stimulus coding since you need only recognize, as distinct from recalling, a stimulus. The problem of decoding explains why psychologists tend to be cautious about the uncritical use of mnemonic devices sometimes recommended by so-called "memory experts."

Mediation

We have already pointed out that associations between stimuli and responses may be developed through mediational activity. *Verbal mediation* is the process by which we link stimulus and response terms by way of implicit verbal responses or associations that we already possess. For example, consider learning a pair of items such as PRT-Good. If, to the syllable PRT you have the association "pretty," then you can easily associate the two terms as "pretty"-"good." More generally, in learning to associate two events, *a* and *b*, a third term *c* may serve to bridge the gap between the two events.

Mediational links can be used in learning foreign language vocabulary. Consider the following set of English-Spanish pairs, with a mediating word between each:

English	Mediator	Spanish
sea	marine	mar
book	library	libro
water	aqueous	agua

There is no immediate connection between *sea* and *mar*. Yet *mar* is the root for *marine*, which in turn enables the connection between *sea* and *mar*. The student is nevertheless cautioned in the uncritical use of mediators, since they may sometimes require more effort than direct association between two words.

The point to remember is that mediation is an important process in human learning. It operates not only in associative learning, but in transfer, concept formation, and thinking. We shall consider this process in later chapters dealing with these events.

The Learning of Connected Materials

Many of the factors that we have discussed in the learning of single items also affect the learning of connected materials, such as sentences. Two factors, sequential dependencies and grammatical structure, are particularly important in the learning of connected materials.

Consider the problem of trying to read someone's poor handwriting. Even if you cannot read all of the letters you can likely understand the meaning of the sentence because you can correctly guess at the unclear letters. You can guess correctly because of the *sequential dependencies* that exist in the English language. Certain letters are known to follow others with high frequency, whereas others follow with low frequency. Similarly, certain kinds of words are likely to follow other words with high frequency. For example, if a sentence begins, "The dog and . . .," certain kinds of words are more likely to follow than others. Another noun, such as "boy," or an article followed by a noun is most likely to occur. A verb or another conjunction is most unlikely to follow. What we do is to make use of the redundant features of the English language. The important point is that this redundant property of the language is what makes our recall of connected materials much greater than our recall of discrete items.

Another factor that helps you to retain verbal materials is the grammatical structure of the language. Consider the statement, "The gegub is smart." You can readily recognize that "gegub" functions as a noun in the sentence because of its position, despite the fact that it is a meaningless item. The position of words as well as properties of words, like ending in -*ing*, serve as grammatical cues which identify structural properties of sentences. The presence of these grammatical cues or tags serve to make sentences easier to learn and remember than single items.

Motivation and Verbal Learning

What is the role of motivation in verbal learning? We know in the case of animal learning that motivation is necessary for performance but not for learning. Although motivational variables have been studied extensively in animal learning, much less attention has been given motivational variables in human learning.

Let us note why this has been the case. In studies of animal learning it is usually essential to deprive the animal of food or water in order to get him to perform. Such is not the case with human subjects. Usually, the instructions are sufficient to motivate the subject to perform the task. Moreover, the subject usually arrives at the laboratory setting with at least a fair amount of motivation. By the time the subject has received his instructions, motivation is usually at such a level that it is difficult to produce large changes in motivation otherwise. Thus, it is not because of disinterest in motivation that it has not been extensively studied in verbal learning but because the learner is typically well-motivated in laboratory studies of learning.

Intentional versus Incidental Learning

Consider the issue of intentional versus incidental learning. Psychologists have long pondered the question of whether intent to learn is essential for learning. The answer is no! REGARDLESS OF OUR INTENTIONS, WE

LEARN SOMETHING ABOUT THOSE THINGS TO WHICH WE ARE EXPOSED. Indeed, there is no reason to maintain the distinction between the two kinds of learning, which really amount to two kinds of instructional operations in verbal learning tasks. If differential responses are made to stimuli, they will be learned without regard to intent. If differential responses are not made, then learning will not occur.

Anxiety and Learning

Motivational factors do affect performance, as has been shown in studies of the effects of anxiety on verbal learning. Where the task is fairly complex or difficult, motivation in the form of anxiety actually interferes with performance. AS THE TASK BECOMES MORE COMPLEX, LESS MOTIVATION IS NECESSARY FOR ACHIEVING OPTIMAL LEARNING. This simply emphasizes the point that you can be too motivated for effective performance, an all too frequent occurrence on the part of the student.

Frequently a student complains that he is doing poorly in a course despite the fact that he likes the course and is highly motivated. Leaving out matters of intelligence and good study habits, the likely possibility is that the student is too highly motivated for efficient performance. A high motivational state may act to energize many responses so that the student becomes confused. In studying, he may fail to think through relationships even though he has memorized many facts. In the test situation, he may have difficulty, therefore, in distinguishing between subtle alternatives that he faces in the usual multiple-choice test.

Not only does anxiety affect your studying but it also affects your performance in the classroom. Highly anxious students tend to think more about irrelevant details of the class, such as the crack in the wall, the mark on the desk, the instructor's dress, manner, or appearance, and what other people are doing. Consequently, such students think less about the topic of discussion and hence learn less. What high anxiety appears to be doing is producing a general energizing effect so that a large number of irrelevant environmental stimuli gain the student's attention. Thus, you may find your attention wandering from the lecturer during the classroom period if you are in an anxious state.

Handling Anxiety

Everyone gets anxious at specific times. Moreover, a little anxiety is useful because it can serve to energize performance. Therefore, the problem is not so much the matter of avoiding anxiety, which is virtually impossible, but of handling or coping with our anxiety. The problem is one of dealing with anxiety so that it does not cripple our everyday performance in learning situations.

Consider first anxiety in test-taking situations. It is normal to be a little anxious just before taking a test, expecially if you are unfamiliar with the instructor's tests. Suppose, however, that you characteristically become quite anxious prior to and during a test so that your performance is poor. What can you do? One approach that I have used with students is to give them "practice tests" which they must take in the regular classroom at some period when the classroom is not being used. In some instances, I have arranged for a faculty colleague to prepare a practice test typical of one the student is likely to receive. In other cases the student has made up his own test. The logic of this approach is to have the student practice taking tests in the very environment that he will take the real test. The test must be taken during the same amount of time allotted for the classroom period, and the test is graded immediately so that the student can check his performance. *If*, under these circumstances, the student can perform well, he tends to reduce his anxiety about test taking.

Consider anxiety in the classroom. This may be the result of general anxiety that you possess, or anxiety specific to certain features of the class, such as the instructor asking questions of students. As we noted, if you are anxious, you tend to think about other things than the lecturer's topic. You may tend to daydream about other events. A little daydreaming is normal but you can see that daydreaming in the classroom is quite nonproductive. What you must do is learn to recognize when you are daydreaming, and redirect your attention to the lecture. Sometimes this can be accomplished by verbal self-instruction in which you occasionally monitor your thinking in the classroom; if you discover that you are daydreaming, you refocus your attention to the lecture. This requires that you develop the habit of occasionally "looking at" what you are thinking. Another approach is to reward yourself if you carefully attended to and thought about the lecture. For example, you may schedule a coffee break after class *only if* you have listened attentively and thoughtfully in class.

There are many specific things you can do in handling anxiety. Regardless of what approach you take, the effectiveness of any approach must be viewed in terms of the extent to which you can avoid paying attention to distracting, irrelevant stimuli, and the extent to which you can attend to the main issues of the class.

Summary

This chapter was concerned with an examination of fundamental processes in verbal learning. Verbal learning was described as a fairly complex affair consisting of a number of processes. The basic processes of verbal learning were described in the context of paired associate learning. Two important processes were those of response learning and associative learning. The response learning process refers to the stage in which verbal items became available for recall, and the associative stage refers to the phase in which the "hook-up" of stimuli and responses occur. This distinction describes what is called the two-stage theory of paired associate learning.

Paired associate learning was also seen to be composed of additional processes, including stimulus discrimination, selection, and encoding. These processes emphasize the importance of the learner coming to perceive each stimulus in a fairly consistent fashion.

Association formation was seen to depend upon the possession of mediating links; however, some association formation can occur by virtue of the contiguity of two events. On the surface, association formation appears to be a gradual process. Nevertheless, a more detailed analysis of this process suggests that association formation may be both a gradual and an all-or-none affair. At present no definitive answer to this issue is clear. Finally, we saw that associations may be learned in both directions in a paired associate task.

Organizational processes also operate in verbal learning. These include changes in the order of presentation, such as clustering in recall, change in specific items which is coding, and the development and use of mediating links between verbal items. Clustering in recall may be on an associative basis or may be in terms of categories. Subjective organization, the development of one's unique basis for clustering, can also occur. The learning of connected materials depends upon many of the same factors as does the learning of discrete materials, but in addition depends upon sequential dependencies and grammatical structure of the language.

Motivation in the form of anxiety was seen as an important factor in affecting performance in verbal learning tasks. In general, we saw that as a task increases in complexity, less motivation is necessary for efficient learning. Practical procedures for the reduction of excessive anxiety during test taking are known. One such procedure requires the student to practice exam taking as part of his regular study procedures. Controlling anxiety in the classroom was seen as dependent upon your ability to focus and maintain your attention on the topics under discussion and to develop habits of monitoring your classroom thinking so as to avoid daydreaming.

True-False Items: Processes in Verbal Learning

1. In learning Spanish vocabulary, that is, Spanish-English equivalents, the response learning component is recalling the Spanish word and the associative component is hooking-up the Spanish word to its English mate.

(Learning foreign language vocabulary is similar to a paired associate task. The Spanish words must be learned to a recallable level, and they must become associated with the appropriate English equivalents. True.)

2. Having to distinguish between highly confusable stimuli, such as identical twins, emphasizes the significance of response learning.

(This example calls attention to the importance of stimulus discrimination, not response learning. A component part of any paired associate task is the process of discriminating among the stimuli, and the importance of this process increases as the stimuli become more confusable. False.)

3. Humans use all aspects of stimuli to which they are presented.

(Humans frequently select and use only a fraction of the entire stimulus presented, if that fraction will validly cue a response. This process is called stimulus selection. False.)

4. The nominal stimulus is what you use as a stimulus, whereas the functional stimulus is what is presented by the experimenter.

(Just the reverse is the case; the nominal stimulus is the experimenter-presented stimulus, while the functional stimulus is what the learner uses. False.)

5. In the course of learning we tend initially to use the most salient or meaningful elements of a stimulus to cue a response. With overtraining, however, weaker or secondary cues may gain some strength.

(This process occurs not only in paired-associate learning, but appears to operate generally. True.)

6. If a learner fails to regard [perceive] a stimulus in a relatively consistent or stable fashion, that stimulus cannot come to signal a particular response.

(The stimulus of the moment must, during the course of learning, come to be regarded as it was on previous trials if it is to serve as the occasion for a particular response. True.)

7. If two verbal items are jointly exposed, some associative strength between the items may develop even though the task demands no association between the items.

(Some association formation can occur simply on the basis of contiguity. True.)

8. Associations are formed from stimulus to response but not from response to stimulus.

(In the course of learning paired associates, backward associations, that is, response-stimulus associations, may be formed. False.)

9. Organizational processes occur in learning of sentences and paragraphs but not in ordinary free learning or paired associate learning of lists of items.

(Organizational processes, which refer to activity by the learner in reorganizing or restructuring the materials, can readily occur in free and paired associate learning. False.)

10. The development and utilization of verbal links to hook up items is called verbal mediation.

(When two items are not easily associated, the learner may think of some verbal mediator which helps hook the two items together. True.)

11. Your solution of complex mathematics problems is more likely to suffer

from high anxiety than the memorization of biological terms, such as the structure of plants.

(In general, anxiety is likely to interfere with more complex tasks. In this instance, we would regard mathematical reasoning as more complex than the learning of biological terms. True.)

12. One way of dealing with test anxiety is to practice taking tests or quizzes.

(The effect of such practice is to familiarize yourself with exams, making them less traumatic when you take the actual test. Moreover, practice in taking exams may "desensitize" you to the aversive features of exam taking. True.)

5

Transfer of Training

American visitors to England may experience some confusion in driving on the left side of the road because of their established habit of driving on the right. What happens is the tendency, especially under conditions of stress, to revert momentarily to driving on the right side of the road even though the rules of driving in England are clearly understood. Momentary confusion, in which the driver vacillates between driving on the right or left, has also been reported. In this illustration we see that previously learned habits can affect our performance in new situations, which is an instance of transfer of training. Similarly, a common experience of many individuals just learning to drive a car with an automatic transmission, *after* having driven only cars with a standard transmission, is to attempt to depress a nonexistent clutch pedal. Alternatively, if a person first experiences driving a car with an automatic transmission and then shifts to a car with a standard transmission, he may on occasion fail to use the clutch pedal when shifting gears. Here again, we see that earlier learned habits and skills can affect the way we perform in new situations.

Instances of transfer occur in more formal learning situations as well as in our everyday experiences. For example, having thoroughly mastered the principles of algebra we find it easier to grasp concepts in advanced mathematics. Similarly, having mastered one foreign language such as Spanish, we find it somewhat easier to master a second and related language, such as French. Proficiency in one athletic skill can affect performance in other athletic skills. For example, the experienced tennis player usually reports that playing squash "hurts" his tennis game. This can occur because tennis requires the player to maintain a stiff wrist, whereas squash requires flexible wrist movements. This example emphasizes that the concept of transfer applies regardless of whether prior learning aids or hinders new learning. Another instance of transfer is seen when skill in playing one musical instrument helps you in learning to play a new instrument. The influence of transfer is pervasive throughout your life and is found not only in intellectual activities and athletic skills but is seen in emotional reactions and attitudes of individuals.

A good deal of teaching is based upon the assumption that what is taught in the classroom will transfer to new learning situations. Students may be taught basic physics with the assumption that portions of what is taught, such as elements of the scientific method, will transfer to the solution of problems in biology, perhaps to the social sciences, and to advanced topics in physics itself. Similarly, students may be taught psychology with the similar assumption that at least certain features of the subject matter, such as scientific method and the development of some systematic way of viewing man's behavior, will transfer to more complex studies. Sometimes, of course, less than the desired transfer occurs. For example, students of mathematics may fail to recognize relationships among equations that are critical for their understanding of the topic. Likewise, similarities among languages may remain undetected, resulting in less than maximal transfer in foreign language learning.

Despite instances in which transfer is minimal, the assumption of transfer underlies much of what is taught in the American classroom. Obviously, there must be some transfer or every new learning situation would involve starting from "scratch." Since we frequently do not start from scratch in each new learning situation, but rather benefit (or suffer) considerably from much of our prior experience, our interest is focused on the factors that affect such transfer. Therefore, the issue is not *if* transfer occurs, but rather the *conditions* under which transfer occurs.

The phenomenon of transfer is extremely important. From a very early period in life much new learning is affected in some way by previous learning. For example, the responses that young children make when entering a new school may be influenced by previous experiences in school. Similarly, the attitudes of a college student toward a particular course may be determined in a large part by his previous experience with similar courses and with the kinds of expectations he has about the course. Indeed, it is difficult to think of any adult learning that is not, at least in some minimal way, influenced by earlier learning.

The Concept of Transfer

Transfer of training refers to the influence of prior learning on performance in some new situation. Transfer effects may be positive, negative, or there may be no observed effect, which defines zero transfer.

Positive transfer occurs in situations in which prior learning aids or *facilitates* subsequent performance. An instance of positive transfer is seen when mastery of Spanish facilitates your learning of French. What is meant is that you are able to master French faster or more skillfully as a result of having learned

Spanish. *We frequently see instances of positive transfer where the learner first masters an easier task and then moves on to a more difficult task.* For instance, the young child exhibits positive transfer when, having first learned to ride a bicycle with training wheels, he then readily learns to ride skillfully when the training wheels are removed. Similarly, the young child becomes skillful in discriminating among difficult letters, such as *d* and *b*, by seeing distinguishing features of the letters exaggerated, perhaps color coded, or made more discriminable in some fashion during his early training.

Negative transfer, in contrast, refers to situations in which prior learning *interferes* with new learning. An instance of negative transfer is seen when playing squash interferes with performance in playing tennis, because of the different kinds of wrist activity required. A GENERAL PRINCIPLE IS THAT NEGATIVE TRANSFER RESULTS WHEN YOU HAVE TO MAKE A NEW RESPONSE TO AN OLD STIMULUS SITUATION, ESPECIALLY IF THE RESPONSES ARE INCOMPATIBLE OR ANTAGONISTIC TO EACH OTHER. For example, the automatic transmission in one of my cars is arranged so that the lever must be pulled all the way down for the car to be placed in reverse. My second car has just the opposite arrangement, requiring that I push the lever up to go in reverse. On some mornings, especially if I am in a hurry and not paying too much attention to which car I am driving, I inadvertently push the lever in the direction opposite from reverse, placing the car in drive. The scars on my garage wall stand in mute testimony to this transfer event. An obvious solution to the problem would be for automobile manufacturers to standardize the arrangement of controls so that they would be reasonably comparable on all cars. This problem of reversed controls also occurs with commercial aircraft and has been known to lead to landing accidents.

Zero transfer, a third outcome, is one in which there is no effect of prior learning on new learning. Zero transfer can occur either as a result of prior learning having no effect on subsequent performance, or as a result of combined effects of positive and negative transfer which cancel. The latter situation emphasizes that sources of *both* positive and negative transfer operate in many learning situations and that what is observed is some *net* effect.

The Study of Transfer

Although transfer has been described in a general way, the concept of transfer is more fully understood by looking at the way in which it is studied. Consider the question: Is there transfer from having a mastery of French to becoming skillful in Spanish? Offhand you might suspect that there would be some positive transfer from French to Spanish based on the similarities between the languages. Suppose, however, that you wanted to know if such transfer occurred. The procedure for answering this question is quite straight-forward and is outlined below.

Design of Transfer Experiments

One group of subjects, an *experimental* group, is first given extensive training in French until they reach some level of proficiency; they then are given the second task of learning Spanish. A second group, identified as *control* subjects, receives no training in French but learns Spanish. The two groups are then compared on their performance in learning Spanish. Some measure of achievement is obtained such as, for example, how long it takes to learn Spanish to some arbitrary level of proficiency. If those subjects who studied French learn Spanish at a faster rate than the control subjects then we con-clude that there is positive transfer from French to Spanish. On the other hand, should those subjects who studied French actually learn Spanish slower than the control subjects, then this would be evidence for negative transfer. Should this latter outcome occur, we would conclude that in some way the study of French interfered with the subsequent learning of Spanish (or at least inter-fered *more* than it aided).

The study of transfer can be schematized as shown below. The experimen-tal group learns an initial task, Task A, and then learns a second task, Task B. The control group learns only Task B, without experiencing the initial task.

	Initial Task	*Transfer Task*
Experimental Group:	Learn Task A (French)	Learn Task B (Spanish)
Control Group:		Learn Task B (Spanish)

As noted above, we compare the experimental and control groups in their performance on Task B. If performance of the experimental group is superior to that of the control group, in the sense of fewer errors, more correct responses, faster rate of learning, etc., this defines positive transfer from A to B. If, on the other hand, the experimental group's performance is inferior to the control group, then this defines negative transfer. Finally, if the two groups are equiva-lent in Task B performance, then we define zero transfer.

The above schematic illustrates the study of *gross* transfer. It tells us only if there is transfer from A to B. It does not tell us anything about what processes are involved in such transfer, but only that a transfer effect does or does not occur. Similarly, in our example of transfer from French to Spanish, if the experimental group did perform better than the control, all we would know was that positive transfer was obtained. We would know that a gross transfer effect occurred, but we would be unable to specify what factors were respon-sible for transfer. For example, positive transfer from French to Spanish could be due to specific similarities between the languages. For instance, some words common to both languages have very similar spellings. On the other hand, there can be positive transfer as a result of *general* language skills acquired in studying French that transfer to Spanish. Study habits, modes of organizing the material, etc., may thus provide a source of positive transfer.

In many transfer studies, the interest of the psychologist is in distinguishing between *general* and *specific* sources of transfer. In our example above, if we wished to know if there were *specific* factors producing transfer from French to Spanish, as distinct from general factors, we would need another kind of control group. In this case, we would have control subjects learn some "unrelated" language, such as Chinese or Navajo, prior to learning Spanish. In this fashion, we have a control for the processes that are involved in learning-how to learn a language in general, as distinct from transfer effects specific to the relationship between French and Spanish. Schematically, this new control group (Control group 2) is shown below, in which the control subjects learn Task X prior to learning Task B. In general, Task X represents some task that is minimally related to Task B, but does provide for practice in learning how to learn tasks of the same class.

	Initial Task	*Transfer Task*
Experimental group:	Learn Task A (French)	Learn Task B (Spanish)
Control group 2:	Learn Task X (Chinese)	Learn Task B (Spanish)
Control group 1:		Learn Task B (Spanish)

The same comparisons are made as before, but now we have more information. Previously, we had only information about a gross transfer effect. Now, we can determine if transfer from A to B (or French to Spanish, as in our example) is *specific* to the similarities between Tasks A and B. Returning to our example, only if the experimental group performs superior to this new type of control can we conclude that transfer from French to Spanish is *specific* to communalities and similarities between Spanish and French.

If, on the other hand, there is as much transfer from Chinese to Spanish as from French to Spanish, and both groups are superior to a control group that learns only Spanish (Control group 1), then whatever is transferring from French to Spanish is *not* specific to the two tasks, but is some general kind of activity that occurs simply as a result of studying another foreign language.

Now that the concept of transfer and the procedures for studying transfer are clear, let us turn our attention to the study of paired associate transfer.

Basic Transfer Paradigms

The study of transfer in verbal learning typically employs the paired associate task. This is so because the paired associate task permits independent manipulation of stimulus and response factors in transfer. Subjects can be given an initial paired associate task, followed by a second paired associate task in which variations in stimuli alone, responses alone, or both, are manipulated by the experimenter. Variations in the relationships between the two tasks describe what are called *transfer paradigms. A paradigm is simply a schematic or shorthand way of describing the task relationships.*

In the *A-B , C-D paradigm*, as in all other paradigms, the subjects learn two successive paired associate lists. The first list is designated as A-B, where A represents the stimulus terms of the list and B represents the response terms. The second list is identified as C-D, where C refers to the stimulus terms and D the response terms. This designation means simply that there is no obvious similarity between the stimulus terms of the two lists (A and C), and no obvious similarity between the response terms of the two lists (B and D). Since both terms refer to verbal units, they are of course similar in this sense. What is meant by no similarity is that neither the stimulus terms of the two lists nor the response terms are formally similar or meaningfully similar.

The A-B, C-D transfer paradigm is illustrated below using three pairs in each list:

Initial List	*Transfer List*
A - B	*C - D*
ZUL - lip	HAF - ice
XEG - sea	BZL - cow
TOF - rug	GQN - sky

The important thing to observe is that the C-D list is essentially unrelated to the A-B list. No obvious or evident similarities exist between the two lists. The stimulus terms of the first list are dissimilar to those of the second list. The items ZUL, XEG, TOG, have few letters in common with HAF, BZL, and GQN; in short, the stimulus terms are formally dissimilar. Moreover, the items are not meaningfully related. The same holds true for the response terms. Therefore, the A-B, C-D paradigm serves as a baseline measure for *general* transfer effects, since specific similarities between the two tasks are removed or at least minimized. Any transfer from A-B to C-D is therefore due to general transfer effects against which specific factors can be assessed using other paradigms.

With an *A-B , A-D paradigm*, the task of the subject is to learn to associate new (D) responses to the same (A) stimuli. The subject learns an initial list (A-B) of paired associates and then learns a second list (A-D) which contains the same stimuli but new and dissimilar responses. The A-B, A-D paradigm produces negative transfer. MORE GENERALLY, LEARNING TO MAKE NEW RESPONSES TO OLD STIMULI IS A BASIC CONDITION FOR PRODUCING NEGATIVE TRANSFER. There is at least one exception to this rule which we shall discuss later; this occurs when the stimuli are very difficult to discriminate.

The A-B, A-D paradigm is illustrated below, again using three pairs in each list. Remember that the first letter in each paradigm represents the stimulus terms and the second letter represents the response terms.

Initial List	*Transfer List*
A - B	*A - D*
ZUL - lip	ZUL - ice
XEG - bat	XEG - cow
TOF - rug	TOF - sky

With an *A-B, C-B paradigm*, the task of the subject is to learn to associate the same response terms (B responses) to new stimulus terms (C). Whereas the previous paradigm varied the responses and kept the stimuli constant, the A-B, C-B paradigm varies the stimuli and keeps the responses constant. This paradigm usually produces positive transfer, so we may generalize by saying that LEARNING TO MAKE OLD RESPONSES TO NEW STIMULI IS A BASIC CONDITION FOR POSITIVE TRANSFER.

The A-B, C-B paradigm is illustrated below, again using three pairs in each list.

Initial List	*Transfer List*
A - B	*C - B*
ZUL - lip	HAF - lip
XEG - sea	BZL - sea
TOF - rug	GQN - rug

Finally, with an *A-B, A-Br paradigm*, we can arrange the lists so that the subjects must repair the same responses with the same stimuli. In the second list, the subject is presented the same stimuli and responses; however, they are completely re-paired, thus requiring him to learn new associations. Hence the designation *Br*, where *r* indicates that the responses are re-paired. *This paradigm is notable because it produces massive negative transfer.*

The A-B, A-Br paradigm is illustrated below:

Initial List	*Transfer List*
A - B	*A - Br*
ZUL - lip	ZUL - boy
XEG - boy	XEG - rug
TOF - rug	TOF - lip

Although it is a bit difficult to think of an everyday situation in which this case might arise, you can easily imagine the negative transfer that might result if our traffic signals *were* reversed. Suppose that instead of stopping the car when the light was red, we had to go when the light was red and stop in the presence of a green light. Confusion and accidents are quite predictable.

A comparison of the four basic paradigms is shown in table 5.1. The table provides a convenient summary of the features that already have been described.

These relationships can also be visualized by comparing performance curves on transfer lists. In this example, an A-B list is initially learned, followed by one of the four possible transfer lists. The transfer effects can be seen easily in figure 10. The curve for C-D represents the control or baseline condition against which the other conditions are compared. The figure portrays the number of correct responses made during list 2 learning for successive trials on the list.

The figure shows that the A-D curve is below that of the C-D curve, indicating that A-D performance is inferior to C-D performance. This simply illustrates the usual negative transfer obtained in this situation. Similarly, the figure shows that the C-B condition is learned faster than the C-D control, which describes the usual positive transfer with this paradigm. Finally, the A-Br condition shows the poorest performance relative to C-D, indicating that this condition produces the greatest amount of negative transfer.

Expansion of Paradigms: Similarity Factor

Keep in mind that the paradigms are simply shorthand conventions for describing the relationship between first and second list learning. As we have described them, the stimuli, responses, or both are changed or kept the same. These paradigms may be expanded if we now vary the *similarity* of either stimuli or responses. For example, in the A-B, A-D paradigm, the responses are quite unrelated. We can, however, vary the similarity of the response terms along some continuum of similarity, and thus produce what is known as the A-B, A-B′ paradigm, where B and B′ represent highly similar responses.

TABLE 5.1

Basic Transfer Paradigms

Paradigm	Stimuli	Responses	Net Transfer Effect
A-B, C-D	Different	Different	(Baseline Control)
A-B, A-D	Same	Different	Negative
A-B, C-B	Different	Same	Positive
A-B, A-Br	Same	Same (Repaired)	Much Negative

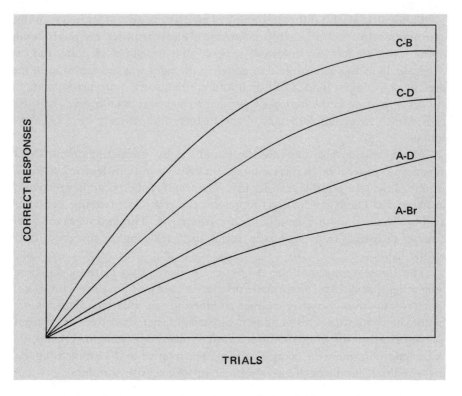

Figure 10. Transfer performance curves for the four basic paradigms. This curve shows the typical superior performance (positive transfer) of the C-B condition compared with the C-D control, and the inferior performances (negative transfer) of the A-D and A-Br conditions compared with the C-D control

Moreover, you can visualize a continuum of response similarity going from B′, where the responses are highly similar to B, to B″ where they are less similar to B, to D, where they are unrelated to B. In a parallel fashion, you can visualize a similar continuum of stimulus similarity going from A′, to A″, to C, which is completely dissimilar.

It should now be clear that a number of task relationships can be studied in transfer paradigms. The basic paradigms, which represent extremes of the similarity continuum, can be expanded to include the dimensions of stimulus and response similarity. If you have difficulty remembering all this shorthand, remember the general point that in paired associate transfer tasks (1) the stimuli in the second list may be changed, (2) the responses may be changed, (3) both stimuli and responses can be changed, and (4) stimuli and responses can be varied along a similarity continuum. With an understanding of how transfer is studied, and in particular of the basic transfer paradigms, we can now turn our attention to general and specific transfer.

General and Specific Transfer

We have already noted that transfer effects can be due to either general or specific sources. They may, of course, be due to the joint operation of both. Let us examine the concepts of general and specific transfer in greater detail.

General (Nonspecific) Transfer

It is frequently observed that individuals improve in their ability to learn new tasks or skills more proficiently as a result of prior practice on a series of related tasks. For example, a parking lot attendant can quickly learn to operate a particular car, even if he has never driven that make or model, based on his long experience in driving various kinds of cars. Similarly, the skilled card player can readily learn a new card game based on his backlog of experience with previous games. Some of this transfer is due to specific similarities between the tasks, but much of it is due to general effects of practice.

The progressive improvement in ability to learn a series of new tasks (that is, at an increase in the rate with which the tasks are learned) is a form of transfer known as *learning to learn*. Learning to learn is observed in a variety of tasks ranging from verbal learning to problem solving and thinking and is one case of general transfer.

Humans show clear evidence of learning to learn paired associate verbal materials. If we learn successive lists of paired associates, say one new list each day for several days, we will gradually improve our performance in terms of the number of trials required to learn the list. This is simply to say that it will require fewer trials for us to learn each successive list. Figure 11 indicates such a relationship, one in which humans are given a number of successive lists over successive days of practice. The figure indicates that we require fewer trials to learn each list on successive days, and that performance begins to level off after extended practice. In other words, some level is reached at which very little improvement over the previous day's practice occurs. New and quite different lists of materials, conforming to successive C-D paradigms, are used each day so that the improvement in performance is not due to specific items in the list.

Similarly, learning to learn is seen in tasks of discrimination learning. For example, we can present young children with a task requiring them to respond to one of two stimuli, such as a circle and a triangle. Arbitrarily, we arrange the situation such that a response to one of the stimuli, say the circle, is rewarded by giving the child a small toy or piece of candy. A response to the other stimulus is followed by no reward. This task will be readily learned by

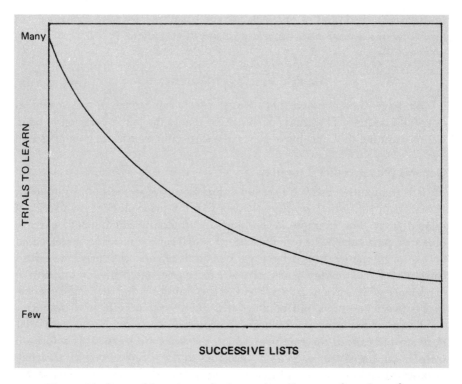

Many

Few

TRIALS TO LEARN

SUCCESSIVE LISTS

Figure 11. Ease of learning paired associate lists as a function of practice on successive lists. Curve shows steady improvement in performance—that is progressively fewer trials to learn the successive lists.

the child. Now, if we increase the difficulty of the task by making the stimuli very similar, or by using stimuli with several dimensions, such as size, shape, and color, with only one dimension being relevant (followed by reward), then the task becomes more difficult to learn. If we give the child practice in a series of such tasks, we will nevertheless observe that the child will learn successive discriminations faster, even if we use new stimuli on subsequent series of tasks. Again we have an instance of learning to learn. Our ability to transfer general modes of attack, to adopt appropriate "sets" in new learning situations, and to use appropriate strategies provides the basis for learning to learn.

A second source of general transfer is *warm-up*. Warm-up is related to learning to learn; however, the basic difference between the two is that warm-up is a much more transitory or short-lived effect. Whereas learning to learn effects are long term, warm-up effects are quite brief in duration, usually no longer than an hour. Warm-up refers to postural adjustments and general "attentive" adjustments that carry over from one task to another and facilitate learning. The facilitation of performance due to warm-up effects is readily seen in a variety of situations. After you have played several games of pool in immediate succession, the next game in the series benefits from the general motor and postural adjustments necessary for optimal performance. Similarly, once you have started studying, you benefit from warm-up effects when you shift to studying new materials. If, however, you take an extended break, you will lose some of the benefits associated with warm-up because of its rapid dissipation over time.

Specific Transfer

Transfer depends not only upon general sources which we have just described, but also upon the presence of certain specific sources. For example, the stimuli in the initial and transfer tasks may be highly similar, the consequence of which is to produce positive transfer if the responses are new. Thus, transfer in this case would be dependent upon the specific factor of stimulus similarity. Likewise, transfer may also depend upon the relationship between the responses in the two tasks.

Transfer can depend upon many specific sources. The similarity of the two tasks is an example of a major specific source of transfer. For example, the fact that there are international traffic symbols makes it relatively easy to obey traffic signs when traveling in foreign countries using these signs, even though you may be unable to read the language. The international stop sign is a hexagonal (six-sided) sign. It is not, therefore, necessary to know the Spanish word for "stop" (which is "alto") when traveling in Mexico. All you need do is recognize that any hexagonal sign means stop.

We shall briefly examine a few specific sources of transfer. They will all be illustrated in the context of paired associate transfer paradigms. These sources stem directly from "what is learned" when one learns a paired associate list. In the previous chapter we noted that several processes operate when we learn paired associates. These included discrimination among the stimuli, response learning, and the establishment of both forward and backward associations. Once these processes are achieved during first list learning, their effects can transfer to second list learning, depending upon the particular paradigm involved. Let us see how this is the case.

Transfer of Stimulus Discrimination

Recall that during A-B learning, that is, the learning of a paired associate list, that part of what the learner must achieve is the discrimination among the stimulus terms. If the stimuli are highly similar, then this process requires more time for completion than if the stimuli are low in similarity.

Now, what happens if the learner transfers to an A-D list where the stimuli are identical to those of the first list? Since the stimuli were discriminated during first-list learning, then the learner should profit from already having learned to distinguish among the stimuli. He could thus begin the second task with this aspect of learning already achieved. This source of transfer, known as the transfer of stimulus discrimination, produces a source of positive transfer. Although the A-B,A-D paradigm usually produces *overall* negative transfer, AS THE STIMULI INCREASE IN INTRALIST STIMULUS SIMILARITY, THEN RELATIVELY GREATER POSITIVE TRANSFER OF STIMULUS DISCRIMINATION WILL RESULT.

This process can be illustrated by considering a hypothetical situation. Suppose that you had to learn arbitrary names to a set of facial photographs consisting of highly similar people. Assume that all photographs were brunette women about the same age, with the same hair style, and with similar facial features. Once you had learned to identify each person by giving her correct name, A-B learning is completed. Now, suppose that you had to learn to identify the same photographs with a new label, such as a letter of the alphabet. This, of course, is the analogue to A-D learning. Having already learned to discriminate the highly similar photographs, the learned discrimination among them would transfer to second task learning.

It should be emphasized that the stimuli must be difficult to distinguish, that is, high in intralist stimulus similarity, for stimulus discrimination to be a potent source of transfer. If the stimuli are initially easy to distinguish, then there will be virtually no transfer from this source. For instance, if the stimuli are familiar and already discriminable events, such as primary colors, discrimination of the stimuli will be an unimportant part of the total set of processes that operate in initial paired associate learning and hence provide for little transfer effects.

It also follows that a parallel process on the response side occurs. IF THE RESPONSES ARE DIFFICULT TO DISCRIMINATE, THEN THERE WILL BE A SOURCE OF POSITIVE TRANSFER TO THE SECOND TASK WHEN THE RESPONSES ARE IDENTICAL. Thus, we find in the A-B, C-B paradigm a source of positive transfer, called the *transfer of response differentiation*, when similarity among the response terms is high.

Transfer of Response Learning

Another specific source of transfer is due to response learning. Recall that one component of A-B learning is response learning. This is the process by which the responses become integrated as a unit so that they are available for recall. We noted that if the responses are low in meaningfulness or are difficult to pronounce, much of your effort will be devoted to integrating the responses into available, recallable units. Thus, *response learning* refers to making the response terms available as recallable units, whereas *response differentiation* refers to the reduction in confusability of initially similar responses.

Now, what happens if you transfer to a C-B list where the responses are identical to those of the first list? Since the responses were made available during first-list learning, you should profit from the response learning that has already occurred. You begin the second task with this aspect of learning already achieved. This source of transfer, known as the *transfer of response learning*, produces a source of positive transfer. More generally, THE LESS MEANINGFUL THE RESPONSES, THUS REQUIRING MORE RESPONSE LEARNING, THE GREATER IS THE SOURCE OF POSITIVE TRANSFER DUE TO RESPONSE LEARNING WHEN THE SAME RESPONSES ARE REQUIRED.

Transfer of Forward Associations

Whenever you learn an A-B association, this association can transfer to the second association and produce interference or negative transfer. This is the case when the stimuli are the same but the responses are new or re-paired. Thus negative transfer in the A-B, A-D and A-B, A-Br paradigms can result because of the carryover of now inappropriate associations.

This negative transfer can be illustrated by recalling the example cited earlier involving the reversal of controls on my two automobiles. Recall that in one car the lever was pulled down to place the car in reverse, whereas in the other the lever was pushed up. Thus to highly similar situations I must make opposite responses. We saw that under such circumstances I would occasionally make the inappropriate response. In other words, the old association would intrude and momentarily displace the appropriate association.

In verbal paired associates, however, actual intrustions of the B responses during A-D learning are infrequent. Rather, the arrangement appears to produce a suppression of the B responses during A-D learning. It is as if one "sets aside" the first list responses during second list learning in the sense of regarding these responses as now coming from an inappropriate list.

Transfer of Backward Associations

We have also seen that during A-B learning you may acquire *backward* as well as forward associations. Backward associations are weaker than forward associations, but they also serve as a source of negative transfer.

Consider the A-B, A-Br paradigm. We have already seen that interference is produced by the transfer of forward associations. In a similar vein, the backward association acquired during A-B learning, which we designate as the *B-A* association, can interfere with the *Br-A* backward association of the second list. Since we have interference stemming from *both* forward and backward associations in this paradigm, we would expect a large amount of negative transfer, which is the case.

In summary, we have examined four specific sources of transfer. Two of these, stimulus discrimination (as well as response differentiation) and response learning produce positive transfer. The remaining two, forward and backward associations, produce negative transfer.

Transfer and Task Similarity

We have already noted that similarity between two tasks is a major factor in producing transfer. Throughout this chapter we have seen instances of transfer based upon the similarity of the two tasks involved. Transfer from French to Spanish, from tennis to squash, from driving one car to another, are all examples that we have noted. In these examples we have not attempted to deal systematically with the separate effects of stimulus and response similarity between the two tasks. We have merely noted that when two tasks possess some similar requirements or features, we may expect some positive transfer from one to the other.

Now, let us examine a more restricted example, one in which we can more closely look at the effects of stimulus similarity alone. Imagine that the laws governing traffic lights in the United States were suddenly changed so that we no longer stopped our car when the traffic light was red but stopped when the light was orange. Would this change be likely to produce difficulty? Most likely not. What we have done is to require our driver to make the *same* response of stopping to stimulus events that are *highly similar*. Given the similarity of red and orange, it would be relatively easy to learn to stop at an orange light. You may recognize this example as an instance of an A-B, A'-B paradigm. The initial association is red-stop (A-B) and the new association is orange-stop (A'-B). This, of course, is a condition for positive transfer.

Now, recall our hypothetical example of an A-B, A-Br paradigm, in which the traffic signals are reversed. Imagine that you must now stop in the presence of green and go in the presence of red. Such a condition, as we noted, will lead to considerable interference, or negative transfer. The negative transfer may, however, occur mainly in the first or first few trials following this change.

Let us now reexamine our example of negative transfer from squash to tennis. Here we observed that the tennis player might experience some difficulty with his game after playing a few sessions of squash. We noted that in this situation the task required a *new* set of wrist responses, responses incompatible with those of squash. What can we say about the stimulus events in the two games? Although there are some obvious differences in size of the courts, rules, and speed with which the ball moves, the essential and common stimulus event in both situations is that of a ball moving towards a player. In other words, both games have a common or highly similar stimulus event but require different responses. If we ignore, for purposes of analysis, the differences between the stimuli and concentrate on the critical stimulus feature, a ball moving rapidly toward a player, this *aspect* of the relationship between tennis and squash *approximates* that of an A-B, A-D paradigm, or at least an A-B, A'-D paradigm, depending on whether we wish to regard the stimuli as identical or as highly similar. In real life, of course, it is sometimes difficult to analyze complex situations and reduce them to an appropriate paradigm. Everyday examples, because of their complexities, may only approximate laboratory paradigms. Moreover, we are less likely to discover stimulus situations that can really be regarded as identical.

These illustrations emphasize the significance of similarity in transfer. Before we examine the relationship between similiarity and transfer we shall again look at the concept of similarity.

The Concept of Similarity

Obviously, if we are to understand how similarity affects transfer, we must first have some reasonable understanding of what is meant by similarity. In chapter 3 we distinguished between formal similarity, meaningful similarity, and conceptual similarity of verbal materials. The basic issue is how does one measure the similarity between two events? Three general approaches to this problem have been made.

One way of specifying the similarity of events is to measure the *number of elements that two events have in common*. This approach is useful when the stimuli or responses contain two or more elements. For example, the formal similarity of trigrams is defined by counting the number of letters held in common by two trigrams. TRM and TRH are high in formal similarity because they share two letters in common; TRM and BKM are somewhat less close in formal similarity because they share only one element in common; TRM and KJC are dissimilar because they share no common elements.

Whereas it is relatively easy to measure the similarity of some laboratory tasks by counting the number of elements in common, it is more difficult to accomplish this with everyday tasks. Nevertheless, you can get an intuitive grasp of the notion of common elements by considering the languages French, Spanish, and Chinese. French and Spanish possess many more common elements than do French and Chinese or Spanish and Chinese. French and Spanish are derived from a common language, Latin; have many words that are similar in spelling, and use the same alphabet. In summary, one way of measuring the similarity of complex events is to count the number of elements in common.

Many stimulus events vary along some *continuous dimension* such as size, brightness, color, etc. Lights can vary in brightness and color; tones can vary in intensity and pitch; objects can vary in size. The closer two lights are in brightness the greater is their similarity. Likewise, the closer two objects are in size, the greater is their similarity. Responses can also vary along continuous dimensions such as speed or force. When dealing with relatively simple stimuli or responses, the measurement of physical attributes is a convenient way of defining similarity.

Since studies of human learning usually use more complex stimuli and responses, common element definitions of similarity are used more frequently than physical dimensions. Only in relatively simple studies of human learning, where the stimulus events vary along a physical dimension, is similarity defined in terms of some measured attribute.

Not only may events vary in terms of physical features, whether this be in terms of common elements or dimensions, but events may vary in their *degree of learned similarity*. For example, words that are meaningfully similar become so not because of the number of common elements, but because they define the same objects or events. The words "icy" and "cold" acquire similarity because they describe the same events. Words that are conceptually similar, in the sense of belonging to the same category, are so because of learned similarity. More generally, stimuli and responses acquire similarity when they are associated with some common event.

Stimulus Similarity and Transfer

Let us now look more closely at the effects of stimulus similarity on transfer. There are two general cases that we must consider. First, we can vary the similarity between the first- and second-task stimuli, keeping the responses identical in the two tasks. Second, we can vary the similarity of the stimuli while simultaneously changing the responses.

In the first case, WHERE STIMULI ARE VARIED AND THE RESPONSES KEPT IDENTICAL, POSITIVE TRANSFER INCREASES WITH INCREASING STIMULUS SIMILARITY. This generalization is illustrated in figure 12, which shows transfer as a function of stimulus similarity. We note that as the similarity between the stimuli increases, the amount of transfer also increases. The stimuli vary along a continuum of similarity beginning with A, which represents identity between first- and second-task stimuli, to A', which represents high between-list similarity, to A", which represents moderate similarity, to C which represents dissimilar stimuli.

A simple illustration will amplify the principle. Consider the games of checkers, chinese checkers, chess, and three-dimensional chess. We would expect considerable positive transfer from checkers to chinese checkers. It would be quite easy to learn chinese checkers, having learned checkers, because of the high similarity of the conditions of the games. The many features of similarity include similar, although not identical, playing boards, only one type of object (checker piece and marble), identical jumping rules, etc. We would also expect positive transfer from checkers to chess, again because of some common features of both games. Both use a common board, similar number of pieces (16 in chess, 12 in checkers, per player), and the *concept* of

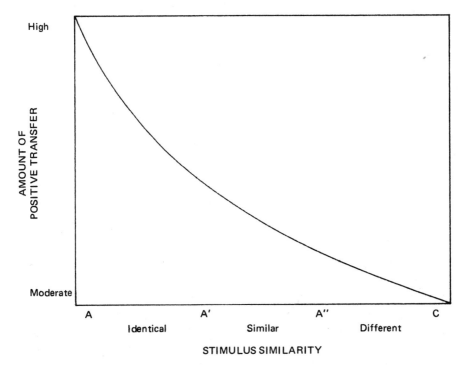

Figure 12. Transfer as a function of degree of stimulus similarity with responses kept identical.

capturing pieces is similar, although the specific rules of capturing differ. The transfer from checkers to chess would, however, be less than our first example because the pieces differ and different playing rules are used. Finally, we would expect even less positive transfer from checkers to three-dimensional chess because the stimulus conditions are even less similar than in the first two examples.

When stimulus similarity is varied and responses also change, we have a *restriction* on the general rule that similarity aids transfer. The rule is: IF THE RESPONSES IN THE TRANSFER TASK ARE DIFFERENT FROM THOSE IN THE FIRST TASK, THEN THE GREATER THE SIMILARITY OF THE STIMULI, THE LESS THE TRANSFER. Indeed, as the stimuli became highly similar, the effect shifts from positive to *negative* transfer. This generalization is illustrated graphically in figure 13, which shows transfer as a function of stimulus similarity when the responses *differ*.

A practical, although hypothetical, example will help make this principle somewhat more obvious. Suppose that the rules governing traffic lights in our society were now changed so that we no longer stopped our car in the presence

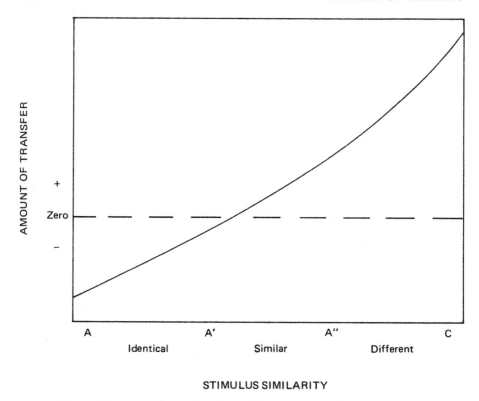

STIMULUS SIMILARITY

Figure 13. Transfer as a function of degree of stimulus similarity when the responses are different.

of a red light and had to learn to go in the presence of an orange light. The situation can be diagrammed this way:

Old Traffic Rule	New Traffic Rule
A - B	A' - D
Red	Orange
light - Stop	light - Go

The situation amounts to making a new (in this case opposite) response D to a very similar stimulus A'. Thus we can regard the situation as like that of an A-B, A'-D paradigm, that of making a new response to a similar stimulus. Now, what is likely to happen? We would, in all likelihood, find it a bit confusing to learn to go when we saw an orange light. We would have some tendency to continue to stop because of an earlier learned response of stopping in the presence of a similar light. Since orange and red are highly similar, we would indeed expect some negative transfer. On the other hand, as the stimuli became less similar, we would find it less difficult to learn the new habit.

Response Similarity and Transfer

We have already noted that, in general, learning to make new responses to the same stimuli is a basic condition for negative transfer. This, of course, is what happens in the A-B, A-D paradigm. We may, however, vary response similarity and ask how this affects transfer.

IF WE KEEP THE STIMULI IDENTICAL IN THE INITIAL AND TRANSFER TASKS AND VARY RESPONSE SIMILARITY, POSITIVE TRANSFER WILL INCREASE WITH INCREASING RESPONSE SIMILARITY. This principle is illustrated in figure 14, which shows transfer as a function of response similarity. Note that the amount of positive transfer decreases as the responses become less similar, and that as the responses become new or unrelated (D), we obtain some negative transfer.

For example, let us compare the transfer from tennis to badminton with tennis to baseball. We would expect greater transfer in the former case because the responses are more similar than in the latter case. Both tennis and badminton are played with racquets, use rectangular courts, and require the habit of

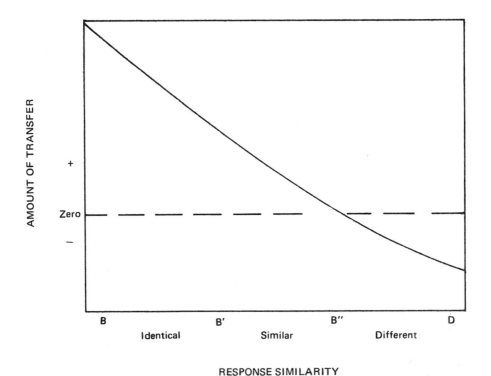

Figure 14. Transfer as a function of degree of response similarity when the stimuli are kept identical.

keeping your eye on the ball. Tennis and baseball are less similar, although they do have some features in common, such as the desirability of keeping your eye on the ball.

Mechanisms of Transfer

Given that similarity between tasks produces a powerful effect on transfer, how do we account for this fact? What kinds of mechanisms or processes underlie the effects due to similarity? There are two mechanisms known to be important: *generalization* and *mediation*.

Generalization

The process of *stimulus generalization* is seen when, having learned to respond to a particular stimulus, we also acquire some tendency to respond to stimuli similar to the training stimulus. For example, having learned to respond to one tone, similar tones also acquire the tendency to evoke the same response. Let us now see how the process of stimulus generalization, as a *theoretical* mechanism, can be used to explain the effects of stimulus similarity on transfer.

Consider the A-B, A′-B transfer paradigm which is known to produce positive transfer. In this situation the same set of responses are learned to new but similar stimuli. If we assume that during the learning of A-B associations there is some tendency for similar stimuli (A′) to develop associative connections with the B responses, then we see that two things are happening. First, the A-B associations are learned and, second, A′-B associations are also strengthened but to a weaker degree. Therefore, when the second list (A′-B) is begun, the learner begins with some of this learning already accomplished by virtue of generalization. Thus he is able to proceed with A′-B learning quite rapidly.

This mechanism can be illustrated with a simple example. Let the stimuli consist of geometric symbols such as rectangles, triangles, etc. During A-B learning, the individual learns to associate a particular geometric figure with a particular response. For example, he learns △-Happy, and □-Increasing as two of several pairs. If we assume the process of stimulus generalization

$A - B$	$A' - B$
△ - Happy	△ - Happy
□ - Increasing	□ - Increasing

during A-B learning, then he learns not only the △-Happy association, but learns to respond in a similar manner to other triangular-shaped stimuli to a weaker degree. Thus the second-list association of △-Happy benefits from considerable transfer based upon stimulus generalization, and is learned with relative ease. Similarly, having learned the association □-Increasing, the second association ☐-Increasing is quite easy to learn because the stimuli are similar, permitting stimulus generalization from one to the other.

A parallel mechanism of *response generalization* can be used to account for the effects of response similarity on transfer. The process of response generalization is seen when, having learned to make a particular response to a particular stimulus, responses similar to the learned response also acquire some strength. For example, having learned to type with a characteristic force, we also acquire some tendency to type with somewhat less and somewhat greater force.

Now consider the A-B, A-B′ paradigm in which new but quite similar responses are learned to the same stimuli. As noted previously, this situation leads to positive transfer. In this case, assume that during A-B learning some strengthening of similar responses (B′) occur so that both A-B and A-B′ associations develop some associative strength. The A-B′ associations are weaker, of course, because they are never directly reinforced. Nevertheless, when the second list (A-B′) is begun, the learner begins with some of this learning already achieved. Thus, the new associations are readily learned because of response generalization.

The use of stimulus generalization and response generalization, as explanatory mechanisms of transfer, stems from the study of conditioned responses in lower animals. In these studies the stimuli are quite simple events, like tones and lights, and thus vary along only a single dimension of similarity such as loudness or brightness. In studies of human learning, the stimuli are usually much more complex, involving at least several components or features. The use of generalization to explain transfer effects due to similarity is therefore most applicable when the stimuli vary along clearly defined physical dimensions. In addition, when the stimuli are formally similar, the generalization explanation is useful. When, however, we deal with *meaningful* and *conceptual* similarity, a second mechanism, *mediation*, is needed to account for some of the findings.

Mediation

It is possible in situations where the response terms are similar, as in the A-B, A-B′ paradigm, or where the stimulus terms are similar, as in the A-B, A′-B paradigm, for transfer to occur on the basis of *mediation* rather than simple generalization. Consider an A-B, A-B′ paradigm in which the response terms are conceptually related, such as *table* and *chair*. We first learn the association CEJ-table and then learn CEJ-chair. Considerable positive transfer will result.

But how is the positive transfer produced? We know from word association tests that table and chair are common associates. Since most people already have this association, they can most likely "use" it in learning the second list. In the first list, the CEJ-table association is established. The second list is easily learned if we use table as a mediating stimulus to think of chair. In effect, we may develop the mediating chain of A-B-B', that is, CEJ-table-chair. Very little new learning is required in the second list if we think about and use the already available associative connection. Thus the process of mediation can account for the effects of similarity on transfer, particularly when the responses or stimuli are meaningfully or conceptually similar.

Some Practical Applications of Transfer

We will now turn our attention to some of the major factors that affect transfer and discuss their implications for the teaching-learning process. From your viewpoint, an important issue is how to study so as to maximize the possibilities for transfer. Similarly, the instructor is concerned with how to teach for transfer. It is useful, therefore, to focus on how knowledge of principles of transfer and of the factors that produce transfer can be applied in educational and daily life activities. We can do no more than state some general guidelines; therefore, the present set of practical suggestions must be viewed as only suggestive of a larger number of possible applications.

Task (Stimulus) Variation

In order to maximize transfer, should you practice extensively on a single task or, alternatively, should you practice on a variety of tasks of the same class? *A factor of considerable importance for producing positive transfer is practice under varied task conditions.* For example, practice in driving different kinds of cars will make it easier to learn to drive a new car compared with an equal amount of practice on only one kind of car. Varied training with different kinds of cars provides experience with different stimulus situations, thus making new learning easier.

In a similar vein, you will find that your understanding of a topic can be improved not so much by repeated rereading of the same text, but by reading another text on the same subject matter. Getting a different slant on the topic, looking at another approach to the issues, and seeing the same ideas presented in a somewhat new context all serve to strengthen your understanding of a topic.

The importance of varied context and examples cannot be overemphasized. Regardless of whether you are learning simple discriminations or more complex concepts, stimulus variation can be helpful. For instance, several examples of a concept will serve to strengthen your understanding so that you are more likely to see potential applications in new learning situations. In contrast, with only one example, you may attend to features unessential to the concept and thus fail to transfer appropriately because of a failure to learn the concept in the first place.

Transfer from Easy to Difficult Discriminations

An important principle of transfer is that transfer is more likely if one first begins with the easier aspects of a task and then shifts to the more difficult aspects. The principle is especially important in discrimination learning, where you must distinguish between two or more stimuli.

Consider the kinds of discriminations that a young child must make in learning the alphabet. To each letter he must learn to respond with a distinctive speech pattern. At a simplified level he must learn twenty-six paired associates, a speech pattern for each visual symbol. Many of the letters are easy to distinguish, whereas others are more difficult, especially *b* and *d.* Two things are important in teaching the child this set of discriminations. First, it is wise practice to begin with the easier-to-distinguish letters such as, for example, *a* and *b.* Only after he has mastered a number of the easier ones should you teach the more difficult ones. Second, when you begin with the more difficult ones, especially *b* and *d,* you should use letters that have been exaggerated or made more distinctive in some fashion. Subsequently you can teach him the *b-d* discriminations with the letters as they normally appear.

The importance of this principle is seen in many situations. For example, in learning to type by the touch method, you first learn the easier discriminations and then move on to the more difficult ones. In learning to discriminate colors, it is best to distinguish the primary colors first and then to distinguish among more subtle differences in varying shades of color. We are, however, unable to specify how easy the initial discriminations should be in order to optimize transfer. This is simply to say that we cannot specify the exact optimal level of difficulty for ensuring transfer. The work of Frank Logan suggests, however, that the "easy" discrimination should not be extremely easy, and that the transfer should be progressive but rapid. Thus the principle of going from easy to more difficult discriminations is a good rule of thumb, given your awareness of these qualifications.

Degree of Original Learning

Variations in the degree of original or first-task learning affect the amount of transfer produced. The effects of degree of learning are somewhat complicated because they depend on the transfer situation or paradigm. With the A-B, A-D and A-B, C-B paradigms, the effect of increasing the degree of learning is first to increase the amount of negative transfer and then to decrease the amount of negative transfer with additional practice. A general rule of thumb is that of a U-shaped function relating degree of learning and transfer. In contrast, with the A-B, A-Br paradigm, negative transfer increases with increasing amounts of original learning.

In situations where one learns successive tasks of the same class, greater positive transfer occurs when extensive practice occurs with the early tasks in the series. Therefore, a good practical rule is to ensure adequate practice with the original task so as to either minimize interference during second-task learning or to maximize positive transfer.

Task Similarity

We have seen that similarity between tasks is a fundamental condition for transfer. From a practical viewpoint this means that one should, ideally, learn under conditions that at least approximate the ultimate testing conditions. But how can this be achieved? How, for example, is it possible to study under conditions that approximate what is required of you during test situations? There are a number of ways that this objective can be accomplished.

Consider the matter of test preparation. If you know, for example, that the test will consist of short essay questions that require both recall of factual information and integration of materials from several sources, then your preparation must include these features. Indeed, you might even practice certain features of this task by asking and *writing* answers to essay questions. You might ask a friend to ask questions of you to which you *write* the answers. By writing short essays, as distinct from merely thinking about or discussing issues, you directly practice the very behaviors required by the test.

In a similar vein, if your exam consists of true-false and multiple-choice questions, you could agree among a small group of friends for each to construct a sample set of test items. The test items could be circulated and you could take the practice test. This has the double advantage of not only practicing an event similar to the forthcoming test, but also of forcing you to think about the important principles and ideas on which you will be examined.

Summary

In this chapter we have emphasized that prior learning can affect the way we perform in subsequent learning situations. The influence of previous learning on performance in some new situation defines transfer of training. Transfer effects may be positive, negative, or zero.

The study of transfer involves the comparison of experimental and control group performance on some transfer task. If the experimental group performs superior to the control, we have positive transfer; if the reverse occurs, we have negative transfer; if the two groups are the same, we have zero transfer. The study of paired associate transfer revolves around four basic paradigms: A-B, C-D (new stimuli and responses); A-B, A-D (old stimuli and new responses); A-B, C-B (new stimuli and old responses) and A-B, A-Br (responses re-paired). Transfer paradigms are simply shorthand expressions for describing the relationship between first- and second-list learning. They may be expanded to include the effects of variations in stimulus and response similarity.

Transfer effects can be analyzed into general and specific sources. General transfer includes learning-to-learn and warm-up effects. Specific transfer refers to transfer based upon similarities between the two tasks. Four sources of specific transfer examined included stimulus discrimination, response learning, forward, and backward associations.

Similarity was seen as a major factor producing transfer. Three approaches to defining similarity were noted: common elements, dimensions, and learned similarity. Formal similarity of verbal materials was seen as an instance of common elements; conceptual and meaningful similarity of verbal materials were seen as instances of learned similarity. We saw that the effects of similarity depended upon changes in stimuli and responses: (1) Where stimuli are varied in similarity between tasks and the responses kept identical, positive transfer increases with increasing stimulus similarity; (2) If the responses in the transfer task are different from those in the first task, then the greater the similarity of the stimuli, the less the transfer; (3) If the stimuli are kept identical in the two tasks and the responses varied, positive transfer will increase with increasing response similarity. Two major mechanisms for accounting for similarity effects on transfer were generalization and mediation.

Some practical points in studying for transfer were noted: (1) practice under varied task or stimulus conditions, such as studying several instances of a concept, is an important factor for positive transfer; (2) arrange learning so as to begin with the easier features of a task before moving on to more difficult features; (3) make sure that sufficient practice with the initial task is obtained before you expect much transfer; and (4) study under conditions that at least approximate those of the ultimate testing conditions, that is, where possible, maximize similarities between study conditions and the ultimate testing situation.

True-False Items: Transfer of Training

1. Transfer of training refers only to situations in which prior learning aids subsequent performance.

(Transfer refers to whatever effect prior learning has upon subsequent performance. Prior learning may aid or interfere with later learning; moreover, there may be both facilitation and interfering effects in the same task which cancel, producing zero transfer. False.)

2. The transfer design that employs a control condition in which subjects do not learn an initial task fails to control for nonspecific (general) transfer effects.

(In such transfer studies, we are unable to interpret the results in any analytical sense, because even if positive transfer is obtained we are unable to estimate how much effect [if any] is due to specific transfer and how much is due to general transfer. True.)

3. The A-B, C-D transfer paradigm is a control condition for measuring transfer effects in other paradigms.

(The A-B, C-D paradigm allows for general transfer effects alone, since both the stimuli and responses in the transfer task differ from and are unrelated to those of the initial task. Hence, any transfer from A-B to C-D is due to general practice effects. True.)

4. Both the A-B, A-D and A-B, C-B paradigms characteristically produce positive transfer.

(The A-B, A-D paradigm typically produces negative transfer, whereas the A-B, C-B paradigm is the usual condition for positive transfer. False.)

> 5. Learning-to-learn is one form of general transfer.

(The progressive improvement in performance when one learns a series of tasks of the same class is an instance of general transfer. In such tasks, neither the stimuli nor responses are identical or similar in terms of common elements; hence the transfer effects cannot be due to specific similarities among the successive tasks. True.)

6. Specific transfer refers to transfer effects that depend upon similarities between the tasks, such as stimulus and/or response similarity.

(Specific transfer refers to transfer effects that occur in situations in which one or more features of the initial and transfer tasks are related, such as identical stimuli and responses, similar stimuli and responses, etc. For example, transfer of response learning is a specific transfer effect because this occurs when responses in the two tasks are identical; having learned the responses in the first task, the person begins the transfer task with this component of learning already achieved. True.)

7. Increasing the similarity of the stimuli in the two lists while keeping the responses identical leads to increasing amounts of positive transfer.

(Stimulus similarity is a basic condition for producing positive transfer when the responses are kept identical. Moreover, the limiting case of similarity is identical stimuli in the two tasks; with identical stimuli and identical responses, we have a continuation of the same task. True.)

8. The two principal mechanisms for explaining transfer are generalization and warm-up.

(The two important mechanisms are generalization, in which there can be either stimulus and/or response generalization, and mediation, which is the development and use of linkages between items. False.)

9. In order to ensure maximum positive transfer, the training (or teaching) conditions should concentrate on keeping stimulus conditions constant.

(On the contrary, stimulus variation is an important factor in facilitating positive transfer. In general, varied experience or practice, and contextual variability, provide for greater transfer than does training under constant conditions. False.)

10. We might expect greater positive transfer from studying biology to psychology than from biology to mathematics.

(We would expect somewhat more transfer from biology to psychology because these two areas are more similar than biology and mathematics. Biology and psychology are both life sciences, use some of the same concepts, and are concerned with the behavior of organisms. True.)

11. In order to maximize the likelihood that your study habits will transfer to exam performance, you should as part of studying include some sort of practice in writing exam questions.

(This example illustrates the principles of attempting to maximize the similarity between the training conditions and the "ultimate" test of performance. True.)

12. Learning to make a new incompatible response to the same stimulus is a general condition for positive transfer.

(This is a characteristic condition for negative transfer. False.)

6 —————————————————————

Memory

Everyone has experienced the frustration of searching for a particular word in memory and not being able to come up with it. Even though you are certain that you know the word, such as a person's name, you cannot recall it at the moment. The word is "on the tip of your tongue," but it does not come to mind. An especially frustrating feature of the tip-of-the-tongue phenomena is the embarrassingly long time it may take to recall a familiar name. This is a case in which we know that the name is stored in memory despite the fact that we are unable to retrieve it. Why this process occurs and how we ultimately are able sometimes to recall an item illustrate basic problems in analyzing memory.

Consider an easy question: What is your home telephone number? For most people the answer simply pops into awareness without much evidence of thinking or search processes. On occasion, however, you may "block" if someone asks your phone number. Similarly, if you move and acquire a new phone number, you may note that the old number will be recalled unless you have had opportunity to rehearse the new number. These kinds of events require explanation in terms of principles of memory.

Consider a somewhat more difficult question: Was your bedroom doorknob in the house in which you lived when you were twelve years old on the right or left? Imagine yourself as being outside your room as you attempt to recall its location. Your recall of this involves several substages. You must first recall the house in which you lived at age twelve; next you will probably "locate" your room in the house; finally, you may be able to recall the doorknob as being right or left. How this process occurs represents another instance of problems in memory. Intuitively, at least, it seems clear that recall of information involves a search process. One problem of a theory of memory is to specify the rules governing this search.

This description of memory will frequently employ the terms *retention* and *forgetting. Retention* refers to the extent to which material that was previously learned is still present or retained. *Forgetting* refers to that portion which is lost. Thus, retention and forgetting refer to two sides of a coin; retention to what is remembered and forgetting to what is lost. The point to note is that each process is defined in terms of the other; *forgetting* is defined as the difference between how much was originally learned and how much is retained, and *retention* is defined as how much is retained.

The examples above are but a few instances of the many kinds of problems in memory. The examples do emphasize that memory is not simply a passive process of storing information and reproducing it when needed. Memory involves reconstruction of events. This is simply to say that in many situations we remember rules and general principles, and from these attempt to recall specific facts and details. Before we examine these issues in greater detail, we shall look at the relationship between learning, transfer, and memory.

Learning, Transfer, and Memory

Obviously learning and memory are related processes. We might say that memory is the result of what is learned, but such a statement would fail to distinguish the processes. It must be first recognized that learning and memory are in some sense continuous processes. This continuity is seen in the fact that any trial during the course of learning some task may be regarded both as a measure of learning and as a measure of what was retained. How then do we distinguish learning from memory?

The distinction is basically a matter of emphasis and convention. It is conventionally agreed that the study of learning focuses on events that occur *during a trial* or series of trials, whereas the study of memory focuses on events that occur *during the interval* between termination of the learning trials and the retention test, that is, the retention interval. Therefore, the operational feature that distinguishes memory from learning is that memory is concerned not only with the factors that affect performance during learning but also those that operate during the retention interval. Another distinction is that learning places principal emphasis on how events get into memory storage, whereas memory is concerned with how events are "recovered" or "retrieved" once they are stored.

In a similar vein, a distinction between transfer and retention can be made. Transfer, as described in the previous chapter, concerns the manner in which prior learning affects the way in which we learn new events. Retention deals with the memory of already-learned events, as distinct from how such events affect new learning. Thus, we can summarize as follows: (1) *learning* deals with how events are acquired; (2) *memory* deals with what gets stored and how we retrieve or recall it; and (3) *transfer* deals with the influence of prior learning upon new learning. Although there are more distinctions that might be made, these are sufficient for our purposes.

Encoding, Storage, and Retrieval

Our current view of memory is one that emphasizes three processes: encoding, storage, and retrieval. Although we referred to these processes in an earlier chapter, let us look at them now with reference to the concept of memory.

For some event to be stored in memory, it must be placed in a "state" such that storage is possible. Regardless of what is stored, the material must ultimately be encoded in some fashion. These encodings may be verbal or imagelike and they represent some kind of transformation of the nominal stimuli impinging on the individual. Encoding is transforming events into some state so that they can be stored and is accomplished during what we ordinarily call learning. We have discussed encoding in previous chapters, so we will only note it here.

Storage and retrieval can be understood by recalling the filing cabinet analogy mentioned in an earlier chapter. As was noted, at an uncomplicated level, memory may be considered as a matter of placing things in a filing cabinet and taking things out when you want them. An item placed in a filing cabinet can be regarded as an event stored. One file clerk, however, might file items in a systematic fashion, whereas another might do so haphazardly. Items filed by either file clerk are considered to be in storage. But consider the difference when the two file clerks try to locate materials: The first clerk will generally be able to locate materials, while the second clerk will have difficulty unless, of course, she develops an elaborate personal system for locating her materials. The business of locating the materials is *retrieval*. The conceptual separation of storage processes from retrieval processes calls attention to the fact that events may be stored in memory even though they are not retrievable. More generally the distinction calls attention to two processes that until recently were treated together.

This description provides only a general understanding of the concepts of storage and retrieval. We shall explore these processes in more detail subsequently. For the moment, this description will allow us to compare two major approaches to the understanding of memory: association theory and information-processing.

Approaches to Memory: Associationism and Information-Processing

Psychologists who study memory usually talk about memory from one of two conceptual viewpoints: either associationistic, or information-processing approaches. These two terms loosely describe a constellation of assumptions and concepts used in the description of memory processes. The older approach is that of associationism, stemming from Ebbinghaus and Thorndike, pioneers in the study of learning and memory. The more contemporary approach is that of information-processing, stemming initially from the work of the British psychologist Donald Broadbent. Since we shall talk about principles that stem from both approaches, we need to describe these viewpoints in more detail.

The associationistic tradition in psychology contends that what gets learned are associations between events. It is usually assumed that stimuli and responses get associated during the course of learning and that this learning is a continuous process. Some learning theorists have contended that what gets associated is some connection between stimuli, that is, a stimulus-stimulus association, but virtually all learning theorists from Thorndike to the present have taken the view that learning is an associative process involving the gradual strengthening of associative connections or bonds.

The concept of "association" refers to some *hypothetical* process and does not imply specific events in the nervous system. It is a descriptive or functional term that, in a neutral sense, merely indicates that event B has some likelihood of occurrence following event A. In other words, a response B has some probability of occurrence upon the presentation of stimulus A, given certain conditions. There are additional meanings attached to the concept of association, but this description characterizes its essential features for present purposes.

An associative conception of the learning process leads to looking at memory in a particular way. If learning is the establishment of stimulus-response associations, memory deals with the problem of "what happens" to these associations over the course of time and under conditions of new learning. The problem of memory becomes the problem of how associations are forgotten with the passage of time and what factors influence the forgetting of associations. From this viewpoint, memory is viewed as the consequence of learning.

The information-processing approach to memory takes a somewhat different attack on the problem of memory. Memory is viewed as dealing with the "flow of information" through the person, from its initial encoding, to storage, and finally to retrieval. An important feature of information-processing approaches is the emphasis on the distinction between storage and retrieval. This distinction, however, can be incorporated into association theory. The associative position places emphasis on the storage process, that is, how events were learned, whereas information-processing approaches ask not only about how information is stored but focus on how information is *retrieved* from memory once it is stored. Associative conceptions of memory have, of course, been interested in recall or retrieval. It is the explicit attempt to distinguish storage and retrieval, using a conceptual language borrowed from computer technology, that characterizes information-processing approaches. Retrieval mechanisms, the business of getting things out of storage, takes on special importance for those psychologists who emphasize information-processing approaches. The focus is more on retrieval than on storage with this approach, because retrieval mechanisms are viewed as the "key" to unlocking memory.

It is beyond the scope of this book to do more than briefly sketch the major differences in emphasis between these two approaches. Both conceptual approaches are in a state of revision and new developments are rapidly occurring. Ultimately, some of the features of stimulus-response associationistic approaches may be translatable into information-processing approaches and vice versa. For our purposes it is important to note that these two approaches represent somewhat different ways of thinking about memory and, consequently have led to different kinds of research in memory. Both approaches have, of course, advanced our understanding of memory.

The Study of Memory

There are many ways in which memory can be measured. As we shall see, these different measures tap different aspects of memory processes, and the amount of retention obtained can readily depend upon the particular method of measurement. Therefore, we cannot talk about the method for measuring memory, but rather of various methods which reflect different features of the process. There are three basic methods: *recall*, *recognition*, and *savings*.

Recall

A straightforward way of measuring what is retained is with the recall procedure. *In recall, you are required to demonstrate what you have learned by producing the correct response(s).* Being able to produce your telephone number, the date of your birth, or a friend's name are obvious instances of recall. Answering questions on an essay examination is another instance of recall.

There is a further distinction, that of *free* and *aided* recall. Free recall simply requires that you produce the items learned in any particular order. We have already discussed this procedure in the context of free learning. Here we noted that you are presented a series of verbal units, one at a time, and required to recall the items in any order. Free recall, therefore, emphasizes simple availability of responses, without any physical cues for recall present. In contrast, aided recall provides some sort of *contextual stimulus* to which you must respond. For example, recall in serial learning can be cued by the previous item, whereas recall in paired associate learning is cued by the stimulus terms.

Instances of free and aided recall are common in everyday experience. Recalling a list of all your relatives or close friends without their being present would be an instance of free recall. In turn, recalling the names of people sitting close to you in a class, while both you and they are present in the class, is an instance of aided (cued) recall. The basic difference is that aided recall has some external stimulus present to cue the response which is not present in free recall.

HUMANS WILL ALMOST INEVITABLY CREATE THEIR OWN CUES IN A FREE RECALL SITUATION. We noted this process in our earlier discussion of organizational processes in learning. The categorization of events seen in free recall is an instance in which we create our own cues for recall. Similarly, "subjective organization" is another instance.

In a number of cases, free recall will show retention superior to that of aided recall. Even though we may be presented stimuli to cue our responses, we may perform poorer than in simple free recall where no physical cues are present. In this case, we are simply better off to create our own cues for recall than to use those presented by the experimenter.

Other variations of the recall method are used. Following the learning of an A-B, A-D paradigm, in which new responses are learned to the same stimulus, the subject may be asked to recall both the B and D responses in the presence of the A stimuli. This method has received extensive use in experiments evaluating the interference theory of forgetting, an issue to be discussed later.

The recall method is also used in the study of memory for visual forms and patterns. In this instance, the subject is shown some form or pattern and is later asked to *reproduce* (draw) it as faithfully as possible. For example, the subject may be shown various geometric designs and then be required to draw the designs on subsequent trials. This variation of the recall method, called *reproduction*, has received extensive use in studies of perceptual memory and learning. One difficulty with this procedure is the problem of judging what a subject has actually drawn, and scoring his drawing in a quantitative and objective fashion.

A principal feature of the recall method is that it can be relatively "insensitive" compared with other methods of measurement. For example, the fact that you are unable to recall a list of terms, say in biology, doesn't mean that there is no effect as a result of memorizing a list of biological terms. All of us have had experiences in which although we were unable to recall certain terms we would still correctly *recognize* them. Let us therefore consider a second method of measuring memory, recognition.

Recognition

A recognition test requires you to select items previously experienced or learned and to reject other items, which are called distractor or filler items. As we noted earlier, there are two basic types of recognition tests: (1) *single-item* procedure and (2) *multiple-item* procedure. The multiple-item procedure is most common, so we will consider it first.

In the *multiple-item* procedure you are shown each item learned, along with one or more distractor items. For example, you might be asked, "Which transfer paradigm yields the greatest amount of negative transfer?"

(a) A-B, C-B   (b) A-B, A-D   (c) A-B, A-Br

If you are *required* to select one of the items in the recognition test, the procedure is called *forced-choice.* This is usually done because of the advantage gained in controlling for possible differences in response bias. In this example, with three choices the likelihood of getting the correct answer just by chance is one out of three. Chance probability assumes, however, that all three choices are, on the average, equally likely. It is usually not the case that all choices are equally likely, principally because you may know enough to eliminate at least one of the incorrect alternatives. Indeed, it is good practice when taking multiple-choice tests to eliminate those items which you know or suspect are clearly wrong and then make your selection among the remaining items, especially if the question is a difficult one.

The typical line-up in a police examination is an instance of a multiple-choice recognition procedure. A suspect is lined up with several other people, all of whom are somewhat similar in appearance. Eyewitnesses to the alleged crime are then asked to identify the suspect. The basic assumption underlying this procedure, as well as all recognition tests of this kind, is that if an item (in this case a person) is remembered, it can be recognized when placed among several alternatives. On the other hand, if an item is not remembered, then it can be recognized correctly no better than by chance in the long run.

With the *single-item* procedure, each item is shown one at a time and you are asked to say "old" or "new" to each item. Some of the items are old, that is, previously experienced, and some are new. Sometimes the subject may instead be asked to say "yes" or "no," with "yes" indicating that he has experienced the item during some previous training session and "no" that he has not. Therefore, the single-item procedure is sometimes referred to as the *yes-no* procedure.

Motivational Factors and Biases in Recognition Memory

Use of a single-item recognition procedure requires an awareness of possible response biases, such as a person's tendency to respond "old" irrespective of the specific stimulus items presented. Assume, for example, that you are shown a series of stimuli such as advertisements from popular magazines and asked to remember them. Later you are given a recognition test in which the old items are shown singly, mixed with new items. Now imagine that the instructions further state that every time you said "old" and were correct you would earn one dollar. Under these circumstances you would have a strong tendency to say "old" and, in fact, would frequently do so even when you suspected that the items were actually new ones. You would, therefore, be unlikely to miss any of the *truly* old items but at the same time you would tend to identify incorrectly many new items as "old." This is simply to say that although you would tend to make a large number of correct recognitions (saying "old" to old stimuli), you would also tend to make many false-positives (saying "old" to new stimuli). The point is quite simple: MOTIVATIONAL-

INCENTIVE CONDITIONS DO AFFECT OUR RESPONSE BIASES IN RECOGNITION MEMORY EXPERIMENTS. And a strong bias to say yes in a single-item test will lead to a high correct recognition score but can be quite misleading as an estimate of our "memory."

Consider a second alternative in our illustrative experiment. If the instructions indicated that every time you said "old" and were incorrect it would cost you two dollars, you would now become very conservative in making "old" judgments. You will say "old" less frequently and tend to reserve that response for items you are absolutely certain are old. In this case, you will miss a number of old items but will rarely tend to identify incorrectly new items as "old." The important thing to note is that your total correct recognition score, the number of truly old items called "old," will be considerably different under these two alternatives, despite the fact that your "memory" for the items is exactly the same.

It should now be clear why consideration of response biases are necessary when recognition is used to measure memory. Forced-choice procedures automatically control for bias by requiring the subject to respond on each trial. In contrast, yes-no procedures are quite subject to bias. Some individuals may be very cautious and conservative, saying "yes" only when very sure. Others may be more liberal, saying "yes" to an item if they think that it's reasonably familiar. Consider the most extreme possibility: If you said "yes" to *all* stimuli presented in a yes-no recognition test, your correct recognition score would be perfect but *only* because your bias was to say yes on every trial.

The procedures for controlling response bias in yes-no recognition tests are beyond the scope of this book. They are derived from signal detection theory and allow a separation of effects caused by decision processes, such as biases, from effects due to memory itself. For our purposes we must remember that any recognition score in a yes-no recognition test is a joint result of both our bias, or criterion for making a yes-no decision, on the one hand, and our "true" memory of the item, on the other.

Performance in multiple-item recognition tests depends upon the *number* of items in the test and upon the *relationship* between the correct item and the set of distractors. A two-item recognition test is quite easy because chance correct recognition on any item is one-half. As we increase the number of items, recognition performance decreases. Similarly, the more similar the distractor items are to the correct item, the more difficult recognition will be.

Recall and Recognition Compared

As we have noted, recognition measures usually show greater evidence for retention than do recall. Successful recall requires some degree of response learning since the material must be produced, not just identified. Response learning is not necessary for recognition since the correct item is always presented in the test along with distractor items. On the other hand, discrimination among items is important in recognition, especially if the items are very similar. Indeed, if we markedly increase the similarity between the distractor items and the correct items, then recognition performance will be about the same as recall performance.

Savings

The third major method is savings. The savings method can be a more sensitive method than recall because it may show some evidence for retention when none is obtained with recall. *With the savings method you first learn some task to a given criterion and subsequently relearn the task.* This procedure permits a comparison of original learning and relearning in terms of a savings score based upon, for example, the number of trials or amount of time required to learn the two tasks. A measure of retention in terms of the percent saved is shown by the formula:

$$\text{Percent Saved} = \frac{\text{Number of trials to learn} - \text{Number of trials to relearn}}{\text{Number of trials to learn}} \times 100.$$

For example, if it requires you 30 trials to learn a list of trigrams and only 15 trials to relearn the list, a savings of 50 percent is obtained. Even if the list is relearned in just one less trial, some savings would be shown.

Many of us have experienced a savings effect in memory. We note first that we are unable to recall something that we have previously learned; yet, if we set about relearning it we are frequently surprised at how quickly we can "pick up" the material we thought we had forgotten. Although we are unable to recall the material, some "residue" was present enabling us to quickly relearn the material.

An impressive demonstration of the sensitivity of the savings method was shown by the psychologist Harold Burtt. Burtt read passages of Greek to a child from age 15 months to 3 years. The child was read 3 passages daily consisting of 20 lines of iambic hexameter which were read to the child for 90 days, followed by another set of passages for 90 days more, and so on, until the child was 3 years of age. The child received no further reading or training in Greek until he was 8. At this time Burtt had the child learn the original Greek passages and compared his performance with the learning of presumably equivalent passages which the child had not experienced. The child learned the original passages faster, showing a 30 percent savings at age 8 but no savings when he was later tested at age 18. Since we have no measure of original learning in this experiment, we are unable to say much about "what" was actually learned in the first place. What is clear is that "something" was retained from this early experience that benefited the child in later "relearning" of the material.

These findings suggest one possible implication for education. Although you may not recall certain things you have learned in school unless you use them, you can rapidly relearn them if the need arises.

Basic Stages of Memory Storage

Let us now turn our attention to some of the fundamental stages of memory storage. Memory is not a single process but is composed of several processes and stages. We have already indicated that an important distinction exists between *storage* and *retrieval* processes. We shall now examine the stages in storing information in memory.

The process by which information is stored is currently viewed as consisting of three stages. These stages are: (1) *sensory* or iconic memory, (2) *short-term* memory, and (3) *long-term* memory. These stages or phases differ in terms of what gets processed into memory. Some memory theorists contend that each stage operates in accord with different laws or principles and, therefore, occupies a different storage system. Other theorists, however, regard at least short-term and long-term memory as more or less continuous processes. Moreover, since there is some evidence that short-term and long-term memory are affected by the same variables, the notion of a continuum between the two stages, as distinct from separate systems, is supported. We may bypass this dispute, however, and turn our attention to the three main phases of memory storage. Let us first consider sensory memory.

Sensory Memory

A stimulus continues to produce its effect upon us even when the external stimulus, such as a light or sound, is terminated. For example, if you stare at a light bulb, you will have an after-image of the bulb for a few seconds after the light has been turned off. This persistence of the stimulus in the individual following removal of the external stimulus is called the *stimulus trace*. The trace is simply a hypothetical notion to account for the persistence of stimulation after removal or termination of the external stimulus.

Sensory memory refers to this quite brief period in which the stimulus trace persists. At this stage of memory the information that is stored is simply some sensory representation of the external stimuli that have impinged upon our receptors. This memory is sometimes called *iconic*, referring to its brief and transient character. Obviously, the after-image of a light disappears after a very brief period; similarly, if you press your skin, you can feel the sensation fade after you remove the source of pressure.

During the sensory stage we take in far more information than we can efficiently process. Thus sensory memory is a large-capacity storage system where information is held for only a brief period of time. We can attend to only a fraction of the total amount of information received in this system. This stage represents the domain where we shift subtly from perception to memory. If sensory memory appears to be more of a perceptual process than one of memory, it is only because memory begins with the reception of information which is perception itself.

Information in sensory memory decays extremely fast. Our best estimates indicate that verbal or pictorial information is retained clearly in sensory memory for about one second, after which most of it becomes unavailable for report. In addition, the presentation of a new stimulus can erase information that is momentarily present in sensory memory. Finally, the fraction of information that we attend to and select for further processing goes to the next phase, the short-term memory system.

Short-Term Memory

How often have you looked up a number in the telephone book only to forget it by the time you start to dial the number? If you have an opportunity to rehearse the number, you usually can retain it. Without opportunity for rehearsal you are almost sure to forget the number if you fail to dial within a few seconds. This can happen if, for example, you look up the number and then are interrupted by someone before you can dial the number. This rapid loss in memory during this short period refers to the short-term memory stage.

If information in short-term memory can be rehearsed or processed in some manner, then it can be transferred to long-term memory, a relatively permanent system. The basic difference between short- and long-term memory is that short-term memory is a small capacity system lasting a very brief period in which information has the opportunity to be processed, whereas long-term memory is a large-capacity storage system containing information that is relatively permanent.

An important feature of short-term memory is that it is a limited-capacity system. We can process only about seven items of information at one time. In other words, our memory span is limited to about seven items or "bits" of information. For example, if I read aloud a series of digits in random order and ask you to repeat them, you can, on the average, correctly repeat up to about seven numbers.

It is obvious, however, that on some occasions you can remember much more than seven items of information. In the digit span test you may be able to "chunk" or group the numbers so that you can recall many more than seven. Nevertheless, your recall is now limited to about seven "chunks" of information. The principle still holds, but the *unit* of information has now shifted from a single item to a chunk.

This limit on how much we can process in short-term memory makes it important that we devise coding and organizational strategies for storing information. Without skills in coding things into categories, the amount of information that can be processed is quite limited. Indeed, a principal feature of people who have good memories is their capacity to code and organize information into larger "chunks," enabling a much larger storage of information.

During short-term memory, information is held for a brief period. The function of short-term memory is to hold information for sufficient time so that it can be used, such as dialing a telephone number, or rehearsed and ultimately transferred into long-term storage. If it is not rehearsed or processed in some fashion, it will drop out of short-term memory. In this manner useless information does not remain in the system.

The rapid forgetting characteristically seen in short-term memory was dramatically illustrated in an experiment by Lloyd and Margaret Peterson. A CVC trigram was read to the subject who then was instructed to count backward by threes from some predetermined number. Counting backwards served to prevent rehearsal of the trigram. Subjects were tested over retention intervals ranging from 3 to 18 seconds. Despite the extraordinary short intervals used, the subjects showed a striking decline in memory, with retention being less than 10 percent after 18 seconds. This finding is especially significant when it is considered that the verbal items were well within the memory span of the subjects. More generally, this rapid forgetting over 20-30 second intervals characterizes short-term memory.

Long-Term Memory

By rehearsing items, then, information can become sufficiently processed that it enters long-term memory. The distinction between short-term and long-term memory is not marked by a sharp and clear temporal division. At best we can say that when the retention interval is more than one or two minutes, long-term memory is involved. Long-term memory deals with information that has entered a more permanent storage system. We must emphasize that memory in this system is "relatively" permanent, which is to hedge somewhat on the meaning of permanence. What is meant is that in contrast to short-term memory, where the information is present for only a fleeting period, information in long-term memory is much more accessible for a longer period of time. Some of this information is always accessible such as, for example, your mother's or father's names. Other information, such as the name of your first-grade teacher, may be accessible only part of the time.

Long-term memory is not some passive process in which information taken in just "sits" there waiting to be retrieved when needed. Rather, information in long-term memory is continually being organized in new ways. As we learn new events, old events acquire new perspective.

The distinction between short- and long-term memory does not necessarily imply that they have a different *anatomical* or physiological locus. Although some memory theorists believe that the two storage systems are located in different parts of the brain, the evidence for this kind of difference has not been unequivocally shown. B. Milner has reported an interesting case history of a brain-damaged patient with lesions in the hippocampus. The patient's immediate and long-term memory appeared to be quite normal. The patient was unable, however, to form *new* long-term memory traces, although he could perform normally on intelligence tests and other tests of brief memory. He could converse normally about topics for a brief period but could not recall the topic of conversation for any long period of time. This kind of finding has led some memory theorists to conclude that the *locus* of the two memory systems is different; however, this type of finding does not *require* that they be regarded as systems having a physically different locus. It could be that their locus is the same but that long-term memory requires additional processes in that particular locus.

In summary, a principal theoretical question raised by studies of short-term memory concerns whether short-term and long-term memory represent two different systems or whether they represent events that occur along a continuum. The strategy of those psychologists who emphasize that the two stages are part of a continuum is to emphasize that short- and long-term memory are governed by similar laws and hence represent continuous processes. The strategy of those who believe in a dual system is to argue that there are behavioral phenomena that require different laws or principles for the two systems. At present we conclude that the issue of dual storage systems of memory is still in dispute.

Organizational and Retrieval Processes

We have already noted that our failure to recall some event does not necessarily mean that it isn't in storage. Events may clearly be stored in memory despite the fact that we are unable to recall the information. The fact that you can recognize certain events that you simultaneously are unable to recall indicates that things can be in storage even though you are unable to get at them.

Practice in Retrieval

A particularly frustrating event is to recall the answer to a test question after you have left the classroom, given that you "blanked" the question during the test. Most of you have probably had a correct answer pop into your awareness after you've handed in a test. Such situations further attest to the fact that information may actually be in storage but that momentarily you may be unable to retrieve it.

One of the principal reasons that retrieval processes may fail, even though information is in storage, IS THAT YOU HAVE FAILED TO PRACTICE THE TASK OF RETRIEVING INFORMATION, that is, you have failed to rehearse the business of retrieval. What this means from a practical standpoint is that much of your study effort should be devoted to formulating and answering questions. Moreover, if the tests require that you write answers, your study habits should emphasize composing written answers, at least at a schematic level, to questions you are likely to be asked. Similarly, if you are to give an oral presentation, direct practice in giving your talk to a small group of friends is good practice. By requiring yourself to practice directly the very behaviors or kinds of behaviors required by the test situation, you rehearse the appropriate retrieval process.

Retrieval Depends Upon Organized Storage

The business of retrieving information from memory is not, of course, independent of how you store it. Obviously, if information is stored in an organized and systematic fashion, it has a better chance to be retrieved. For example, consider the fact that test questions sometimes require you to compare and contrast several theories on, say, several issues. If you have studied each theory as an isolated event, without thinking of the relationship between them, then the test will be difficult. If, on the other hand, you have actually compared each of the particular theories with respect to the important issues, perhaps by constructing a chart with issues across the top and theories down the side, then you will have stored the information in a much more systematic and organized fashion. Thus we see that efficient orderly storage is necessary for good recall.

We have already seen in an earlier chapter how organizational processes influence our ability to recall materials. We noted that humans may organize materials in a number of ways as evidenced by the phenomena of associative clustering, category clustering, and subjective organization when no "objective" basis for organizing the materials was present. In both associative and category clustering, humans are able to use the structure inherent in the material to their advantage. This can occur in two ways: material that has some inherent structure is easier to store in memory, and well-organized material aids the retrieval process in the sense that it has a better chance to be retrieved.

Retrieval Cues

Effective retrieval depends upon the presence of retrieval cues. Earlier we distinguished between cued and free recall, noting that cued recall referred to recall in the presence of some physical stimulus, whereas free recall did not have an identifiable physical stimulus. In the most strict sense, however, all recall is cued recall. Free recall is cued by events that we are not always able to identify. At present, however, we know relatively little about the effectiveness of retrieval cues. One thing is clear: the retrieval cues, if they are to be helpful in the sense of helping us recall information that we otherwise could not recall, must be *relevant* to the way in which we stored the information in the first place. For example, if a test question asks you to compare three theories on four issues, and you had constructed a chart comparing these theories on these four issues, then the retrieval cues in the question would be directly relevant to your organized storage style.

A simple illustration of the importance of retrieval cues can be seen as follows: Suppose that a list of categorized materials is learned by a group of subjects. These categories might include animals, vegetables, minerals, plants, etc. Then, half of the subjects are given a free recall test in which they are given the category labels. The remaining half is instructed to recall as many words as possible, but are not shown the retrieval cues. The first group will of course recall more words than the second group. The importance of retrieval cues is probably recognized implicitly by many instructors when they note that the way a question is written can provide the student with a good deal of information about the answer. Indeed, the student who reads a question carefully can often use informative features of the question to help cue his recall.

In summary, the long-term memory system is not simply a dumping ground of facts, arranged in some random fashion. We are constantly shifting, organizing, and reorganizing our memory storage, particularly so when new information is stored. If we are to store information efficiently, it must be effectively organized in some fashion. The particular organization is unique to each individual and is a result of his own individual learning history. Finally, organized, systematic storage is an important key to good recall.

Reconstruction of Events

Another feature of retrieval processes in memory is that they sometimes show evidence for *reconstructive* activity. Not only do we *reproduce* information at the time of recall but we sometimes *reconstruct* information. The reconstructive character of memory is easily seen in studies of perceptual memory where the events consist of pictorial materials, shapes, or geometric figures. If we are shown ambiguous visual stimuli and associate these with verbal labels, we tend to reconstruct the figure in accord with the verbal label. In other words, when we are asked to draw the figures, our drawings are influenced by the verbal label linked with the stimulus during associative training.

Our memory for stories and jokes also shows this reconstructive character. In repeating a story we may tend to add new features to make it more meaningful and coherent, and to drop out features that seem unimportant. Sometimes elaborate detail may be added, indicating that we make up new features based on whatever limited information we can recall.

Interference in Long-term Memory

Once information is placed in long-term memory it is much more resistant to forgetting. Nevertheless, information in this system can also be forgotten despite the fact that long-term memory is a much more stable system than short-term memory. Therefore, the principal problem of long-term memory is to determine the cause(s) of forgetting after a prolonged period involving no additional practice.

A long-held view was that forgetting occurred because of *disuse*. If we failed to use the material learned, in the sense of no additional practice or rehearsal, then it was thought that disuse would bring about forgetting. A disuse theory implies that forgetting occurs because of the passage of time; however, the passage of time, that is, time per se, cannot be the cause of forgetting. Events do change in the course of time but it is not time that produces the change. Rather, IT IS WHAT HAPPENS DURING THE PASSAGE OF TIME THAT BRINGS ABOUT FORGETTING. Therefore, memory theorists have focused on processes that can produce forgetting.

Memory psychologists have proposed two kinds of theory for explaining forgetting: *decay* theory and *interference* theory. Decay theory contends that hypothetical memory traces, which are representations of events learned, decay or weaken automatically with the passage of time. The memory trace decays autonomously, that is, independently of any additional learning that takes place. This decay or weakening of the memory trace is seen as the result of some built-in property of our nervous system. Therefore, forgetting is the natural outcome of a trace-decay principle.

Interference theory, on the other hand, has emphasized that forgetting occurs because of the interfering effects of new learning and of prior learning. The primary task of this theory has been to formulate the various processes that bring about interference and to demonstrate that these processes do, in fact, account for forgetting. The central point to note about interference theory, without describing its details, is to remember that the reason we forget is because of new learning that "interferes" with memory traces, or because of old learning that gets in the way of remembering more recently-learned events.

The advantage of interference theory is that it has led to experiments that ask how new learning affects our retention of previously-learned events. Interference theory has the considerable advantage of being experimentally testable, whereas decay theory has been difficult to evaluate experimentally. Studies of interference theory have led to examination of the effects of events that occur during the retention interval, that is, events that occur between learning some task and the retention test. The study of these effects is known as *retroactive inhibition*.

Retroactive Inhibition

Retroactive inhibition refers to the fact that an event learned during a retention interval can lead to some forgetting of a previously learned event. Retroactive inhibition is simply the forgetting of an earlier-learned task produced by the effects of learning some interpolated task during the retention interval. Suppose you learned a list of Spanish vocabulary and then learned a list of French vocabulary. Although we might expect some positive transfer from the learning of Spanish to the learning of French, we would also find that if we now tested our retention of Spanish, that some forgetting of Spanish would occur because of the interpolated activity of learning French. What you do during the interval between learning some task and being tested for retention can have powerful effects on what you remember.

The importance of events that occur during the retention interval as a factor influencing forgetting has long been known. For example, in one experiment researchers required human subjects to learn a serial list of nonsense syllables to a criterion of one perfect recitation. Following learning, half the subjects slept and half the subjects stayed awake. Subjects slept in the laboratory so that control over this activity was maintained. Subjects who were awake were allowed to leave the laboratory and to return at appropriate time intervals for a retention test. Both groups of subjects were given retention tests after varying amounts of time up to 8 hours, using different lists for each retention interval. The same subjects were tested under both conditions. The retention test was a free recall test requiring the subjects to produce as many items learned as possible. The results of this study are shown in figure 15, a plot of the percent retained for the sleep and waking conditions. While both conditions showed some forgetting, the sleep condition produced far less forgetting than did the awake condition. Forgetting continued to occur for the awake condition over the retention intervals employed, whereas retention was relatively stable after the two-hour retention interval in the sleep condition.

This study demonstrates that the normal activities that occur while we are awake can produce considerable forgetting. Sleep, on the other hand, prevents interfering activities from producing a comparable amount of forgetting. Why this is the case is not fully clear. Sleep may allow consolidation of the memory traces, protecting them from possible interference, whereas normal everyday activities may provide conditions for interference. In any event, the fact that the waking subjects continued to show forgetting and retained far less than the sleep subjects is evidence in support of an interference theory of forgetting.

The study of retroactive inhibition, like that of transfer, requires an experimental and a control group. The *experimental* group learns an initial task, A, and then learns a second task, B, which is interpolated between the initial task A and the test of retention. The *control* group learns some "unrelated" or irrelevant task during the retention interval so that rehearsal of task A is

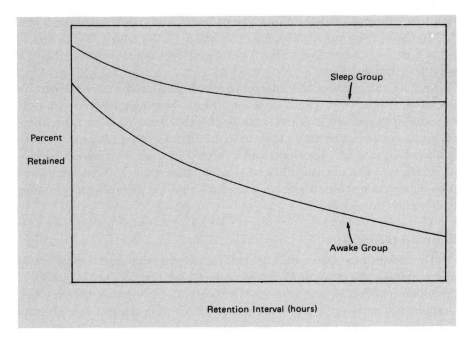

Figure 15. Temporal course of retention of verbal materials following sleep and waking conditions. The figure shows the usual superior retention when subjects sleep after learning a verbal task.

prevented or minimized. The paradigm for retroactive inhibition is shown thus:

Group	Learn	Learn	Retention Test
Experimental:	Learn Task A	Learn Task B	Retention of A
Control:	Learn Task A	Learn "Unrelated" Task	Retention of A

The basic question is: Does the learning of the interpolated task, B, interfere with the retention of task A, compared with the retention shown by the control group? A comparison of the experimental and control groups in their performance on the retention task reveals the amount of forgetting due to the learning of task B. If the effect of learning task B is such that the experimental group retains less than does the control group, then retroactive inhibition is inferred. The logic of this paradigm assumes that the experimental and control groups are comparable or equivalent, on the average, in task A learning. Therefore, any differences in retention of A must be due to the interference effects of task B on the memory traces or representations of task A. The term *retroactive inhibition* does not literally mean that events act backward in time, which is a concept foreign to science. All that is meant is that the interpolated task acts to disrupt, change, or interfere with the current memory-trace of task A. Moreover, the term *inhibition* refers merely to the forgetting that occurs. It is not a theoretical concept in the sense that it does not explain anything; it only describes an effect.

Usually the effect of the interpolated task is to produce interference in retention, that is, retroactive inhibition. It must be noted, however, that the relationship between task A and B can be of such a nature that the experimental group retains more than the control. In this case we speak of retroactive *facilitation*. In the vast majority of cases, interest in this paradigm has been in its interference and not its facilitative effects. Before we look at the factors that produce retroactive inhibition, let us examine a second procedure for studying interference in retention.

Proactive Inhibition

The second procedure which is used for investigating interference effects in retention is one that produces proactive inhibition. *In general*, proactive inhibition *is the loss in retention produced by the effects of some previously learned task.* In this case, however, the effects are due to the learning of a task *prior to* rather than after the to-be-tested task. As shown below, the paradigm for studying proactive inhibition, like that for studying retroactive inhibition, requires a comparison of performance between an experimental and a control group.

The experimental group learns an initial task, B, *prior* to learning task A and is then tested for retention of task A. The control group learns only task A and is subsequently tested for retention of task A. The proactive inhibition paradigm is schematized below:

Group	Learn	Learn	Retention Test
Experimental:	Learn Task B	Learn Task A	Retention of A
Control:	Learn "Unrelated" Task	Learn Task A	Retention of A

The basic question is: Does the learning of the preliminary task B interfere with the subsequent retention of task A? A comparison of the experimental and control group's performance on retention of A reveals the amount of forgetting due to the learning of task B. If the experimental group remembers less of task A than does the control group, then proactive inhibition is inferred. In some fashion, the learning of B interferes with the retention of A.

Factors Influencing Retroactive and Proactive Inhibition

We have already noted that sleep during the retention interval is an important factor in preventing forgetting. Indeed, more recent experiments have continued to show superior retention following sleep with much less forgetting than was obtained in earlier studies. As we indicated earlier, we do not have a complete understanding of this process, although it is clear that sleep reduces the opportunity for interference effects. From a practical view-point, one way of minimizing forgetting is to sleep after learning a particularly important task, such as studying for an upcoming test.

A second factor that affects retention in the retroactive inhibition para-digm is the *degree of original learning*, that is, learning on the initial task. In general, the greater the degree of original learning, the greater is retention of the originally-learned task. In short, if a task is to be made more resistant to forgetting, then ideally it should be well-learned.

A related factor is the *degree of learning of the interpolated (interfering) task.* In general, the greater the degree of learning of the interpolated task, with degree of first-task learning held constant, the less the retention of original learning. Similarly, in the proactive inhibition paradigm, as degree of learning on the prior task increases, forgetting of task A also increases.

Similarity between the two tasks also affects the amount of forgetting ob-tained in both retroactive and proactive inhibition paradigms. We have seen in the previous chapter that similarity plays an important role in transfer, so it should not be surprising that it also is important in affecting retention. With materials low in meaningfulness, such as trigrams, we find that, in general, the more similar the two tasks, the greater the forgetting in both retroactive and proactive paradigms. With more meaningful materials, such as prose passages, far less interference is produced by similarity. This is especially the case where the test task is one of factual retention or substantive content of the passage. Presumably, more meaningful materials can be better organized by the learn-er so as to minimize or prevent interference.

Where the effects of stimulus and response similarity have been separately examined, the picture is more complicated. In the case of response similarity, forgetting increases with a decrease in response similarity where the responses belong to the same class. Consider an A-B, A-B′ transfer paradigm in which variations in response similarity are introduced. The A-B task can be regarded as the original task and A-B as the interpolated task. If we now test for retention of the original A-B associations, we find that retention improves as the responses increase in similarity. If, however, the responses are drawn from *different* classes, as would be the case with an A-B, A-D arrangement, then the more dissimilar the response classes, the less the forgetting of the initial A-B associations.

The effects of stimulus similarity on interference are also complex. In general, as the stimuli are increased in similarity, the less is the interference when the responses are the same. Where the responses are different, then an increase in stimulus similarity is accompanied by an increase in forgetting. We shall shortly discuss one possible explanation of these complexities.

Contextual factors also influence interference. For example, if two tasks that are known to produce interference are learned in different environments, such as different rooms, then less interference is produced. This kind of finding indicates the importance of environmental or contextual cues, and indicates that they can become effective or functional stimuli during learning. Indeed, for this reason students who study in the same room in which they will be tested tend to perform slightly better on tests.

Finally, *instructions* on what to expect can influence forgetting in interference situations. For example, if subjects are told that learning a second task will hinder their performance, they actually show less forgetting than subjects who are told that learning the second task will facilitate learning. This occurs despite the fact that both subjects receiving the two kinds of instructions learned the second task at the same rate. It is possible that subjects told that learning a second task would hinder performance developed some strategy, probably rehearsal of the first task, so as to retain it better than they normally would.

These, then, are some of the important factors in retroactive and proactive inhibition. They show the importance of interference factors in retention, and have led, in turn to the development of interference theory. Let us now turn our attention to some of the salient features of this theory.

Interference Theory

The study of retroactive and proactive inhibition in long-term memory has led to the development of interference theory. Interference theory begins with the fundamental assumption that forgetting is the result of other learning which prevents what initially has been learned from being remembered. Interference theory emphasizes, however, that forgetting can be due to several factors and not just one process. Thus modern interference theory consists of a collection of several assumptions about processes that are viewed as underlying forgetting.

One aspect of interference theory that was formulated early in its development is the notion of *response competition.* According to this view, responses acquired in the original and interpolated learning tasks, and attached to identical (or similar) stimuli, as in the A-B, A-D paradigm, remain available to the learner and compete with each other during the learner's attempt to recall the original (A-B) list. This simply means that the D responses may tend to intrude and displace the B responses at the time of A-B recall. Evidence for response competition is seen when your latency for correct responses is significantly lengthened, when incorrect (D) responses are given, or when response blocking occurs such that no response is given unless you are forced to respond. These intrusion errors, however, occur principally after the first few trials on the interpolated task, indicating that interference is not solely due to response competition.

It was therefore proposed that a second factor must be operating to produce forgetting in retroactive inhibition paradigms, the factor of *unlearning*. The concept of unlearning was viewed as analogous to the extinction of instrumental responses. The unlearning mechanism hypothesizes that the first-list responses in an A-B, A-D paradigm tend to be unlearned, or extinguished, during second-list learning. Theoretically, unlearning takes place in the following fashion: During A-D learning it is assumed that the B responses will tend to be elicited because they have already been associated with the A stimuli. When the B responses do intrude during A-D learning they are nonreinforced, since the D responses are now the correct ones, and hence should undergo extinction in a manner analogous to that of classical or instrumental conditioning. Therefore, a later test for retention of the A-B associations should show some forgetting of the B responses to the extent that they have been extinguished.

The fact that unlearning does occur has been dramatically shown in an experiment by Jean Barnes and Benton Underwood. In their experiment, subjects first learned a list of paired associates and then learned a second list with varying amounts of practice on the second lists. The lists were arranged as an A-B, A-D paradigm. Following practice on the second (A-D) list, subjects were presented the A stimuli and asked to recall responses from *both* of the lists. They found that with increased practice on the A-D lists, subjects recalled fewer A-B associations. It was as if the A-B associations had undergone "extinction" during A-D learning.

It is important to note that this view of unlearning emphasizes the extinction of *specific* stimulus-response associations. Making a new response to an old stimulus leads to a weakening of the originally-learned associative connections, with each specific association itself being weakened. If, however, we extend the analogy to extinction, it should follow that some *spontaneous recovery* of the A-B associations should occur, just as spontaneous recovery is shown in instrumental conditioning. Experimental tests for spontaneous recovery of the A-B associations after relatively long-term intervals have not shown consistent or dependable evidence for the phenomena. Thus, the early conception of unlearning as the extinction of specific S-R associations has been questioned. More recently, the notion of unlearning has been modified by Leo Postman and his colleagues.

Instead of specific S-R associations being necessarily extinguished, Postman has emphasized that unlearning, in the sense of the relative unavailability of the originally-learned associations following interpolated learning, represents a "set" to respond in terms of the list most recently learned. This view emphasizes that the learner restricts himself to the responses of the most current list. Moreover, Postman's modification represents a shift in the locus of interference from individual responses or S-R associations to entire *systems of responses*. The critical feature of this view of unlearning is the shift in emphasis from the extinction of specific associations to the operation of a more "central" selector mechanism. It is as if the learner "suppresses" the entire set of first-list responses at the time of recall.

This tendency on the part of the subject to continue responding on whatever list he learned last has been termed *generalized response competition*. While it is beyond the scope of this book to review the detailed development of this concept, it is important to note that this concept is one of the major developments in the contemporary modification of interference theory. Thus it appears that interference theory has returned to its original emphasis on response competition, but with quite a different viewpoint.

Additional developments in interference theory have occurred in recent years. These additions are too complex to present in an introductory discussion of this topic, but one such addition emphasizes that less interference than might be expected can occur because of a *conservation* principle. Humans may reorganize and transform learned materials which can alter the meaningfulness of the material, thus enabling us to keep interfering materials separate from those to be retained. We have only begun to understand how these organizational processes work to set limits on how much we forget.

Study Habits and Memory

Let us now turn our attention to the matter of study habits and memory. A good deal of what has already been described has clear implications for the way in which you read, take notes, and prepare for examinations. A principal issue is how you can arrange your study activities so as to ensure maximum retention of the material. We shall focus on only a few basic points which are relatively straightforward, and which derive largely from our discussion of learning and memory.

Understand the Objectives of What You Are Studying

A major feature of good study habits is that you UNDERSTAND THE PRINCIPAL OBJECTIVES OR GOALS OF WHATEVER IT IS YOU ARE STUDYING. It is, therefore, good practice before reading a chapter to review the chapter outline if one is given in the table of contents. Note what topics are listed and the order in which they are discussed. In this fashion you will begin your reading of the chapter with fewer misconceptions of what to expect and with a clearer picture of the objectives of the author.

If a detailed chapter outline is not presented, then try to obtain some "structure" by careful reading of the introduction. In addition, read over the chapter, noting the topic headings, in order to get a "feel" of what the author is discussing. Sometimes a summary is given at the end of the chapter which may be profitably scanned before careful study of the chapter is undertaken.

Regardless of how you achieve this overall picture, keep in mind that you are trying to get a good "mental roadmap" of the material before you study it in greater detail. By reading the major headings and the italicized sentences and words, you will obtain what David Ausubel has termed an "advance organizer," or what I term a "mental roadmap" of the assigned reading. At this stage do not try to understand details or fine points. Get the big picture. Just as it is much easier to travel to a new place if you have a good roadmap, it is much easier to comprehend materials when you have a general idea of what the chapter contains. This first step will provide you with a *preliminary organization* of what you will subsequently study more carefully.

Focus Attention on the Study Materials

Once you have decided to study a particular chapter, focus your attention on your task and eliminate irrelevant stimuli. Remove magazines and newspapers from your desk, turn off the television, ignore the poker or bridge game in the next room, and avoid getting in a bull session with friends. If you are to learn the material at hand, you must tune out irrelevant stimuli.

Students sometimes report that they have no understanding of what they have read after finishing several pages. A similar experience is that of holding a book in your hand staring at page after page without any clear comprehension of the material. Chances are in both instances that you have failed to *attend* to the material and perhaps are daydreaming about some unrelated activity. While daydreaming can be pleasant, it simply is a way of avoiding the task at hand.

The matter of daydreaming and thinking about irrelevant activities can be handled if you learn to *monitor* your reading and thinking. As we noted in an earlier chapter, a good practice is the habit of occasionally "looking at" your thoughts while reading. In this fashion you can detect if you have wandered off course and can redirect your attention to the materials that must be studied. Failure to do this may lead to hours of wasted effort in which you neither engage in effective study nor use the time in recreation or other important activities.

Arrange Contingencies of Reinforcement

The business of paying careful attention to what you are reading is a *learned habit*. That is, you can teach yourself to attend by periodically asking yourself questions about what you are reading. Moreover, you can schedule coffee breaks and other forms of rewards if you arrange these rewards such that they occur only *after* you have achieved some goal or subgoal of studying. For instance, you may require yourself to study and outline two chapters *before* you take a break for conversation with friends. By actually planning these contingencies, in the form of rewarding yourself *after* you have completed some agreed-upon segment of study, you will find yourself managing your study habits in a far more efficient fashion. This practice of arranging your study so that you reward yourself only after you have accomplished some subgoal or task is called self-management of contingencies. With practice in the management of reinforcement contingencies, a topic that was discussed in the conditioning chapter, you can become increasingly effective in studying.

Organizing the Materials

An important feature of efficient study habits is the matter of organizing the material into some kind of systematic, useful structure. Some texts will present materials in a reasonably organized fashion, just as some lectures will be highly systematic. In such cases little effort on your part will be required to organize the material. Other materials will be less well-organized. Regardless of the nature of the material, it is good practice to organize it into some kind of useful framework that will enable you to encode it in memory. Indeed, the best organization will be idiosyncratic. As we have already noted, the effectiveness of memory retrieval depends in part on how well the material is organized.

In our discussion of the topics of conditioning, verbal learning, transfer, and memory, you may have noted certain fairly consistent features of each chapter. Each of these topics has been dealt with in a reasonably consistent way and each has a "structure" or format that you may have detected. For any topic you may have noted that the discussion revolves around five central features: nature or characteristics of the concepts, methods of measurement or study, major processes and principles, some theoretical issues, and finally, implications and applications of the principles discussed. Therefore, a good way to ask yourself questions about any chapter, for purposes of review, is to focus questions around these five central features. In this fashion you organize your studying around identifiable issues and are more likely to avoid directionless study.

If structure is not immediately evident in the material, then you must seek structure or *create* some kind of useful system for organizing the materials. This is simply to say that you must impose some kind of organization upon the materials if none is readily evident. Keep in mind that the organization that you develop or impose will be useful to the extent that it can provide efficient *retrieval* cues. Thus the usefulness of outlines, tables, charts, etc., that you construct in notetaking depend on how well these cues work in enabling you to recall the materials.

Practice Retrieval

We have already emphasized the importance of practicing retrieval, so we shall simply reemphasize this point. You must practice or rehearse *output* as well as concentrate on *input* of information. Too often the student concentrates on how many pages were read as an index of his study effort. THE FINAL AND VITAL KEY TO EFFECTIVE MEMORY IS DIRECT PRACTICE IN THE RETRIEVAL PROCESS, THAT IS, IN PRODUCING THE INFORMATION.

The importance of practicing retrieval activities cannot be overemphasized. How is this accomplished? This requires that you try to anticipate and answer test questions. Moreover, you should construct questions and try writing answers to them as part of your study. In general, let part of your study involve practice in the very kinds of activities that a course exam requires.

Summary

In this chapter we have described some of the major characteristics of memory. The study of memory involves encoding, storage, and retrieval processes. Psychologists have used two conceptual approaches in analyzing memory, one stemming from stimulus-response associationism and the other from information-processing conceptions. Although the latter approach adopts a language derived from computer technology, the approaches are not fully exclusive or necessarily conflicting.

The measurement of retention involves the three basic methods of recall, recognition, and savings. Recall requires the production of responses; recognition requires selection of alternatives; and savings requires relearning. Recall is usually more difficult than recognition because recall requires response learning. Recognition memory is easily influenced by motivational-incentive factors and response biases.

The basic stages of memory storage are sensory memory, short-term memory, and long-term memory. Sensory memory refers to the very short period in which some sensory representation of a stimulus persists after termination of the external stimulus. Short-term memory is the period in which information is stored long enough so that if it is rehearsed it may be transferred to long-term storage. If the material is not rehearsed, it will drop out of short-term memory. In long-term memory, information enters a relatively permanent storage system. Whether short-term and long-term memory represent different storage systems is an issue still in dispute.

Effective retrieval of information in memory depends upon organized storage. Retrieval cues aid recall, especially if the cues are relevant to the way in which the information was stored. The importance of practice in retrieval was emphasized. Humans may reconstruct information during recall, adding information that provides coherence, and dropping out unessential details.

Forgetting in long-term memory was viewed as a result of interference processes. Forgetting is attributed to both retroactive and proactive sources of interference. Modern interference theory was viewed as encompassing several processes, including unlearning and generalized response competition.

Our knowledge of principles of learning and memory have clear implications for effective study habits. Five features were emphasized: (1) understand the objectives of what you are studying; (2) focus attention on the study materials; (3) self-arrange contingencies of reinforcement; (4) organize the material; and (5) practice retrieval.

True-False Items: Memory

1. Once information is stored in memory it can be readily recalled.

(The fact that information is stored does not guarantee that it can be recalled. You may know a person's name and yet not be able to recall it, a finding which emphasizes the distinction between storage and retrieval. False.)

2. If asked to recall the names of all the states in the United States, you would probably tend to recall them in clusters based on geographic regions (e.g., Maine, Vermont, New Hampshire), or in size or population (e.g., California, New York, Pennsylvania, Texas). This clustering of recall is regarded as evidence for organizational processes in memory.

(The fact that the order of output in recall is grouped in some fashion, differing presumably from the order in which the material was presented during learning, is evidence for organizational processes in memory. True.)

3. Reproducing a cross-sectional drawing of some object such as a leaf structure is an instance of recognition.

(Reproducing your memory of some object by drawing it is an instance of recall. In studies of perceptual memory the recall procedure is usually referred to as reproduction or reproductive memory. False.)

4. The typical multiple-choice examination is an instance of the recognition method.

(Since the test items are presented, all you must do is select (recognize) the correct item. True.)

5. A forced-choice recognition procedure controls for possible differences in response bias.

(A choice must be made in every case, so possible differences in the "willingness" of individuals to respond to the recognition-test item is kept constant. True.)

6. Two people are shown a set of 20 advertisements, each for a brief period of time. Then they are shown these advertisements, one at a time, mixed in with 80 new advertisements and asked to correctly recognize the old items.

Individual A correctly recognizes all 20 items, while B correctly recognizes only 12 items. A has a better recognition memory than B.

(With this information we cannot say anything definitive about differences in recognition because we don't know anything about possible differences in their response biases ["willingness to say yes"]. Individual A may have been more willing to say that he recognized items, and thus obtained a better score principally because of his response bias. False.)

7. Humans can typically hold about seven "bits" (units) of information at one time in short-term memory.

(You are limited to about seven "bits" of information; however, if you "chunk" or group information into categories, you can hold a greater amount of information even though you are still limited to about seven "chunks". True.)

8. You may fail on occasion to write a good essay exam, not because you don't know the material, but because you have insufficiently practiced "getting out" (producing) the material.

(Producing the material is retrieval, and the key to memory output is the matter of practicing the task of retrieving information as well as simply storing information. True.)

9. A good way to practice retrieval of information is to reread the text and lecture notes just before a quiz.

(This practice still emphasizes input of storage. It fails to emphasize output or retrieval processes, which would involve such things as practice in writing answers to questions. False.)

10. A decay theory of memory emphasizes that the memory trace weakens with the passage of time.

(Decay theory stresses that memory traces weaken automatically in the course of time. True.) explains that

11. Interference theory states that forgetting is due to disuse, that is, it is due to a failure to continue rehearsing the material.

(Interference theory does not assume a principle of disuse. Rather, interference theory contends that forgetting is the result of other learning. False.)

12. The following schematic experiment represents the paradigm for proactive inhibition:

Experimental: -	Learn A	Learn B	Recall A
Control: -	Learn A	Learn "X"	Recall A

(This schematic experiment represents retroactive inhibition, in which the effect of learning task B is to produce interference in the recall of task A. False.)

7 ————————————————————————

Concept Learning

Human learning would be a complex and burdensome affair if you had to learn a particular response for every stimulus situation you encountered in life. If each new learning situation was essentially a matter of rote learning, you would be overwhelmed by a mass of specifics in a complex world. Fortunately, you are not reduced to treating each and every situation with such a high degree of specificity. Humans have the capacity to generalize from particular situations enabling the learning of concepts.

Concepts provide you with a certain kind of stability in interacting with your environment. Concept learning allows you to rise above the specific and infinitesimal variability of your environment and to treat events that have common properties as members of a class. For example, a young child, in learning the concept of dog, learns to classify a variety of specific instances as members of a set. He learns that the label "dog" may be applied to specific instances, but more importantly he learns that "dog" refers to a *class of instances* which have certain properties or features in common.

If a child applies the concept of dog only to a specific dog, such as his own, then he has not really developed the concept of dog. It is only when he can apply the term to a number of specific instances in a reasonably accurate fashion that one can say that he has acquired the concept. Moreover, it is important that he not only apply the term appropriately in the presence of instances but that he recognize other events or objects that are properly not part of the concept. Thus, for example, he must properly exclude instances such as cats, rabbits, and other animals. More generally, then, the formation of concepts refers to *both* the *selection* of appropriate instances and the *rejection* or exclusion of inappropriate instances.

The development and refinement of some concepts probably takes place over an extended time period. Moreover, it is true that the learning of many concepts involves progressing from some gross, diffuse state to a highly refined condition in which fine-grain distinctions can be made. Thus, it is reasonable to say that you may have only a general concept about some things or events and a quite precise concept about others. In addition, you may be in the process of refining some of your more vague concepts. It is known that in the course of formal learning, students' concepts of things such as "justice," "freedom," and "integrity" constantly grow and change as they are exposed to new experiences and knowledge. Similarly, you have probably experienced the condition in which your understanding of a particular concept has sharpened and expanded with additional experience, advanced training, or new knowledge.

A good deal of teaching is directed toward the development of concepts because concepts are necessary for more complex behaviors such as the learning of principles, problem solving, and symbolic activities such as thinking. One of the principal objectives of formal education is the teaching of basic concepts that enable individuals to function in our society, and to teach also the notion that concepts can be revised, altered, and amended on the basis of new knowledge and experience. The ability to handle concepts as they currently exist and to deal with them in a flexible and changing fashion is a joint objective of school learning.

Concept learning, as a topic in the psychology of learning, stands roughly midway between the simpler processes of stimulus discrimination, response learning, and association formation, on the one hand, and the more complex processes of thinking, reasoning, and problem solving, on the other hand. It is the juncture at which one shifts from the development of simple one-to-one associations to the development of many-to-one associations. This feature will be amplified when we compare concept learning with paired associate learning.

Finally, concept learning represents no clear and sharp break from the simpler processes involved in verbal learning. Even in verbal learning tasks such as paired associate and free recall learning, you saw that humans may engage in conceptual activity. Indeed, it is doubtful that one can devise a learning situation that entirely prevents the human from forming concepts, adopting strategies, or engaging in thinking. Therefore, this chapter on concept learning in no way implies that you have not already been dealing with conceptual behavior. The thrust of this chapter, however, is most exclusively on these activities that are typically labeled conceptual.

Nature of Concept Learning

Concept learning has already been described in an informal way. More formally, however, *concept learning refers to any activity in which the learner must learn to classify two or more somewhat different events or objects into a single category.* The fact that you can learn to classify events in a reliable and consistent fashion is taken as evidence for the development of a concept. Thus, concept learning involves learning to make a common (classification) response to a group of stimuli which have some features or properties in common. This is *not*, however, all that is involved in knowing whether a person has acquired a concept.

What is a concept itself? A concept is the cognitive basis for assigning a category label or term, which in turn, refers to a number of specific instances. For example, Richard M. Nixon is not a concept; he is a particular instance of a concept. Nor is John F. Kennedy a concept. Nixon, Kennedy, Johnson, Eisenhower, and Truman are instances of the concept, American President. The concept *President* includes Nixon, but it also includes those individuals mentioned as well as Washington, Jefferson, and all the other instances. Thus, more generally, A CONCEPT REFERS TO A CLASS OF STIMULI OR EVENTS THAT SHARE IN ONE OR MORE COMMON CHARACTERISTICS.

Let us consider the difference between concept learning and paired associate learning. As we have seen, paired associate learning requires learning a particular response for a particular stimulus; that is, the ratio between stimuli and responses is one-to-one. Concept learning, on the other hand, involves learning a single response for two or more stimuli; that is, the ratio between stimuli and responses is several-to-one. This distinction is illustrated schematically below in which a paired associate task consists of six pairs, whereas a concept learning task contains two concepts (R1 and R2) with three stimuli for each response.

```
     PAIRED ASSOCIATE        CONCEPT
        LEARNING            LEARNING
         S1 - R1            S1 ⟍
         S2 - R2            S2 ⟶ R1
         S3 - R3            S3 ⟋
         S4 - R4            S4 ⟍
         S5 - R5            S5 ⟶ R2
         S6 - R6            S6 ⟋
```

It is possible, however, for someone learning a conceptual task to learn in a "rote" fashion. This is simply to say that one can treat the situation as if it were essentially a paired associate task rather than a classification task. Even though one can classify the stimuli S1, S2, and S3 as instances of the category R1, one may be doing so simply by learning each stimulus-response pair as a separate association. For concept learning to have genuinely occurred, we want to be able to say that the person has classified S1, S2, and S3 on the basis of some common feature, and that he treats them as an instance of a class.

Therefore, the true test of concept learning is to present the learner with *new* instances of the concepts and determine if he appropriately classified them.

Consider, for example, teaching elementary color concepts to children. A child is shown a specific instance of a white object, such as white paper, and told that it is white. He is then instructed to repeat the response "white" in the presence of the sheet of white paper. This, of course, in no way ensures that he has learned the concept of white; he may simply be responding to the size or shape of the piece of paper, or to some other property. Therefore, we continue to present the child other objects that contain the property of whiteness, such as a white sweater, piece of chalk, etc., requiring that he say "white" to each of the objects presented. Even though he correctly says "white" to all of the objects, you still cannot be sure that he has learned the concept. He may simply be learning associations between specific stimulus objects and the response of saying "white."

To ensure that he has, in fact, learned the concept of white, two additional things are necessary: (1) he must be presented with additional objects that are *instances* or exemplars of the concept to see if he appropriately classifies these as white, and (2) he must be presented *noninstances* or inappropriate exemplars to see if he excludes these as part of the concept. If he can *both* appropriately include instances and exclude noninstances, we then infer that he has learned the concept. In the actual practice of teaching concepts, one typically includes both instances and noninstances so that the concept becomes sharpened and well-defined for the student. The test of whether one has learned the concept requires, as has been said, the presentation of *new* instances and noninstances.

Our discussion so far has indicated that one must come to classify events in terms of common features or properties if concept learning is to occur. This means that the learner responds to the relevant features of the set of events and comes to ignore other features. For example, in learning the concept of a circle, a child is shown a number of circles that differ in size, in color, and in other features that might be systematically varied. The child learns, however, that the *only relevant* feature is the round-circular property of the event, and that size and color are irrelevant properties or dimensions. By "relevant" is meant simply the feature or features that are pertinent to the concept.

In order to refine the concept further, other shapes such as triangles and squares are presented so that the child also learns that shape is the only relevant dimension that distinguishes circles, triangles, and squares. Again, he learns that size and color are irrelevant to these concepts. Thus, IT IS SEEN THAT CONCEPT LEARNING REQUIRES THAT THE LEARNER COME TO RESPOND TO THE RELEVANT DIMENSIONS OF THE CONCEPT AND TO IGNORE THE IRRELEVANT DIMENSIONS IN CLASSIFYING EVENTS.

Concept Learning, Generalization, and Discrimination

So far, our description of concept learning makes it appear as a special case of generalization and discrimination. Indeed, psychologists who adopt a stimulus-response associationistic approach to learning characteristically view conceptual behavior as involving primarily the processes of generalization and discrimination. With this approach, LEARNING OF CONCEPTS IS SEEN AS A COMBINATION OF (1) DISCRIMINATION BETWEEN CLASSES OF EVENTS AND (2) GENERALIZATION WITHIN CLASSES OF EVENTS.

An illustration of this viewpoint can be seen by examining how one might teach the concepts of "circle," "square," and "triangle." A child is shown several exemplars of each concept which vary not only in the relevant dimension (shape) but in irrelevant dimensions (such as size and color). For example, the exemplars of "square" are very large, large, medium-sized, small, and very small; they also are colored differently; they may have shadings or hash-marks on them; in general, the exemplars vary in several ways. The same is true for the exemplars of "circle" and "triangle." The child can be said to have learned the three shape concepts when he *generalizes* within the exemplars for each class, that is, correctly categorizes instances of each, and when he *discriminates* between each class. This is simply to say that he classifies correctly all exemplars of "square" regardless of size, color, or other irrelevant dimensions. Likewise, he does this for the exemplars of "circle" and "triangle," respectively.

This view of concept formation is reasonable under conditions in which there is some element or dimension that is common to all the examples. In the illustration above, the common element was shape. The child could thus be said to be discriminating among classes of shapes and generalizing within instances of the class. There are, however, other instances of concept learning in which no element or dimension is common to the instances. For example, tacos and ice cream belong to the class foods, but no obvious *elements* or physical dimensions are common to both. They are members of the same conceptual category because of what we do with them. Thus things may become members of the same conceptual category because we make *common responses* to the exemplars.

The development of a concept, based upon some common response to the exemplars not directly attributable to some common dimension, leads to a *mediational* view of concept learning. Here we postulate some intervening link between the external stimuli (the exemplars) and the overt response made to the stimuli. Mediational approaches to concept learning will be discussed subsequently and compared with a major alternative view, that of hypothesis testing. For the present, we need only note that concept learning is a process akin to generalization and discrimination, and can be described as a special case of the two processes *when* the exemplars have clear-cut dimensions or attributes. When the situation becomes more complex, however, the analogy with these two processes is less straightforward.

The Study of Concept Learning

Although the study of concept learning has been described in a general way, it is more fully understood by examining some of the details of laboratory experiments in concept learning. In this section we shall briefly describe the principal features of any concept learning experiment. Some of these features have already been illustrated in our examples cited.

Features of Concept Learning Tasks

As in other human learning tasks, the typical concept learning study involves *stimuli, responses,* and some form of *feedback* to the learner. Stimuli consisting of both positive instances (exemplars) and negative instances (non-exemplars) are presented to the subject. These vary in several *dimensions,* one or more of which may be relevant to the concept while others are irrelevant. Each dimension may take on two or more *values.* For example, we may have shape, size, and color as dimensions, with two values of each dimension: circle and square for shape; large and small for size; and red and green for color. This arrangement produces eight stimuli as shown in figure 16.

The particular concept to be learned is arbitrarily determined by the experimenter. If the concept to be learned is "square," then the "square" instances enclosed by the dotted line are positive instances of that concept. If the concept to be learned is "green," then the "green" instances enclosed by the dotted line are positive instances of that concept. A similar arrangement could be made for the size concept. Moreover, various combinations could be used such as "small red" and "large green" things, which designate a more complex kind of concept.

The category response used in this case is quite simple. The experimenter can instruct the subject to give the category name or the subject may simply say "yes" or "no" in the presence of each instance. Sometimes subjects press switches to designate whether or not the stimulus is an instance of the concept. Finally, the subject is given feedback as to the correctness of his responses.

Basic Paradigms in Concept Learning

Psychologists have adopted two basic procedures in the laboratory investigation of conceptual behavior. The first of these employs the *reception paradigm* in which the stimuli are presented in some random or predetermined order by the experimenter and the subject attempts to classify each stimulus when it is presented. If only one concept is being learned, the subject classifies each

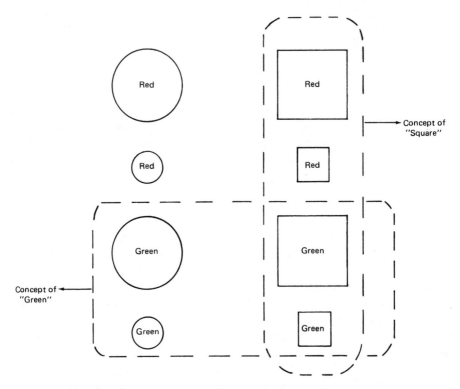

Figure 16. Schematic diagram showing instances of objects relevant to the concept "square" and to the concept "green."

stimulus as a positive or negative instance of the concept. As soon as the subject classifies a stimulus, he is given informative feedback. Usually only one stimulus is presented at a time, thus requiring the subject to depend upon his memory of the events over a series of trials.

The second procedure is known as the *selection paradigm*. As the name implies, the subjects select the stimuli, one at a time, from a set of stimuli placed before him. The subject is presented the entire set of stimuli at the onset of the experiment and thus selects the stimulus, trial after trial, on which he wants to obtain feedback. An obvious advantage of the selection paradigm is that one may gain information about how the subject "solves" the problem. There are several variations of these two procedures, but most concept learning studies fall into one of these two categories.

Attributes and Rules

A concept has two critical features: attributes and rules. We have already seen that concepts possess *attributes*, which are those features or characteristics of the stimuli that are relevant to the concept. Simple concepts may involve only a single attribute, such as color. In a similar vein, "sweet" and "sour" are essential attributes of the Chinese dish, sweet and sour pork. The concept of "student" refers to someone who is engaged in study, either formally in the sense of being enrolled in course work, or informally in the sense of self-directed study activities. Whether or not such a person is tall or short, young or old, or has long or short hair, are attributes irrelevant to the concept. The important thing is that in learning concepts you learn to focus on the relevant attributes and to disregard irrelevant features.

Attributes may be combined in several different ways which define a conceptual rule. In our example above, the Chinese dish consists of sweet *and* sour pork, that is, *both* the attributes of sweetness and sourness along with pork must be present. In this case we have an instance of a conjunction (joint-presence) rule.

Other concepts may employ a disjunctive rule where the combination is *either or*. For example, the concept of a "person" may refer to either a man or a woman. The concept includes, of course, people of all ages. There are several rules for combining attributes of which conjunctive and disjunctive rules are instances. Thus, in describing a concept, we must refer to its attributes and to how the attributes are combined (rules).

Factors Which Affect Concept Learning

Let us now turn our attention to some important factors which influence concept learning. In general, these factors can be classified into two categories: *task* variables and *learner* variables. Instances of important task variables include positive and negative instances, relevant and irrelevant attributes, stimulus salience and abstractness-concreteness, feedback and temporal factors, and conceptual rules. In a parallel vein, examples of learner variables known to be important are intelligence and memory.

Positive and Negative Instances

A question of interest is whether humans learn concepts faster from positive than from negative instances. This issue focuses on the *nature* of the instances as a factor in concept learning. The answer to this question is somewhat complicated by the fact that, at least in our society, we are more accustomed to dealing with positive instances and are, therefore, more likely to learn concepts faster from positive than from negative instances. This, however, is not the complete picture.

Early studies of concept learning found that humans make little or no use of negative instances. This was the case, however, because the negative instances typically carried far less information than did the positive instances. In laboratory situations where the negative instances can be controlled or constructed so as to carry more information, there is a corresponding increase in their use.

Another reason why humans tend to prefer positive over negative instances in concept learning tasks, as noted above, is that they are much more likely to encounter positive instances in their everyday experiences. Rarely are concepts in everyday life formed by negative instances alone. One close approximation is medical diagnosis, where a physician may judge a disease category by the absence of certain symptoms and by negative laboratory tests. This is because different diseases may have similar symptoms and the way they may be distinguished is by the absence of a particular symptom or pattern of symptoms. Thus, it is not surprising that humans generally learn faster from positive instances. Yet some parents try to teach the concept of "honesty" principally by identifying instances of "dishonesty"; such teaching may produce only limited effects. If, however, humans are trained to learn concepts from negative instances alone, they can learn to become almost as proficient as people who use positive instances alone. The fact that differences in the facility with which humans use positive and negative instances can be largely eliminated through training indicates that such differences are not immutable. Nevertheless, in your everyday experiences you are much more likely to use positive instances, principally because the number of negative instances is much larger than the number of positive instances and are, therefore, less useful in carrying information.

Relevant and Irrelevant Attributes

What happens to the efficiency of concept learning when the number of relevant and irrelevant dimensions is varied? First, in any concept learning task, the number of irrelevant attributes or cues may be increased, which means that the proportion of relevant attributes will decrease given that the total number of attributes remains constant. THE LARGER THE NUMBER OF IRRELEVANT ATTRIBUTES IN A CONCEPTUAL TASK, THE MORE DIFFICULT IS THE TASK. This is not hard to understand, because by doing so it becomes more difficult for the learner to discover the relevant attributes that are correlated with the correct response. Putting it simply, the more irrelevant cues that you must learn to discard or ignore, the longer it will take to latch on to the relevant cue.

Second, the number of relevant *redundant* attributes can be increased, thus increasing the relative proportion of correct cues. A relevant redundant attribute refers to features that are perfectly correlated so that either feature validly predicts the concept. For example, if every circle is blue, every square is red, and every triangle is yellow, and if these attributes are relevant to the concept to be learned, then we say that shape and color are redundant. Thus, in this example it is possible to obtain a solution of the concept on the basis of either shape or color, or both features. The principle regarding the role of number of relevant redundant attributes is quite simple: THE LARGER THE NUMBER OF RELEVANT REDUNDANT ATTRIBUTES, THE EASIER IS CONCEPT LEARNING. Intuitively, this principle is easy to understand, because by increasing the number of relevant redundant cues the likelihood that you will discover one or more of the cues is increased. This principle is recognized by many lecturers who repeat a point, but in a slightly different way, in order to ensure that the audience grasps the central idea.

Stimulus Salience and Abstractness-Concreteness

The salience or distinctiveness of the relevant cues determines, in part, the ease of learning concepts. Young children tend to learn color concepts more readily than form concepts which may, of course, be related to differences in previous experience with these dimensions. Similarly, concrete concepts such as, for example, house, dog, and car, are learned more readily than abstract concepts that involve, for example, spatial form. The difficulty of abstract concepts is apparently related to the difficulty in giving them a mediating label and in the fact that you are less likely to have image-like mediators for them.

The salience or distinctiveness of the relevant cues is related to the degree of similarity among the cues. As the cues increase in similarity, which in effect reduces their distinctiveness, concept learning becomes more difficult. Moreover, since cues related to abstract concepts may be more similar to each other, the effect of greater difficulty in concept learning with more abstract concepts may be due to the greater similarity of such cues. For example, more abstract concepts such as "circle" and "elipse" may be more difficult to learn than concrete concepts such as "tree" and "house," because instances of the abstract concepts may be more similar or confusable. Even more abstract concepts such as "democracy" or "socialism" may be difficult to distinguish because of their several overlapping features.

Feedback and Temporal Factors

Feedback, in the form of indicating whether a response is correct or not, provides the learner with information about the correctness of his responses. Moreover, feedback can serve to guide subsequent responses in conceptual tasks. At one level feedback can be viewed as somewhat analogous to reward in instrumental learning situations if the learner's response is correct. At another level, feedback is important because of the *information* that it provides the learner, both with respect to what hypothesis seems to be correct as well as to the elimination of incorrect hypotheses. The learner must, however, utilize the information in the stimulus in conjunction with feedback in order to achieve efficient solution to the problem. Merely being told that you are "right" or "wrong" on each trial is insufficient for concept learning unless you simultaneously attend to and use the information in the particular exemplars presented. This means, of course, that you must remember something about the particular exemplars, noting and remembering from trial to trial what feature(s) is present when the response is confirmed as correct.

One aspect of feedback that has been examined is the time delay between the learner's response and informative feedback. Although it might be expected that *delay of feedback* would exert a pronounced effect on concept learning, this factor has been found to have very little effect on performance. This finding stands in striking contrast to studies with lower animals, where delay of reward produces a marked effect on performance.

In contrast, another kind of delay called postfeedback delay produces a potent effect on performance. Postfeedback delay refers to the delay between feedback on one trial and the next presentation of a stimulus. AS POSTFEED-BACK DELAY IS LENGTHENED, CONCEPT LEARNING IS FACIL-ITATED. This is not difficult to understand when you consider that by lengthening the postfeedback interval the learner is given more time to "think about" what he learned, or to process the information that he obtained from that particular trial. On the other hand, simple delay of feedback, as described previously, exerts little effect, apparently because the learner cannot process the information fruitfully until *after* he has been given feedback.

These effects of feedback can be intuitively appreciated if you think about them in the context of an ordinary conceptual game such as "twenty questions." In this game you are allowed to ask twenty questions in order to solve a problem, asking only categorical questions (that is, questions that can be answered by a "yes" or "no"). You ask one question at a time, trying to "zero in" on the correct concept. Each question is answered "yes" or "no" by the person with whom you are playing the game. The more time you are given to think about the information you have gained from your question following his yes or no response, the more rapidly you are likely to solve the problem. Indeed, for this reason the twenty-questions game is sometimes played at a particular pace so as to control the rate at which information is being conveyed.

Conceptual Rules

The manner in which particular attributes are combined, that is, the conceptual rule, also determines the ease with which a conceptual task is learned. This is simply to say that there are several basic conceptual rules, and they differ in ease of learning. At the simplest level, concepts that merely *affirm* the presence of an attribute, thus conforming to an affirmation rule, are the easiest to learn. This rule simply means that all stimuli with a given attribute are members of that concept. For example, all people who currently breathe can be said to be alive. Conversely, people who have ceased to breathe (after some brief but specified time interval) are dead. The converse of an affirmative rule, which is the lack of a given attribute, is the negation rule.

Concepts which employ a conjunctive rule are also relatively easy to learn. *Conjunctive rules* refer to conditions in which both attributes must be jointly present, which can be described as A and B. For instance, a "black cat" is a conjunctive concept since two attributes, "black" and "cat" must be jointly present. In contrast, concepts which employ *conditional* rules (if A, then B) and *biconditional* rules (if A, then B; if B, then A) are much harder to learn.

Memory and Intelligence

Conceptual learning depends not only upon characteristics of the task but upon characteristics of the learner as well. Both memory and intelligence are individual-difference variables which are known to affect the ease with which we learn concepts. The role of memory is reasonably obvious in conceptual tasks in which a series of instances are presented over successive trials. In order to achieve a particular concept, the learner must remember information over several trials because a single trial usually does not present sufficient information for the concept to be learned. Thus, memory for specific instances increases the ease with which concepts will be learned.

In a similar vein, it is most reasonable to expect that intelligence is an important factor in concept learning. Indeed, more intelligent children will solve conceptual tasks consistently faster than less intelligent children. The explanation of this relationship apparently lies in the greater ability to construct hypotheses by the more intelligent children and in their greater skill in using verbal mediating responses. Mediational responses are implicit responses that are in some way symbolic of or representative of the class of instances; these responses enable humans to respond to instances in terms of their common properties. Mediational responses may not necessarily be verbal, but may be perceptual in nature.

Theories of Concept Learning

Two general approaches have been taken in trying to account for the process of concept learning. One approach stems from stimulus-response associationistic conceptions of the learning process, and adopts principles of conditioning to explain conceptual behavior. With this approach, concept learning is thought to develop in a manner like that of simple discrimination learning, and is regarded as a special case of the processes of generalization and discrimination. In contrast to S-R association theory, a second approach to concept learning emphasizes the importance of hypotheses and strategies and adopts, therefore, a cognitive approach. Here emphasis is placed upon the active role of the learner in developing concepts and the manner in which he tests various hypotheses.

There is no single S-R theory and there is no single cognitive hypotheses-testing theory. Rather, there is a constellation of approaches that can be roughly classified as S-R and there are several approaches that adopt an hypothesis-testing approach. These approaches have been modified over time, are still evolving, and it is our intent therefore to characterize only their typical features. Many nuances of detail will, therefore, not be considered, since the focus will be on the essential and characteristic features of these approaches, looking at them in bold-relief.

S-R Association Theory

In general, S-R association theories of conceptual learning regard the process as akin to, or a special case of, discrimination learning. We have already noted certain features of this approach in the discussion of concept learning, generalization, and discrimination.

A conceptual task is seen as consisting of a series of instances or exemplars, each instance consisting of both relevant and irrelevant features of attributes. The learner must respond on each trial, sometimes being correct and sometimes being incorrect. Each response to a positive instance is reinforced in the form of being given feedback. S-R theories contend that associative strength between the relevant dimension and correct response is gradually built up to some point at which a person can be said to have acquired the concept. In turn, response strength to the irrelevant dimension is gradually weakened because it is not consistently reinforced. Thus, concept learning is similar to discrimination learning in that a discrimination between relevant and irrelevant cues is gradually developed by differential reinforcement.

With this approach a concept is viewed as a learned association between a class of stimuli having some common element and an overt response. The associative strength is, however, between the common element and the response. For example, in learning the concept of "green," associative strength develops between the property of greenness in the various stimulus objects presented and the response "green" made to these various objects.

In this connection, the reader must be cautioned not to confuse the *manner* in which concepts are taught with *theory* about what is learned. Our previous illustrations about how concepts are typically taught may superficially look like theory. Theory refers to the conceptualization about *what* gets learned, which in this case, is an association between stimulus elements and a response.

When a person responds to new stimulus objects that contain the relevant feature or cue, he is said to generalize. Thus, once a concept has been acquired it may be applied in new situations. This occurs if the new situation contains the relevant features because of the already built-in associative strength between the features and a response. Thus, referring back to our previous example, new objects that are green will tend to evoke the correct response by virtue of a generalization process.

S-R Mediational Theories

As we noted in a previous section, an S-R associative conception of concept learning is reasonable when the stimulus examples contain elements common to all of the examples. There are, however, many situations in which no element or dimension is common to the examples. As we noted, tacos and ice cream are members of the same conceptual class—namely, foods—not because of common dimensions but because we make responses common to these events.

Mediational S-R theories assume that concept learning develops because of mediating responses made to the stimulus instances. For example, the common response of "eating" is made to the following stimuli:

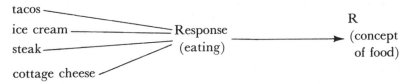

Thus, we don't *directly* identify tacos as an instance of the concept of food because of some physical dimension such as their color, or the fact that they may be hot, but because of our response to them. Thus, things that are edible are called *foods*. We may further require that these things have "food value," in the sense of having vitamins, minerals, or caloric value if they are to be called foods. This, however, represents simply a further refinement of the food concept. The point to note is that a mediational view emphasizes an association between a common response to a class of stimuli and the overt response.

The mediational response can be characterized in several ways. Frequently it is regarded as a verbal response or some kind of verbal label is given to the stimulus instances. It may also be regarded as some kind of perceptual response or attentional response that involves images. More generally, we may think of mediating responses as symbolic events that serve to represent particular aspects of external stimulus events.

The more general importance of mediational views of concept learning is that an intervening step is introduced between stimuli and responses. Instead of thinking of connections between the relevant attributes of stimuli and overt responses, we think of connections between mediating responses made to stimuli and overt responses. Mediational theories are therefore more complex than simple S-R association theories. Moreover, mediational theories are more flexible in their ability to handle certain kinds of conceptual behaviors.

Hypothesis-testing Theories

Hypothesis-testing theories of concept learning emphasize the human as more active in the task in the sense that he is actively selecting and testing possible solutions. These theories emphasize the importance of the selection of hypotheses, of the decision-making character of the task, and are therefore cognitive theories in the sense that implicit decision processes are involved.

The essential difference between S-R and hypothesis-testing theories is that S-R theories emphasize that the human is under control of the properties of the stimulus environment, or of mediating responses made to the stimuli. In contrast, hypothesis-testing theories emphasize an additional set of processes, namely, what the learner himself does in the conceptual task. The particular hypotheses and strategies that he may employ are seen as important.

Formal models of hypothesis testing, such as those proposed by Gordon Bower and Frank Restle, emphasize that the subject samples from some population of hypotheses on each trial. The population of hypotheses consists of both relevant and irrelevant hypotheses and the subject is viewed, theoretically, as sampling at random from such a population. If the subject samples an irrelevant hypothesis, this must eventually lead to an incorrect response, leading the subject to sample a new hypothesis. The subject continues to sample hypotheses until one leads to continuous correct responding.

Other types of models have been developed which emphasize the information-processing character of concept learning. These models derive from computer analogies and view concept learning in terms of a sequence of decisions made by the learner. Information-processing models assume hypothesis-testing by the learner in which hypotheses are generated and then tested.

S-R associative, S-R mediational, and hypothesis-testing models can be thought of as being along a continuum of complexity going from the simplest to the most complex. It is not necessary to regard them as mutually exclusive or contradictory. All three are useful in the sense that they can adequately account for some range of findings about concept learning.

Some Practical Principles of Concept Learning

It is reasonable to ask what is known about concept learning that may be usefully applied by yourself. Psychologists know about many of the factors that affect concept learning and have formulated some principles regarding efficient concept learning. Therefore, it is appropriate to examine some of these factors and principles and note some of their potential implications. The focus of this section will be on only a few of these, with the objective of seeing how they might apply in familiar learning situations.

Think of New Examples of Concepts

A moment's reflection on your part may lead you to recognize that much of classroom instruction involves going from concepts to examples and from examples back to concepts. Frequently, an instructor introduces a concept by briefly defining it and then proceeds to illustrate the concept by giving one or two examples. After a few illustrations he proceeds to refine and clarify the concept, developing it to some level required by its inherent complexity. Similarly, many textbooks reveal this characteristic feature.

In order that a concept be fully grasped and understood, *it is important that you think of additional examples beyond those presented by your instructor.* The instructor typically has time to present only one or two examples, perhaps a few more at best, and depends upon these examples to provide you with sufficient information to abstract the essential features of the concept. Unfortunately, you may fail to understand the concept with only one or two examples, or at best you may achieve only a "general idea" of the concept. Your instructor, however, may expect you to achieve a much more detailed and elaborate concept, one that you cannot obtain unless you continue to think of additional examples that will aid you in refining and enriching the concept.

Obviously, your examples must be pertinent to the concept. If you are in doubt about the adequacy of your examples and hence your full grasp of the concept, you must check these by talking with other students, or by continued reading in other sources, or by asking your instructor about the adequacy of your ideas.

Generating new examples not only helps to sharpen and refine the particular concept, but also provides practice in retrieval of information, a process important for memory. Test questions frequently ask the student to produce new examples or illustrations, as distinct from those given in a lecture. Thus, thinking of new examples not only sharpens, refines, and enriches the concept but also provides practice in the important process of information retrieval.

Use Both Positive and Negative Instances

The sharpness and precision of a concept develops as we process both positive and negative instances of a concept. In learning a particular concept you must discriminate between instances of the concept and those instances which fail to fit the category. If all of your examples are positive instances of the concept, then you have certainly minimal opportunity to compare positive and negative instances and, hence, to zero in on the essential attributes or features.

Consider teaching a young child the concept of dog in which all the examples are positive instances. Assume that he is shown pictures of a collie, fox terrier, miniature poodle, and German shepherd. To each of these he learns to say "dog." But what are the relevant attributes of the concept? What features of these examples control his response? Obviously, we cannot be entirely sure in this situation. Moreover, if we show him a picture of a cat or rabbit, we cannot be sure of his response unless we have additional information about his experience with these animals. Indeed, he may well regard a picture of a cat as another instance of dog. It is for this reason that the inclusion of carefully selected negative instances is helpful in developing a concept.

In order to develop a sharply delineated concept, negative instances must contain, toward some latter stage of training, irrelevant attributes that are likely to be found in the positive instances. Both dogs and cats are four-legged animals, so the property of four-leggedness is an irrelevant feature. Cats are frequently smaller than dogs, but obviously not always. Hence size is not a predictable feature. Nor is the presence of a tail, paws, or coat of fur. It is clear that differences between cats and dogs are based on the presence and absence of several features in combination. Features like head shape and presence or absence of claws help to distinguish the two. Even with head shape we may have difficulty when we first show a child a picture of a Pekingese.

The more general point is that if you teach concepts only by the use of positive examples, or try to learn concepts with only positive examples, you may fail to respond to the *essential* features of the concept and respond instead to some superficial or unessential feature.

The Importance of a Variety of Examples

The previous sections implicitly emphasized the importance of a variety of examples in learning concepts. This point has also been emphasized in the discussion of transfer. With only one example you may easily attend to some nonessential feature of the concept and erroneously assume that you have learned it.

How many examples should you use? No simple answer can, of course, be given to this question because concepts vary in difficulty and complexity. Perhaps the best answer is that examples should be selected so that they encompass the *range* of the concept. Practical limitations will prevent you from considering all possibilities, but by sampling examples along some range you are likely to include highly pertinent ones.

Highlighting Relevant Features

From the viewpoint of teaching, a major task is to highlight or emphasize the relevant features of concepts. One objective is to make the relevant aspect or essential parts of a concept more distinctive than the nonessential features. In a similar vein, you can help to highlight the essential features of concepts by *verbalizing* these features to yourself. This effort can involve trying to define the concept in your own words, as distinct from memorizing formal definitions of concepts.

Relevant features of concepts can be made more distinctive by the *simultaneous presentation* of both positive and negative examples. This simply means that in teaching a particular concept, a positive as well as negative instance should be presented to the learner at the same time, allowing him to compare the instances. For example, in teaching the concept lake, a picture of a lake, a stream, a river, and an ocean are all shown together. By leaving all of these in view, the burden on memory is minimized and the discrimination between the relevant and irrelevant features is made easier. This superiority of simultaneous over successive presentation of stimulus examples holds for simple discrimination learning as well as for concept learning.

Similarly, by comparing and contrasting concepts and principles, you can emphasize the feature of simultaneous presentation in your own study habits. Comparison of concepts stands clearly in contrast to concentrating on each idea as an isolated event.

[Every subject area in the curric (except those which are primarily for teaching motor skills) The teachers' major task in is the teaching of concepts]

Summary

This chapter has described some of the major characteristics of concept learning. Concepts serve to reduce the complexity of one's environment, provide one with tools for thinking and for learning principles, and reduce the necessity for constant learning in each new situation. One objective of formal education is concept learning coupled with the notion that concepts can be revised and amended with new experiences and knowledge.

Concept learning is any activity that requires you to classify two or more events or objects into a single class. A concept is a class of stimuli that share one or more common features. Concept learning differs from paired associate learning in that the ratio of stimuli to responses is several-to-one. Concept learning requires both learning to respond to one or more relevant aspects and learning not to respond to irrelevant features. At a simple level, concept learning is akin to generalization and discrimination.

Experiments on concept learning have three principal features: stimuli, responses, and feedback. Stimuli consist of positive and negative instances, and stimuli may vary in several dimensions. Each dimension, in turn, can have one or more values or attributes. Concept learning experiments employ, typically, either the reception or selection paradigm. A concept has two essential features: attributes and the rules by which the attributes are combined.

Factors which affect concept learning include both task and learner variables. Important task variables discussed were positive and negative instances, relevant and irrelevant attributes, stimulus salience and abstractness-concreteness, feedback and temporal factors, and conceptual rules. Learner variables described were memory and intelligence.

Theories of concept learning divide into S-R theories and hypothesis-testing theories. S-R theories may be simple association theories and may include the process of mediation. Hypothesis-testing theories are cognitive-type theories emphasizing the importance of decision-making by the learner.

Several practical principles for effective concept learning were described. These emphasized the importance of (1) thinking of new examples of concepts, (2) using both positive and negative examples, (3) having a variety of examples, and (4) highlighting the relevant features of concepts.

True-False Items: Concept Learning

1. Your understanding of abstract concepts such as "honesty," "democracy," "cognition," or even the concept of a "concept," can change, grow, and become refined as the result of new knowledge and experiences.

(Concepts need not be fixed; they may be modified or amended as we gain additional information. True.)

2. Classifying a set of facial photographs into the categories "attractive" and "unattractive" is an instance of concept learning.

(The individual is presumably sorting the photograph on the basis of an already-learned concept of attractiveness. Here he is *using* a concept, as distinguished from learning a concept. False.)

3. Concept learning is defined as the process by which you both learn to include exemplars and exclude nonexemplars of the concept.

(Concept learning involves both responding to instances and not responding to noninstances of the concept. True.)

4. Concepts are distinguished by their attributes and by the rules for combining the attributes.

(The concept of a "red barn" is defined by its attributes [redness and its barn-like structure] and by the rule of joint presence, that is, the object must be both red and a barn. True.)

5. Humans characteristically learn concepts from negative instances about

as fast as they do with positive *examples* ~~instances~~.

(On the contrary, we typically learn concepts faster from positive instances. False.)

6. In general, the greater the number of relevant redundant attributes in a concept, the easier it is to learn the concept.

(This is the case because with more relevant redundant attributes your likelihood of discovering any one attribute is greater. True.)

7. Concepts such as "justice," "fair play," and "gravity" are generally easier to learn than concepts such as "desk," "chair," or "house."

(Abstract concepts are typically harder to learn than concrete concepts. False.)

8. The longer the delay of feedback, that is, the interval between a response and feedback, the harder it is to learn the concept.

(Delay of feedback produces no systematic or marked effect on concept learning. This is distinguished, however, from the effect of postfeedback delay, whose increase tends to retard concept learning. False.)

9. Stimulus-response association theories differ from stimulus-response mediation theories of concept learning, in that the latter are somewhat more complex.

(Stimulus-response mediational theory introduces one additional step, that of a mediating link between the stimuli and responses. True.)

10. Hypothesis-testing theories place considerable emphasis on conditioning principles in concept learning.

(Hypothesis-testing theories emphasize what the learner does [e.g., use of strategies] in the task. False.)

11. In learning to refine your concept of "learning," it is helpful to distinguish between instances and noninstances of the concept "learning."

(Concept learning is facilitated when you can compare and contrast both positive and negative instances. True.)

12. A variety of examples which illustrate the *range* of a concept are more likely to ensure that a concept is well-learned.

(With a greater number of examples, you are more likely to focus on the essential features of a concept. True.)

8

Perceptual Learning

The skillful automobile driver has learned to make reasonably precise judgments about distance, objects in space, and the speed of approaching vehicles, as a result of considerable practice. In a similar vein, some drivers become proficient in reading city maps as a result of practice. The novice map reader may experience difficulty in relating things on the map to city streets or freeways, whereas the skillful map reader can quickly see the relationship between the map and where he actually is at some moment as well as where he wants to be. In both instances perceptual judgments are observed to improve with practice. The fact that such perceptual judgments do improve with practice is one kind of evidence for the process known as perceptual learning.

There is considerable evidence which indicates that our perceptions are influenced by our past experience and that our perceptions can be modified or changed by various practice conditions. Thus, in a general sense, *the term perceptual learning refers to various changes in perception that can be brought about by learning.* Instances of perceptual learning are common in your everyday experience. You learn, for example, to recognize a particular melody even though it is played by different bands using different musical instruments. Indeed, you may recognize a Beethoven Symphony when played by a rock band. The fact that you can pick out a common set of features (melody) regardless of large changes in musical context is one instance of the process called perceptual learning.

Another instance of perceptual learning is seen when you become skillful in identifying objects under a microscope. The beginning student occasionally has difficulty in seeing what he is supposed to see, and indeed may even describe his own eyelashes or some other irrelevant object. With practice, however, one becomes quite proficient in identifying objects and in describing their important features. Similarly, one learns to make certain perceptual adjustments when first wearing eyeglasses. This is particularly the case if one has to wear bifocals which require somewhat separate adjustments for close and distance viewing.

We have already referred to the significance of perceptual processes as they relate to learning in earlier sections of this book. For example, in paired associate learning the related processes of stimulus discrimination, stimulus selection, and stimulus coding were described. It was emphasized that if a particular stimulus was to become reliably associated with a particular response, the stimulus of the moment must come to be *perceived* in a relatively consistent fashion on each trial. This process called attention to the significance of perceptual processes in associative learning. Likewise, the "relaxation of attention" on a single dominant stimulus and the strengthening of weaker or secondary cues during associative learning represents another instance of perceptual-attentional processes operating in learning. Similarly, in our discussion of memory we emphasized the role of organizing materials in some fashion for purposes of efficient storage and retrieval. In order, however, for the learner to organize the material in some fashion, he must *perceive* some kind of "structure" by which the material can be organized or construct some sort of structure if it is not evidently apparent. In a similar vein, the use of concepts like stimulus discrimination in concept learning calls attention to processes akin to perception in concept learning. Thus, throughout this book perceptual processes have been seen to operate in learning. *This chapter focuses, however, on the manner by which learning influences perception as distinct from the way in which perceptual processes influence learning.*

Nature of Perceptual Learning

Perceptual learning has already been described in an informal way. As you saw, PERCEPTUAL LEARNING REFERS TO ANY MODIFICATION OF PERCEPTION WHICH CAN BE ATTRIBUTED TO LEARNING. Such a definition requires that both *perception* and *learning* be distinguished and the relationship between them described. Let us therefore turn our attention to some of the properties of the concept of learning and then distinguish it from perception.

At the beginning of this book learning was defined as a relatively permanent process that is inferred from performance changes due to practice. Four features of this definition are important: (1) *learning is an inference* which means that it is not something directly observed. Thus learning is an inferred or hypothetical concept like gravity or electricity. We never see gravity directly; we observe falling objects and therefore infer that such a process exists. (2) *The concept of learning is tied to performance, but is not the same as performance.* Hence a distinction is made between learning and performance. Various performance indicators are employed to infer learning such as number of correct responses, errors, percentages of correct responses, response rate, response speed, etc. (3) *The concept of learning is tied to conditions of practice* which serves to distinguish learning from performance changes attributable to other conditions such as fatigue, maturation, or drug states. This simply emphasizes that the conditions antecedent to learning are *practice* conditions as distinct from other kinds of conditions. (4) *Learning is a relatively permanent process*, which is an assumption which is useful in order to distinguish learning from other more temporary processes such as sensory memory or short-term memory.

Schematically, learning can be described as an intervening or inferred process as shown below:

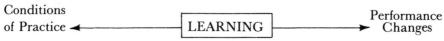

The phrase "conditions of practice" refer to the various conditions which might be varied in some experimental setting. These include, for example, such conditions as number of practice or training trials, reward and or punishment conditions, feedback, distributed practice, intralist similarity, and meaningfulness. In general, they refer to the various training and task conditions which might be manipulated in order to see how they affect performance changes. These comments only amplify what has been explicitly stated or implicitly indicated in previous sections but do serve to formalize the concept of learning in somewhat greater detail.

In a parallel vein, *perception is a process that is inferred from performance changes due to conditions of stimulation.* Thus perception, like learning, is an inferred or hypothetical process which is also tied to performance changes. A principal difference lies in the nature of the antecedent conditions; antecedent to perception are *stimulus* conditions whereas antecedent to learning are *practice* conditions. Some perceptual theorists may wish to make *additional* distinctions regarding the nature of the inferred process. We need, for present purposes, only emphasize the differences in antecedent conditions.

The fact that you detect a change in light intensity when you flick a light switch on is, of course, an instance of perception. Detection of an increase in brightness is a performance indicator, and "turning the light on" produces an increase in stimulus energy. Thus perception, like learning, is a relational concept inferred from both performance changes and stimulus input. The performance change in this example is going from a report of no detection to detection of the light.

The concepts of learning and perception can now be more formally compared as illustrated below. As the diagram shows, both concepts are tied to performance changes and both concepts are inferences from performance tied to some class of antecedent conditions.

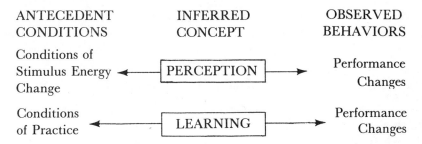

ANTECEDENT CONDITIONS	INFERRED CONCEPT	OBSERVED BEHAVIORS
Conditions of Stimulus Energy Change	← PERCEPTION →	Performance Changes
Conditions of Practice	← LEARNING →	Performance Changes

We can now define perceptual learning by showing how learning and perception relate. Consider first a simple instance of perception. Imagine that two points of pressure about the size of a pencil point are applied to your forearm. The points, which are initially very close together, are gradually moved apart at greater distances until you report at some stage in the test sequence that you feel two distinct points. This report defines what is called the *two-point threshold* for cutaneous sensitivity. In general, the minimal distance between two stimuli pressing on the skin which yields a report of "feeling like two" defines the two-point threshold. Here is an instance of *perception* which, by the above definition, involves a relationship between stimulus energy impinging on the skin receptors (varying the distance between the two points) and some performance indicator (a report of a feeling of "twoness").

Once a two-point threshold is determined, however, you may be given extended practice in making this perceptual judgment. With extended practice the threshold will gradually decrease, which is simply to say that you can detect progressively smaller distances between two points as you are given more practice in making this perceptual judgment. In this instance, decrease of the two-point threshold with practice would be an instance of perceptual learning. Thus the definition of *perceptual learning as a change in perception due to practice* becomes quite clear. It is a change in perception because the threshold value becomes smaller, and the observed change is due to practice factors. This does not, of course, specify what processes might operate during practice but merely emphasizes that perception can become modified as a result of practice conditions.

This example is, of course, but one of many instances of perceptual learning. It serves principally to illustrate in fairly precise terms what is meant by the phrase, perception can become modified by learning.

Categories of Perceptual Tasks

The study of perceptual learning focuses on how practice conditions produce changes in perception. To get at changes in perception psychologists must have certain performance indicators or responses that presumably index changes in perception. A taxonomy of perceptual tasks relevant to perception has been developed in recent years, a taxonomy which categorized the various kinds of behaviors observed in studies of perception and perceptual learning. The five basic response categories are *detection, discrimination, recognition, identification,* and *judgment.* Let us consider each of these briefly.

Detection

An observer watching for "blips" on a radar scope is engaged in the task of detection. Similarly, when you respond to the ring of the telephone you do so because you have detected a stimulus. *A detection study is one in which the observer reports the presence or absence of a stimulus.* The stimulus might be a brief flash of light, a tone, or a target stimulus embedded in a complex as found, say, in hidden puzzles. All that is required in a detection task is the reported presence or absence of some specified target stimulus.

Discrimination

A wine taster reporting that he distinguishes between two wines is engaged in discrimination. He does not have to name or identify the wines to be engaged in discrimination; all that he must do is report that they are different. Similarly, being able to perceive the difference between two identical twins is an instance of discrimination. Thus the term *discrimination refers to the reporting of a difference between two stimuli.* In an experimental setting a subject is presented two stimuli, either simultaneously or successively and asked to report whether they are "same" or "different." Noting that the warmed over roast tastes different from when it was first cooked, that your girl friend has changed her hairstyle, or that a change in the temperature has occurred are all instances of discrimination.

Recognition

In recognition the observer must report if a particular test stimulus is "old" (familiar) *or "new"* (unfamiliar) *following a training series in which the observer looked at one or more stimuli.* Recognition differs from discrimination in that the judgment required is one based upon the familiarity of the stimulus. As we noted in a previous chapter, an example of recognition tests is the typical multiple-choice examination. The task of the subject is to designate which item he thinks he has previously seen or experienced.

Identification

An identification task goes essentially one step beyond that of recognition in that an identifying response must be made in the presence of the stimulus.

This is simply to say that the *task of identification requires a unique response be made to each stimulus.* Producing the name of each individual shown in a photograph is an instance of identification. It is not necessary that a name be used as such because arbitrary labels, letters of the alphabet, or numbers could also be used as identifying responses.

Judgment

Judgment, as a perceptual response indicator, refers simply to the placing or ordering of stimuli along some scale. The subject is typically presented with a series of stimuli and asked to make judgments about them in accord with some scale. For instance, beauty contest judges are asked to rank contestants in accord with some scale of beauty. Similarly, observers may be given some visual patterns and asked to rate them in accord with some scale of complexity going from simple to very complex patterns.

Categories of Perceptual Learning

In this section we shall examine several representative categories of perceptual learning. We can do no more than illustrate a few of the various kinds of changes that have been studied, changes which illustrate the process of perceptual learning. Six categories of perceptual learning studies will be examined: (1) Effects of practice on perceptual skills; (2) Reward and punishment factors; (3) Adaptation to transformed stimulation; (4) Cross-Modal transfer; (5) Verbal labels and perceptual learning; and (6) Schema learning.

Effects of Practice on Perceptual Skills

An earlier section illustrated one kind of improvement in perceptual skills with practice. The example described the reduction in two-point thresholds with practice. Other kinds of perceptual skills also are known to improve with practice. In general, improvements in all five perceptual tasks, detection, discrimination, recognition, identification, and judgment do occur as a result of practice.

A typical example of improvement in perceptual skills associated with practice is seen in a search task. A typical search task requires you to scan a group of stimuli such as letters, numbers, or visual patterns and to detect some prespecified target stimulus or stimuli. For example, you might be shown a series of letters presented in scrambled order and asked to locate all the m's. Similarly, you might be shown several paragraphs of prose material and asked to detect the number of words misspelled in which the misspelled words are experimentally built-into the passage. In any event, the materials can be presented so that humans detect either single or multiple targets. Figure 17 shows the typical improvement in performance when humans are given search tasks on successive days. The figure shows that search time, that is, time to locate either single or multiple targets, progressively decreases with days of practice.

Not only does search time decrease with practice, but also the number of targets detected increases with amount of practice. In general, the improvement in search task performance appears to a phenomenon very much like learning-to-learn. The individual is learning something about efficient scanning habits, perhaps learning to reduce the search down to a few critical features of the stimuli in the case of multiple targets.

Similar kinds of improvements are seen in recognition and identification tasks. Here the task is to recognize or identify stimuli in successive tasks. Both recognition time and recognition accuracy, as well as identification accuracy improves with sustained practice.

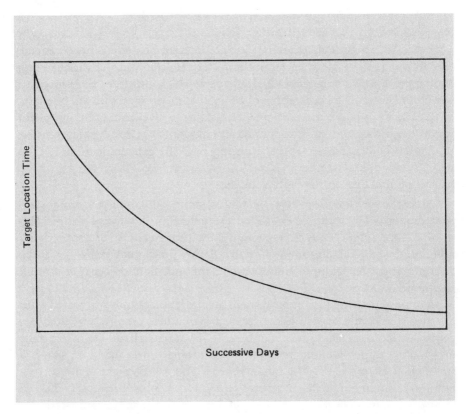

Figure 17. Gradual improvement in target location on successive days of practice.

Reward and Punishment Factors

What humans tend to perceive is governed in part by the conditions of reward and punishment. This is simply to say that under certain conditions we are more likely to perceive those stimuli which have been associated with reward. The role of reward factors has been demonstrated in studies using ambiguous stimuli, either of which can be perceived as a facial profile. In such studies, subjects have been shown each profile separately, and rewarded when they responded to one profile and not the other. In the test situation, they are shown both profiles together and asked to report what they perceive. Typically, subjects report that they tend to perceive the rewarded profile more frequently than the nonrewarded profile. We cannot conclude, however, that perceptions themselves are being modified as such. It appears that what is being modified is the subject's *response bias*, that is, his likelihood of making a particular response. In this connection, you saw earlier in the memory chapter how response bias could influence recognition performance. Here again we have an instance of response bias which is separate from perception itself. Therefore, reward appears to affect response tendencies (performance) but not necessarily perception as such.

Similar kinds of effects have been found in studies of perceptual recognition. Subjects have been shown so-called taboo words such as "whore," "kotex," and "rape," intermixed with non-taboo words such as "apple" and "cigar." The words have been presented for extremely brief durations and the task of the subject is to identify each word. Usually it takes somewhat longer for subjects to identify the taboo words, suggesting to some psychologists the operation of a *perceptual defense* mechanism. By this is meant that the human organism tends to protect himself against stimuli that he perceives as potentially threatening. A simpler interpretation, however, is that humans are simply more likely to withhold responding until they are sure they have seen a taboo word, indicating that longer recognition times are a matter of response bias rather than any perceptual process as such.

Adaptation to Transformed Stimulation

Another type of perceptual learning is seen when one adapts to stimulation that is transformed in some fashion. For instance, you have learned to perceive the world in a particular orientation. If, however, you now wear eyeglasses constructed such that the world is perceived upside down you have the problem of readjusting to your perceptual world. The world, of course, has not changed but your perception of it has. In particular, your ability to locate objects in space is seriously disturbed. The meaning of objects doesn't change, as people are still seen as people, houses as houses, etc., but one must learn to reorient oneself to this new stimulus input.

A simple example of adaptation to transformed stimulation requires that the subject manually locate a target while looking through a prism at his hand. The prism has the effect of displacing the image of his hand, and the subject is allowed to observe his hand movements alone, or the target alone, but not both together. The subject attempts to repeatedly localize the target under the condition of transformed stimulation and gradually improves in his performance. This type of task has been used most extensively by Richard Held and his associates, and the results indicate that perceptual learning, in the form of improved localization skill, depends upon active movement of the subject's hand rather than no movement or passive movement by an experimenter.

Cross-modal Transfer

Cross-modal transfer refers to the fact that learning in one sensory system such as the visual mode, can transfer to another sensory system such as the tactual mode. For example, if you learn a paired associate task consisting of visual patterns as stimuli, then such learning will transfer to a second task if the same stimuli are now presented tactually. In the second task you are not allowed to see the stimuli but only to feel them. Such learning is an instance of perceptual learning and implies to some perceptual theorists, such as James Gibson, a kind of "unity of the senses". This notion implies that there are certain properties of stimuli such as shape, which have invariant features regardless of the sensory system in which they are learned. Thus when you learn something about stimuli in one system you tend to automatically pick up some information in another system. Despite the fact that there is considerable evidence for cross-modal transfer, we understand very little about the mechanisms that produce the effect.

Verbal Labels and Perceptual Learning

A longstanding view in psychology has been that language or verbal labels can aid humans in distinguishing otherwise confusable or highly similar stimuli. The basic notion has been that if distinctive verbal labels are associated with confusable stimuli, that this process will serve to make the stimuli more distinctive or less confusable. At the outset it should be noted that there is evidence indicating that if humans are trained to associate distinctive verbal labels with stimuli, that such stimuli become more recognizable, or are more easily learned in new situations, under *some* conditions. The point to note, however, is that the *mechanisms* by which such an effect occurs are not fully understood.

In these studies, subjects are usually trained to label stimuli in paired-associate fashion with distinctive verbal labels. Their performance is sometimes compared with subjects who are merely shown the stimuli without instructions to label, or who are trained in labeling other stimuli which are unrelated (or irrelevant) to the stimuli used in the test task. Presumably, if the verbal labeling task makes the stimuli more distinctive in some perceptual sense, then they should be more easily discriminated or recognized in a test task when compared with subjects who only looked at the stimuli. The evidence indicates that verbal labeling does produce this effect, but principally when the stimuli are fairly complex. With simple stimuli there is usually little if any effect due to verbal labeling practice. A simple stimulus is a visual shape, for example, with few sides or angles, whereas a complex shape is a many-sided figure.

The most complete explanation of such an effect lies presumably in relating stimulus complexity to the *codability* of the shapes. Henry Ellis has proposed that complex visual patterns are more difficult to code verbally, and, therefore if subjects are given verbal labels which are "representative" of the shapes, that such a label helps the person to more rapidly or efficiently encode the pattern. On the other hand, if the shape is simple and easily encoded, then association of a verbal label is unlikely to do much in addition to what the individual can do for himself. Simple shapes easily suggest verbal codes and hence are unlikely to benefit from the additional effects of labeling.

The effect of verbal labels on subsequent recognition memory of shape stimuli is thus seen, according to this formulation, as one of providing the subject with a rule or verbal instruction for encoding the visual shape. If the verbal label is representative of the shape, it tends to encourage the individual to attend to those distinctive features which are suggested by the label. In effect, the verbal label can suggest to the person certain features of the stimulus to which he should attend, thus allowing a more rapid encoding of the stimulus.

Other investigations of verbal labeling effects have been conducted in which common labels have been associated with different but similar stimuli. Here the object has been to see if associating a common response to different stimuli makes these stimuli less distinctive, an effect sometimes referred to as *acquired equivalence of cues*. In general, stimuli become less recognizable when common labels are attached to them. Again, this process seems to be the result of the common label encouraging the individual to look for common features, much as he might do in a concept learning experiment.

Not only can verbal labels facilitate perceptual performance but they may also mediate or bring about changes in the way in which humans respond to stimuli. For instance, learning to attach the same labels to dissimilar stimuli may make them less distinctive or more equivalent. Indeed, verbal labels serve to mediate or facilitate the learning of new responses to stimuli in a number of everyday situations. You may, for instance, respond to a particular person in some particular way because he has been labeled as a "conservative" or as a "radical" without additional information about the individual's belief system. Or you may tend to regard an entire group of people in a particular way simply because they have been labeled in some specific fashion. The phenomenon of racial and other prejudices appears to be basically a matter of generalizing to a class of stimuli (in this case, people), that is, a matter of responding to groups of humans by virtue of the verbal labels associated with them.

Schema Learning

Another kind of situation which appears to involve perceptual learning are tasks that fall under the rubric of schema learning. A *schema* is a kind of concept that presumably is abstracted (developed) from studying a series of similar or related stimuli. For example, you may be said to have acquired a schema for the human face, which refers to some abstracted representation derived from your experience with faces. Moreover, if asked to draw a representative "American" face, your representation will be different from that of a "Chinese" face, for instance. A schema, then, represents some abstracted central tendency of the sample of stimuli to which you have been exposed. In this sense, a schema is somewhat like an image in that it may represent some "visual picture" of a typical member of some class of events. Thus, we may have schema for a variety of events such as trees, houses, people, faces, cars, and books. So far, this use of the term schema is basically that of an inferred concept, based upon the responses that are made to classes of stimuli. It remains hypothetical, unobserved, and something inferred from behavior.

More recently, however, investigations by psychologists such as Selby Evans and Michael Posner have attempted to *define* the schema in advance of an experiment rather than *infer* its existence. Visual patterns are generated in accordance with statistical rules such that the central tendency or "average" figure is determined. In this fashion the most representative figure of some population of visual figures is known prior to an investigation.

Schema learning researchers have been interested principally in how humans acquire schemas and how they use them to classify additional stimuli once the schema is learned. In the latter case, subjects are shown visual patterns that belong to two or more classes (schema categories) and asked to sort them according to their own judgments. Subjects do learn to classify patterns in accordance with rules built in to the stimuli, that is, they do learn to sort stimuli in accordance with the statistical schema. Moreover, they seem to do this without the benefit of external reinforcement in the form of knowledge of results.

What is Learned in Perceptual Learning?

Let us now turn our attention to the issue of "what is learned" in perceptuallearning. We have illustrated several kinds of situations in which perceptual learning occurs but we need now to ask what gets learned in these situations. The most explicit attempt to identify what is learned in perceptual learning has been outlined by Eleanor Gibson and the following description is a summary of her account. Gibson's description emphasizes three aspects: (1) an increase in specificity of responding; (2) the detection of distinctive features; (3) the detection of properties and patterns.

Increase in Specificity of Responding

First, perceptual learning is seen as involving an increase in the specificity of responding to stimuli. Perceptual learning is not the learning of responses per se, but is seen as the responding to variables of stimulation not previously responded to. At the onset of some learning situation there are many aspects of stimulation to which the learner may fail to respond. For instance, the wine taster may respond to only one or a few features at first but later responds to many features such as body, aroma, clarity, etc.

Detection of Distinctive Features

Closely related to the first process is what Gibson calls detection of distinctive features. Consider learning to distinguish between a pair of twin Siamese cats. Upon first contact they are difficult to distinguish on the basis of any single quality or characteristics. Indeed, many complex stimuli must be distinguished on the basis of a bundle of characteristics rather than one alone. This detection of critically distinctive features appears to be another aspect of perceptual learning.

Detection of Properties and Patterns

Finally, Gibson has proposed that the detection of *regularities* is another aspect of perceptual learning. Consider the earlier example of recognizing a melody regardless of the context in which it was played. Here is an instance of detecting a pattern or regularity in stimulation. More generally, this process involves the detection of invariant properties of stimulation as they appear in various settings.

Some Practical Implications

The study of perceptual learning focuses attention on the *properties of stimuli* in learning tasks. Emphasis is placed on how initially confusable and complex stimuli become distinguished and on the role of structural characteristics of stimuli in learning. The most extensive application of perceptual learning principles have been made by Eleanor Gibson in the analysis of reading skills. Reading skills are seen to consist of at least four distinctive stages. The first phase, which lasts for several years, is learning to speak. This phase precedes the others, involves much response learning, but is part of the total skill of reading. Next the child must learn to discriminate among the printed letters because they are the smallest units of the writing system. While this may seem like a relatively simple task, imagine learning to distinguish the symbols in Chinese or Arabic languages. The third phase involves decoding the letters to sound, that is, learning letter-sound combinations. Finally, the learner must learn higher-order units such as whole words, and then phrases or sentences.

Many other practical skills clearly involve perceptual processes. Map reading is an obvious example. Architects and engineers must learn to read and interpret three-dimensional drawings. Structural properties of mathematical concepts such as equality, symmetry, and transitivity are instances of concepts that must be made perceptible to the learner. How to make structure, order and equivalence distinctive events for the learner is a major task for perceptual learning research, an endeavor which focuses its effort toward the stimulus properties of the learning task.

Summary

This chapter has described some of the principal characteristics of perceptual learning. Perceptual learning refers to changes in perception that can be brought about by learning. Although there is somewhat less agreement about the concept of perception than there is about the concept of learning, perceptual learning can be easily understood in functional terms.

Important categories of perceptual tasks are those of detection, discrimination, recognition, identification, and judgment. To a large extent the study of perceptual learning is the study of how changes in these performances are related to conditions of learning.

Six categories of perceptual learning studies were described. These were: (1) Effects of practice on perceptual skills; (2) Reward and punishment factors; (3) Adaptation to transformed stimulation; (4) Cross-modal transfer; (5) Verbal labels and perceptual learning; and (6) Schema learning. An examination of what is learned in perceptual learning suggests at least three aspects: an increase in the specificity of responding, the detection of distinctive features, and the detection of properties and patterns.

Applications of perceptual learning principles have been made most extensively to the reading process. Perceptual learning focuses attention on the properties of stimuli as important determinants of learning.

True-False Items: Perceptual Learning

1. Your perceptions of events, objects in space, as well as coded stimuli may be modified as a result of learning.

(This is simply to say that the process of perceptual learning occurs. True.)

2. The fact that perception can be modified by learning implies that learning is uninfluenced by perceptual processes.

(The interaction between perception and learning is a two-way affair. Not only is perception modifiable by learning but learning is influenced by perceptual and attentional processes. False.)

3. Both perception and learning are inferred processes. *can be actually observed nor actually measured*

(Neither are directly observed but are inferred from some relationship between performance changes and antecedent conditions. Thus both are relational concepts in that they are defined by the relationship between two classes of events. True.)

4. The antecedent conditions of perception are changes in stimulus energy.

(Perception is dependent upon changes in light or sound intensity, contour information in patterns, contrast, color, all of which are instances of changes in stimulus energy. True.)

5. The fact that you can barely hear a tone is an instance of detection whereas recognition means that you can tell the difference between two tones.

(Barely hearing a tone is detection but being able to tell the difference between two tones is an instance of discrimination. False.)

6. Identification is similar to recognition except that in identification you are able to name or label the stimulus in some fashion.

(Recognizing a stimulus only means that it is familiar; identifying the stimulus means that you can give its appropriate name or label. True.)

7. The fact that your proficiency in locating hidden objects improves with practice is an instance of perceptual learning.

(Here you are learning something about efficient search habits, in effect, how to scan in a proficient fashion. True.)

8. The fact that we tend to perceive with greater frequency events or objects which have been associated with reward means that your perceptions have been modified.

(We cannot be sure that our perceptions have actually changed; all that may have occurred is a change in response bias. False.)

9. Verbal labels associated with visual stimuli can make the stimuli more distinctive in the sense of becoming easier to recognize.

(This process does occur but principally when the verbal labels are "representative" of the stimuli and when the stimuli are somewhat difficult to encode. True.)

10. A schema is very much like a concept.

(The basic difference is that a schema is usually not tied to a single feature or dimension but to a bundle or complex set of dimensions, some

7 *Perceptual learning focuses attention more on the kinds of responses rather than the properties of the stimuli*

of which may not be easily specified. In contrast, a concept may be tied to a defined single dimension, such as the concept of redness. True.)

11. Learning to recognize a melody regardless of the musical context in which it is played would be best described as an instance of response learning.

(Learning to recognize a melody regardless of the context would be an instance of detecting an invariant pattern of stimulation. False.)

12. Applications of principles of perceptual learning have focused largely on analysis of the stimulus properties of learning tasks.

(Perceptual learning places its main emphasis on properties of stimuli. True.)

9

Language, Thinking, and Problem Solving

The one kind of behavior that most clearly distinguishes man from other animals is his facility with language. Although it can be demonstrated in the context of controlled laboratory situations that lower animals can think, learn concepts, and solve problems, language is frequently said to be a distinguishing feature of man. Recent investigations of language behavior in chimpanzees suggest, however, that man may not be the sole possessor of language. These animals have been shown capable of using language at a simple level. Language is closely related to thought and other cognitive processes such as problem solving. Indeed, for this reason the topics of language, thinking, and problem solving are dealt with jointly in this chapter.

Thinking represents man's most complex and advanced activity. This "mental activity" results from man's ability to manipulate symbols and concepts and to use them in new and different ways in order to solve problems. The importance of thinking is clearly evident in our daily activities. Humans are urged to "think carefully," sometimes to "think fast," sometimes to "think systematically" or "clearly," and sometimes just to think. Indeed, the widespread importance of thinking is reflected in the forceful motto "THINK!" used by a major international corporation. In a similar vein, the importance of thinking is attested by the fact that it is a frequently expressed objective of education.

Teachers may exhort students to think clearly without, however, complete understanding of how one engages in this activity. Although teachers have a reasonably clear understanding of how to help one write systematically and speak clearly, it is more difficult to specify how one thinks logically. In part this is because thinking refers to *covert* activities, events that we do not directly observe or measure, whereas writing and speaking are overt language behaviors which are directly observable.

Much of your thinking is directed toward solving problems of practical importance. Certainly you are more likely to think when your old habits, skills, and routines are inappropriate for the particular task at hand. In such situations you are forced to search for and try out new solutions. Moreover, thinking ranges from relatively simple events to quite complex activities. If you play the game of categories and are asked to think of instances of the category "tree," numerous examples come to mind immediately. This represents a case of the simplest kind of thinking which involves the direct association between some conceptual category and an instance. Only when you exhaust the immediately obvious instances do you begin a more careful search of the various possibilities. Perhaps you first think of subcategories such as evergreens, deciduous trees, and overlapping subcategories such as tropical vegetation, and then think of instances of each subcategory. This aspect of thinking involves a two-stage process in which specific words are produced only after you have thought of two or more categories that serve to mediate specific words.

In summary, language, thought, and problem solving are intimately related activities. In this chapter some of the characteristics of language are first described, followed by a consideration of thinking and problem solving.

Language

Language is the basic tool with which humans think. Jean Piaget, the distinguished Swiss psychologist, has made an interesting analogy in pointing out that language is to thought as mathematics is to physics. Just as we use mathematics as the "language" of physics, ordinary language bears a similar relationship to thought.

Language is composed of words combined according to certain rules. Words themselves represent symbols which are composed of basic vowel and consonant sounds. These sounds are called *phonemes* and represent the basic unit of language.

At a more general level, language represents the major system of *symbols* available to the human for communication. Other symbol systems are, of course, available. For example, the deaf can communicate with sign language, small children can count by raising their fingers, mathematical formula can convey information, and signs can convey emotional feelings of the carrier. All of these are symbols in the sense that they convey meaning. They provide some kind of information which, in turn, allows some kind of response by other humans. The symbol ☮ represents "peace" but the symbol is not peace itself. Rather, it stands for the concept of peace and for the hope of peace by the person who uses the symbol. It communicates a set of feelings and attitudes by the user of the symbol; it clearly conveys meaning.

Functions of Language

Language, as the most important symbol system for humans, serves at least three identifiable functions: (1) First, language can be *instrumental* in the sense that verbal behavior can lead directly to reward. For instance, the young child may learn that by saying "please" he obtains a reward such as candy or a cookie from his parents. Commands such as "stop" and "be quiet" are instrumental in that they may lead to the cessation of unpleasant stimuli. (2) Language serves as *stimuli* or signals for other behaviors. This is to say that language aids us in thinking and in mediating behaviors that ultimately may achieve some kind of reward. (3) Language serves as a vehicle for communication with others. This communication may, of course, directly achieve some kind of reinforcement for the speaker.

Basic Units of Language: Phonemes and Morphemes

All languages are made of basic sounds called *phonemes*. Adult humans can produce approximately 100 phonemes and the English language is made up of about 45 phonemes. Languages vary in the number of phonemes, ranging from as few as 15 to as many as 85. One reason why it is difficult for some Americans to learn foreign languages is that different phonemes are used. For instance, there are phonemes in Germanic and Slavic languages that are never used in English.

Phonemes are in turn composed of about 12 *distinctive features*. The linguist Roman Jakobson has constructed a classification of distinctive features by which phonemes differ. For example, a given phoneme (speech sound) may be sounded nasally or orally. Another feature is the explosive or tense character of some sounds, as seen when you pronounce letters like *p* or *f*.

Another unit of language is the *morpheme*, which is the smallest meaningful unit in a language. Morphemes usually consist of combinations of two or more phonemes, and roughly correspond to the most elementary words. The words *good, put,* and *go* are single morphemes. *Goodness, putting,* and *going* consist of two morphemes. Thus, single morphemes may be root words of a language; they may also consist of prefixes or suffixes.

At about two years of age the young child begins to combine two words to form the most rudimentary kind of sentence. The combination of words into sentences is referred to as *syntax*. A young child will frequently use sentences like "want cookie," "where ball?" or "drink Mommy," which clearly convey meaning. These sentences are quite systematic, are usually understood by the parent, and are similar to adult English sentences with the unessential words omitted.

Phrase Structure in Sentences

In order to understand language in the adult, it is necessary to examine the structure of sentences. At one level of analysis a sentence can be simply regarded as a string of phonemes. The single phoneme, however, is not a particularly useful way of analyzing sentences since this would be looking at a sentence as a series of isolated speech sounds. At another level, a sentence can be regarded as a series of morphemes, which are groupings of phonemes. From this viewpoint, however, the sentence is viewed as a string of words. Linguists have found it more useful to describe a sentence in terms of *phrases*, which are groupings of words.

Analysis of a sentence into its various phrases describes the *phrase structure* of a sentence. A sentence is regarded as composed of two basic phrases, a *noun phrase* and a *verb phrase*, which are in turn composed of subcomponents. Figure 18 shows the phrase structure of a simple sentence, "The boy rode the bicycle." The noun phrase is composed of a determiner and a noun, and the verb phrase is composed of a verb and noun phrase; the latter noun phrase is also composed of a determiner and a noun. The relationship between the two phrases is portrayed in the tree-diagram of figure 18. Our pauses in speech are defined by the phrase marking. For example, we would be most likely to say, "The boy—rode—the bicycle," pausing ever so briefly after *boy* and *rode*. We would not be likely to say, "The—boy rode—the bicycle," grouping *boy* and *rode*, or, "The—boy rode the—bicycle," grouping *boy*, *rode*, and *the*. While in normal speech we may search and grope for a particular word, and thus alter the pauses, the listener would still tend to understand the message.

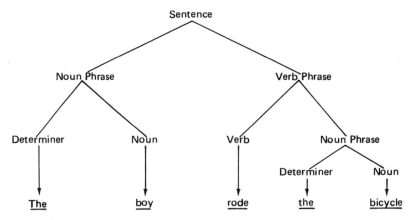

Figure 18. Phrase structure of the sentence, "The boy rode the bicycle," represented by a tree diagram.

Surface Structure and Deep Structure

Linguists distinguish between surface and deep structure of sentences. The *surface structure* is the actual sentence as it is sounded and reflects simply the relationship among the parts of the sentence. In contrast, deep structure refers to the meaning of the sentence, that is, to the specification of the logical relations between the words in the sentence.

Consider the sentences, "John threw the ball," and "The ball was thrown by John." Both sentences convey the same meaning despite the fact that they sound differently. Hence their deep structure is the same. But consider the sentence, "They are eating apples," which can have two meanings. "Eating" may serve as a verb or it may modify the noun "apples." Thus, the deep structure can vary with the same sentence depending on what meaning the speaker wishes to convey.

These illustrations indicate the necessity of distinguishing between surface and deep structure. The deep structure of a sentence conveys the basic or underlying information in the sentence. By applying certain theoretical rules of grammar, it is possible to link the surface structure of a sentence to its deep structure. Rules for the specification of this linkage process, called *transformational* rules, have been developed by Noam Chomsky and other linguists. These transformational rules are the rules by which ideas (deep structure) are transformed into understandable sentences (surface structure).

Transformational rules have clear implications about what features of sentences humans do store in memory. If the sentence is very simple, so that its deep structure approximates its surface structure, then features of the surface structure may be stored. As sentences become more complex, what is stored is some underlying base structure or schema, plus one or more "footnotes" that serve as rules necessary to regenerate the sentence in its original surface form. This is simply to say that what is stored is some coded representation of the complex sentence.

This brief description only begins to sketch some of the complexities of language. What is clear is that young children have an enormously complex task in learning to speak, read, and use language in a meaningful fashion. The fact that humans can acquire and use language emerges as a remarkable achievement. Let us now turn our attention to the matter of how humans develop language.

Language Development

Language development follows a fairly orderly course. The beginning of language is evidenced in babbling, which is an elementary type of vocalization. Children do produce sounds earlier than six months, but babbling, which is the repetition of speech sounds, is most clearly evident beginning around six months. Between six and nine months, infants are able to produce all of the basic speech sounds that make up a language.

The emission of speech sounds, even at this early age, can be controlled to some extent by an adult. For example, the rate at which infants emit speech sounds can be increased by having an adult repeat the sound after the infant. These responses, called *echoic responses*, can be shaped in the sense of increasing their rate just like other instrumental responses. Language learning is not, however, simply the result of reinforcement of particular speech sounds and sequences. Language involves maturational processes as well as learning. Moreover, the structure of language is sufficiently complex to require principles beyond those of S-R formulations in order to account for its development.

Making speech sounds is only the first step in acquiring language. The sounds must come to represent objects, symbols, and events in the child's environment. This is simply to say that the sounds must acquire meaning for the child. Moreover, the child must learn to *associate* particular sound symbols with particular aspects of his environment. The child is familiar with many aspects of his environment before he learns to speak. His parents are familiar stimuli; toys, pets, siblings, and household objects are also familiar stimuli. His task, at this early stage of language development, is one of learning to associate particular environmental stimuli with particular responses. For example, he must learn to associate the sight of mother with the sound of "mama." Similarly, the sight, feel, and taste of a cookie must become associated with the sound of "cookie." Only when such associations are acquired can the speech sound come to represent or symbolize some object or event for the child. Thus, the development of meaning begins with the acquisition of associations between objects and events, on the one hand, and speech sounds, on the other.

The particular speech sounds a young child makes are shaped by cultural (e.g., parental) reinforcement much the same way other responses are shaped. First, whether or not a particular reward (such as parental approval) is given determines what responses will be strengthened. If, for example, a parent thinks it important for the child to say "please" when asking for something, the parent will arrange to reward the response when the child says "please" and will omit reward if the child fails to say "please." Thus, the particular responses that a child may make are under some control of external reinforcing events.

In a similar vein, properties of verbal behavior such as its loudness and rate are also influenced by reinforcement. If members of the family characteristically talk loud or fast, the child is likely to do the same. In addition, these properties of verbal behavior may be reinforced if the parent chooses to do so. For example, the parent may withhold a reward until the child speaks sufficiently loud, as judged by the parent. Moreover, as the child approximates a desirable pronunciation, the response may achieve rapid reward from the parent. Thus, properties of speech such as its loudness, rate, and quality of pronunciation can be shaped by their careful reinforcement.

The association of speech sounds to environmental stimuli is, of course, only a part of language development. Once the child has acquired a rudimentary vocabulary, he must then begin to form sentences. At first the young child will form quite simple sentences, usually consisting of two or three words, such as "want drink." Even as his vocabulary expands, short sentences continue to be used.

Gradually, however, the child begins to construct more complex sentences that take on the characteristics of adult language. This is an enormously complex task, far more complicated than associating sounds with environmental stimuli. He must learn to construct increasingly complex sentences, many of which he has never heard. His task is not only that of understanding complex sentences but of constructing sentences that are grammatically "correct" in the sense of being understood by the listener.

What the child is now learning are sets of *grammatical rules* for constructing sentences. Usually, of course, the child is unable to verbalize the rules. Indeed, many adults who speak grammatically acceptable English are unable to specify the rules they employ. Thus, you learn to recognize and use (operate in accord with) grammar appropriately even though you are frequently unable to specify the rules.

It is at this level of language learning that principles of conditioning and reinforcement appear less applicable. There are an enormous number of possibilities in constructing sentences, so many that it is difficult to regard sentence construction as resulting simply from some S-R associative process. Rather, humans learn grammatical rules in learning to use language, rules that enable them to generate a large number of different kinds of sentences.

Language and Thought

Language and thought are related events. The ability of children to handle concepts is related to their language development. Indeed, children who can verbalize relationships such as "nearer than" or "larger than" are better able to deal with problems involving relationships among stimuli than children who do not yet verbalize such relationships.

Nevertheless, language does not seem to be *essential* for complex mental processes, despite the fact that language facilitates problem solving. For instance deaf children, who are deficient in language, are able to handle many concepts. Thus, although language is a facilitating factor in thought, it does not appear to be essential in some critical sense for the development of cognitive capacities. As noted, this is the case because deaf children can develop other modes of communication by acquiring symbol systems other than conventional language.

The most explicit attempt to relate language and thought is seen in the *linguistic-relativity hypothesis* developed by Benjamin Whorf. Whorf's hypothesis contends that the structure of one's language leads one to conceive of the world in particular ways, ways that differ from someone using a different language. This is simply to say that a person's language imposes a particular view of the world. Presumably, cognitive processes are in some way inevitably affected by the structure of language. The notion of linguistic *relativity* is emphasized because thought is presumed to be relative to the particular language used.

Vocabulary differences provide one instance of how language is presumably related to thought. For instance, Eskimos have several different words for labeling snow, depending upon its characteristics, whereas only one is widely used in English. Skiers, of course, do distinguish between several kinds of snow. Some cultures have many words for the various colors, others have only a few. For Whorf, the range of words or labels available influences the range of cognitive activities with which humans may engage. If a person has a number of different descriptive labels that he can apply to a range of events, presumably he is able to think about these events in more alternative ways than one who has only a few labels.

There are two versions of Whorf's hypothesis. The *strong* version emphasized that language *invariably* influences thought, whereas the *weak* version emphasized that language affects thought when the particular task directly depends upon properties of the language system. There is little support for the strong version of the hypothesis but a reasonable amount of support for the weaker version.

Thinking and Problem Solving

In this section we shall turn our attention to important issues of thinking and problem solving. Consideration of the nature of thinking and problem solving, general features of problem-solving tasks, and factors influencing problem solving are given. Subsequent sections deal with theories of thinking and problem solving and some practical principles of problem solving.

Nature of Thinking and Problem Solving

Thinking refers to *covert* processes not directly observable by the psychologist. Thinking is something that psychologists *infer* from the behavior of individuals but it is not something directly seen. In general, THINKING REFERS TO A CLASS OF COVERT ACTIVITIES THAT INVOLVE THE MANIPULATION OF SYMBOLS. For man the most important symbols are language and concepts.

You may observe thinking *indirectly* when you watch a young child at play attempting to construct some object, such as a swing. At each stage of construction you may observe some characteristic pause in which the child appears to be making decisions about the next stage. The pauses may be very brief, but they are typically followed by a burst of fairly continuous activity until the next phase of the task is completed. It is assumed that the child is "thinking" during these pauses between activity, and this inference is made, in part, because the child continues to carry out productive sequences in reaching his desired goal.

Like overt behavior, thinking ranges from simple to complex levels. As noted earlier, at a very simple level, thinking involves little more than making an association to some conceptual category. If I ask you to think of an example of transportation, "automobile," or "plane" immediately come to mind. On the other hand, if I ask whether it is less expensive to fly or go by train from Chicago to Los Angeles, the answer depends on several considerations. At a simple level you may directly compare the cost of air fare versus train fare. But then you must include the cost of meals and incidentals if you travel by train. Finally, you must weigh the "cost" of the added travel time if you go by train. Clearly, this problem requires more complex thinking than the first.

The term *thinking* refers to numerous kinds of situations. A small girl *decides* that if she is especially pleasant to her father he will buy her a desired toy; a small boy *figures out* how to reach the cookie jar; a student *works* a math problem; a teacher *organizes* his lecture; a housewife *plans* a shopping list. The terms *decide*, *figure*, and *plan* all refer to the activity of thinking; however, we can only infer that thinking has taken place when we observe an outcome. Whether or not the outcome is successful is not critical for inferring thinking. What must be observed is some change in behavior in relation to some specified set of conditions, such as instructions to do something, that were present prior to the change in behavior.

The study of problem solving typically involves observing the way in which a learner arrives at a solution to some particular task. Psychologists usually make no attempt to distinguish rigorously between problem solving and thinking because it is assumed that thinking occurs during problem-solving activity. Moreover, problem solving is one class of activities that allows the psychologist to infer the process of thinking. Finally, the two terms are frequently used synonymously and, therefore, no attempt is made to distinguish them here. One activity appears to involve the other and to overlap to such a great extent that they will be used interchangeably in this book.

General Features of Problem-solving Tasks

The typical problem-solving task presents the learner with a situation in which he must discover a solution to some problem. The task frequently allows many alternative responses to be made, thus making problem solving relatively complex in the hierarchy of activities studied by psychologists. Whereas in concept learning and paired associate learning relatively few response alternatives exist, problem-solving tasks characteristically allow many response alternatives. Sometimes only one response is correct and sometimes several responses are correct in the sense that they are acceptable solutions to the problem.

A large number of experimental procedures have been used in the study of problem solving. Moreover, there is no "standard" problem-solving task in the sense that the paired associate task is standard in verbal learning. Laboratory problem-solving tasks do, however, possess certain common features. These can be more easily seen by examining several examples of problem-solving activities. In the next section several types of problem-solving activities are examined, with a focus on factors which affect problem-solving efficiency.

Persistence of Set in Problem Solving

One type of problem-solving task examines the tendency of humans to persist in inappropriate or less adequate ways of solving problems when simpler, more direct ways exist. The *water jar* problem is an example of this type of task. This task requires a person to determine how to fill a jar of water in order to obtain a specified amount. All problems are of the form: "You will be given three empty containers, A, B, and C, and your task is to describe how to obtain a specific quantity of water, Y."

Table 9.1 illustrates a typical problem sequence. Problem 1 is an illustrative problem. Here the solution is to fill jar A, then remove 9 quarts from it by filling jar B three times. Problems 2 through 6 are training problems in which the solution is always to fill jar B first, then from this jar fill jar A once and jar C twice which leaves the exact quantity specified. All problems, therefore, have a general solution of the form Y (the quantity specified)=B - A - 2C. Problems 7 and 8 can also be solved this way; however, there is a much simpler and direct solution in which you fill jar A first and pour off into jar C once leaving the exact amount required for problem 7, and add A and C for problem 8. Problem 9 requires the simpler solution.

If humans receive no instructions about the change in problems 7 and 8, they tend to persist in solving these problems just as they did in problem sequences 2 through 6. This simply illustrates the more general principle, namely, that most humans have a strong tendency toward *persistence of set. Once you have learned a rule that works, you may tend to continue applying that rule even when a simpler solution is possible.* This means that our old habits continue to be used, even when they are less efficient, if we fail to perceive that the situation has changed.

Many instances of the persistence of set can be seen in everyday life. For example, you may continue to try to solve mathematics problems by a rule no

TABLE 9.1

Water Jar Problem

		Size of Jars (in quarts)			Quarts of Water Desired
	Problem	A	B	C	Y
Example ⟶	1	29	3	—	20
	2	21	127	3	100
"Training" Problems ⟶	3	14	163	25	99
	4	18	43	10	5
	5	9	42	6	21
	6	20	59	4	31
"Test" Problems ⟶	7	23	49	3	20
	8	15	39	3	18
	9	28	76	3	25

longer appropriate to the situation. The math problem may require, for instance, a combination of two rules or principles while you may be using only one of them. Similarly, the inexperienced chess player may continue to make the same type of moves even when they are no longer strategic or efficient. Only when he can "break" his set will he have the opportunity to consider a new mode of attack.

Functional Fixedness in Problem Solving

Another kind of problem-solving task which also measures persistence of set are tests of functional fixedness. *Functional fixedness* refers to the tendency to think of objects as functioning in one certain way and to ignore other less typical ways in which they might be used.

A typical problem is described below. The subject is given a set of objects and asked to arrange them as a stand capable, say, of supporting a vase of flowers. Some of the objects are appropriate to solving the problem, while others are inappropriate or irrelevant. The point of such tasks is to require you to use a familiar object in a novel fashion. In this example, the objects consist of a rectangular piece of plywood which has a wooden bar wired to it, pliers, and two L-shaped metal brackets. The first step is to use the pliers to loosen the wire and detach the wooden bar. The wooden bar can be used as a support for the plywood board but this, in itself, is not sufficient. The L-shaped metal brackets appear reasonable to many subjects but they will not support the board. In order to solve the problem, the subject must use the pliers in an unusual way as "legs" for the plywood stand. This is accomplished by opening the pliers and placing them under the stand. The weight of the stand keeps the pliers steady at one end, while the wooden bar supports the stand at the other end.

As emphasized, the principal interest in this kind of task is to see if the subject will use the familiar object in a novel and unusual way to solve the problem. The ability of humans to solve this kind of problem is hampered to the extent that they tend to think of the pliers in terms of its typical function. In effect, you must be able to break an established set in order to deal with this type of problem. Like the water jar problem, here is another instance of negative transfer in the sense that persistence of old ways of doing things or viewing objects hampers problem solving efficiency.

Set in Verbal Anagram Problems

A third class of problems that has received wide use is the anagram problem. The anagram is a scrambled series of letters, such as BOLREMP, which, when rearranged, makes at least one word such as PROBLEM. The subject may be asked to form only one word, or he may be given an anagram which allows several possible solutions and is asked to produce as many words as possible. Usually the former procedure is used. Either the number of correct solutions achieved in a fixed time period, or the time to obtain a solution is measured.

Anagram problems can be used in a fashion directly analogous to the water jar problem. Subjects can be given a series of anagrams such as:

"Training" Problems	APMR OSYB AEVH OTAG AFIW
"Test" Problems	LCAM OFRT

The first five of these anagrams can be solved by the formula 4-1-3-2, where 1-2-3-4 is the presented order of the letters. For example, unscrambling OTAG yields GOAT. During training the subject learns a particular rule, although he may not verbalize it. During the next part of the sequence, the subjects are given "test" anagrams which require a new rule for solution. The problems are presented in a continuous series so the subject does not know, of course, that the rules have changed. Under this circumstance, subjects have a strong tendency to persist in trying to use the old rule, taking longer to discover the new rule than control subjects who did not undergo the initial training.

What is characteristic of all three of these laboratory problems (water jar, functional fixedness, and verbal anagrams) is that HUMANS MAY SHOW STRONG PERSISTENCE OF OLD HABITS IN NEW SITUATIONS WHERE THEY ARE NO LONGER APPROPRIATE. Indeed, the typical study of problem solving characteristically looks like a negative transfer paradigm in the sense that learned behaviors *interfere* with learning of new responses. What is observed is the ease with which humans can overcome interference. Problem-solving tasks can, of course, be constructed so as to reflect positive transfer from one task sequence to another. This amounts to arranging the situation so that the rule or principle learned in the first stage of the task transfers positively to the second stage, facilitating the learner's performance. Much more emphasis has, however, been placed on the interference aspects of problem-solving tasks.

These three tasks provide a small sample of a large number of problem-solving tasks that have been used by psychologists. No attempt is made, however, to catalogue the great variety of tasks employed.

Motivational Factors

A person can bring a particular level of motivation to a problem-solving task and the task itself may induce some motivational state in the person. These motivational states can, in turn, influence the efficiency of problem solving. The general principle noted in an earlier chapter still holds: As the task becomes more complex, less motivation is necessary for achieving optimal learning.

A second important principle is that the relationship between degree of motivation and problem-solving efficiency is U-shaped. AS THE DEGREE OF MOTIVATION INCREASES, PROBLEM-SOLVING EFFICIENCY INCREASES UP TO SOME OPTIMAL POINT BEYOND WHICH INCREASES IN MOTIVATION PRODUCE A REDUCTION IN PROBLEM-SOLVING EFFICIENCY. This relationship is shown in figure 19, which presents a hypothetical curve showing the effect of degree of motivation on problem-solving performance.

What this means is that excessive motivation interferes with problem-solving efficiency. Moreover, if failure to solve a problem induces frustration, then this motivational state will further hamper your effectiveness. One important implication of this principle is that children must be taught to deal with problems without reacting in an overly emotional fashion which can be destructive of personal efficiency.

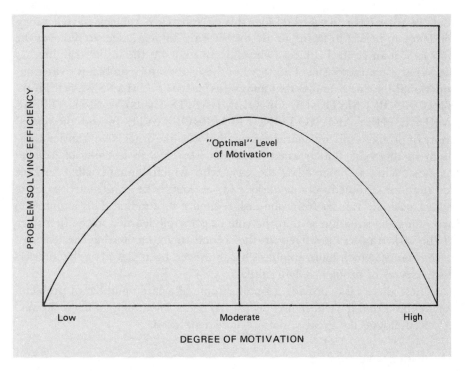

Figure 19. Relationship between degree of motivation and efficiency in problem solving.

Theories of Thinking and Problem Solving

Three theoretical approaches have been developed in accounting for the events of thinking and problem solving. In general, theories of thinking and problem solving are less formal than are theories of the less complex processes of human learning. One class of theories involves the extension of stimulus-response associationistic conceptions to the processes of thinking and problem solving. This class of theories is very similar to stimulus-response theories of concept learning and adopts the same fundamental assumptions. A second class of theories stems from Gestalt psychology and has emphasized the importance of insight in problem solving. This class of theories views thinking and problem solving as a matter of reorganizing one's perceptual world. Finally, a third class of theories use information-processing conceptions to understand thinking and problem solving.

Stimulus-response Theory

Stimulus-response conceptions of thinking regard it basically as an associative process. Thinking is viewed as *covert* or implicit trial-and-error behavior, just as there is overt trial-and-error behavior in many simple learning situations. It is assumed in any problem situation that the learner brings to the task a number of possible habits. These habits are assumed to be already available, in the sense of being associated to some degree of strength to the particular task situation. Not only do these habit tendencies vary in strength to the particular task situation but they are arranged in what Clark Hull termed a *habit-family hierarchy*. This is simply to say that the learner enters a given situation with a hierarchy of habits varying in strength.

The theory contends that in a problem-solving situation, the available habits would be run off in the order of their strength until some particular response was successful. So far, this account is just like that of trial-and-error behavior of lower animals in solving simple problems. In order to account for thinking, however, S-R association theory does not need to assume that the responses are run off overtly. Rather, the theory assumes that these responses are run off *covertly* until one achieves success. The process is basically that of first trying (covertly) one response, then another, until you finally discover the correct response.

S-R theories, emphasizing covert activity, have been used to account for certain kinds of performances that require discovery of the optimal or correct response. Consider, for example, "doing" a complicated picture puzzle. According to S-R theory, your approach to the puzzle could be characterized as one of implicitly trying out several alternatives while holding a piece of the puzzle in your hand until you discovered a solution that appeared to work. The principal point is that your problem-solving behavior is interpreted as a matter of running off covert responses until you achieve a solution. In a similar fashion, S-R theory could characterize games such as chess as involving trying several alternative responses implicitly until you discovered one that would optimize your position.

Gestalt Theory

Gestalt psychologists have approached thinking and problem solving from the viewpoint of how the organism perceives his world. Thinking is regarded, theoretically, as a matter of perceptual reorganization, that is, as the process of coming to "see" environmental stimuli in new and different ways. Thinking is thus viewed as some "central" perceptual-cognitive process. Like S-R theory, thinking involves covert activity; however, thinking is not conceptualized as a matter of running off available habits.

The characteristic approach of Gestalt psychologists, such as Wolfgang Köhler, has been to place a subject in a problem-solving setting and observe how he goes about solving the problem. A typical problem setting has been the *detour* task in which a barrier is placed between a subject and goal object. Usually small children or animals such as chimpanzees or dogs are used as subjects, and the barrier is constructed so as to prevent the subject from *directly* obtaining the object. The animal or child must detour by going around the barrier to obtain the goal object. With this kind of problem, chimpanzees and dogs achieve fairly rapid solutions, whereas chickens tend to rush headlong into the barrier, usually failing to solve the problem. Presumably the performance of chickens represents their inability to perceive the stimulus features of the task that would enable a more insightful solution.

Other problem settings, have required animals to use two sticks, joining them so as to form a rake for obtaining food. Descriptions of the behavior of animals solving problems emphasize such features as their observing the objects for some period of time followed by rapid solution of the problem. As the Gestalt psychologists contend, this rapid problem-solving activity implies that the animal was able to reorganize his perception of the world, thus achieving "insight" into the problem.

These examples can only briefly serve to illustrate the kind of tasks Gestalt investigators have used. These tasks usually allow the subject to perceive most aspects of the problem in its entirety. In contrast, problem-solving tasks used by S-R theorists have typically not been of this nature. Thus it is not too surprising that different theoretical conceptions should have developed. Stimulus-response and Gestalt conceptions of thinking have had a long and controversial history. Our concern is not with this history but with noting that different views of the process have, in part, stemmed from different experimental attacks on the problem.

Information-processing Approaches

Information-processing approaches to theorizing about psychological events are fairly new with developments accelerating since 1960. Just as there are information-processing approaches to concept learning and memory, as noted in previous chapters, there are information-processing conceptions of problem solving, pattern recognition, language translation, perception, and learning.

Information-processing approaches to psychological events attempt to formulate a "flow-chart," or sequence of events, using the format of computer programs. A computer program consists of a series of steps or rules that tell the computer what to do. In a similar vein, the basic idea of information processing is to identify the steps involved in some psychological activity, list these steps in proper sequence, and then see if the computer can simulate these activities. To the extent that the computer can simulate the actions of a human, the psychologist may gain some understanding of what must go into a theory designed to "explain" such actions.

Clearly, of course, a human being is much more than a computer. Basically all that is implied by information-processing approaches to behavior is that a program which can simulate some psychological process can, in turn, serve as a highly abstract model of the kinds of events that must make up the process. Thus, a theory of some process becomes essentially a statement of the rules of operations, restrictions placed on the rules, how the rules combine, and how much information the program must contain.

Several kinds of programs for problem-solving activities have been developed. An example of one type is seen in letter-series completion tasks used by Herbert Simon and K. Kotovsky. These problems contain a series of letters and require that the subject fill in the next letter.

A simple example would be:

$$B \; D \; F \; H \; \_\_$$

Here the rule is very simple and can be solved by children seven or eight years old. Another series could take this form:

$$B \; T \; C \; T \; D \; T \; \_\_$$

And a more difficult series could take this form:

$$P \; X \; A \; X \; O \; Y \; B \; Y \; N \; Z \; \_\_$$

This type of task can be made even more difficult so that most college students are unable to solve the problem.

A problem-solving program of this type must contain a number of features. It must be able to recognize and distinguish letters. It must be able to detect regularities in the pattern by looking for repeatable periodicities in the sequence. More generally, it must be programmed to discover whatever regularity is intrinsically built into a particular letter series. Finally, if the program can successfully solve a given class of problems, then the psychologist gains some conception of the kind of rules that must be present in any theory of problem-solving activity.

Some Practical Suggestions

What can be summarized about thinking and problem solving that can be useful to you in everyday problem situations? In this section, five general principles will be outlined that are useful in virtually all problem situations. Many additional practical rules of thumb can be cited, but these five principles focus on central aspects of problem solving.

Understand the Problem

Before you can solve a problem you must first be sure you understand it. Perhaps this appears so obvious as to sound trite. Yet all too frequently the basic difficulty you have in solving a problem is a failure to have a clear conception of its components. One of the frequent reasons that students do poorly on exams is that in their haste to answer the question they fail to analyze and reexamine the question itself. An all too familiar experience of students is to discover that they have written an answer to a question other than the one asked by the exam. Thus, not until you understand a problem can you attempt to answer it. Moreover, once you have clarified a problem, it is good practice to check again to see if your initial understanding is still correct.

Remember the Problem

Another source of difficulty arises if you fail to remember the problem accurately. On occasion students produce incorrect answers on essay exams because they failed to remember the problem as it was formulated. Somewhere in the course of writing an answer the student may veer away from the central issue and deal with irrelevant issues. You may, so to speak, shift in midstream from the main thesis to trivial, secondary, or utterly unrelated topics if you fail to keep the problem in mind. Therefore, periodically recheck your memory of the problem to ensure that you stay with the particular issue.

Identify Alternative Hypotheses

Problem solving requires, of course, that you produce hypotheses. Rather than fixate on one or two hypotheses, try to identify and classify several hypotheses that appear reasonable. It is generally advantageous to try the easier or simpler hypotheses first and, if these fail, then to shift to more complex hypotheses. Finally, avoid the premature selection of a particular hypothesis until you have had opportunity to evaluate reasonable alternatives, that is, generate a list of hypotheses.

Acquire Coping Strategies

Coping strategies refer to ways of dealing with difficulties, failure, and frustration encountered in problem situations. Frustration and difficulty are inevitable accompaniments of problem solving. Since frustration cannot, in the long run, be avoided under all circumstances, a major task is to learn how to *cope* with such difficulty.

Blind persistence in using old rules and excessive motivation, particularly in the form of frustration, were seen as barriers to successful problem solving. Therefore, you should attempt to recognize rigidity in yourself and to avoid inflexibility when solving problems. One way of doing this is to cultivate a general plan of using variable modes of attack as the situation demands. The colloquial expression "hang loose" captures much of the meaning of what is required for effective problem solving. Thus, it is important to remain open for new options, alternatives, and approaches.

Evaluate Your Final Hypothesis

Once you have decided on a final hypothesis, reevaluate your choice. Consider the issue of implementing your choice. Even though it may be a good one on rational and logical grounds, is it practical and feasible? In summary, take one final look before you commit yourself to a particular sequence of action.

Summary

This chapter has described some of the main features of language, thinking, and problem solving. Language, thinking, and problem solving were described as closely related activities.

Language was seen to have three functions: It achieves reward, it serves as stimuli for other behaviors, and it is a vehicle for communication. The basic units of language are phonemes and morphemes. In order to understand adult language, sentence structure must be examined. Sentences possess both surface and deep structure. Language development is a progressive and orderly process in which the child learns general rules of language so that he can communicate.

Thinking and problem solving were treated as interchangeable topics. Thinking refers to a class of covert activities that involve manipulation of symbols. Problem-solving performance was seen as strongly dependent upon set and motivational factors. Typical problem-solving tasks were the water jar problem, tests of functional fixedness, and anagram problems.

Three theories of problem solving and thinking were described: S-R theory, gestalt theory, and information-processing approaches. Finally, five practical principles for efficient problem solving were noted: understand the problem, remember the problem, identify alternative hypotheses, acquire coping strategies, and evaluate your final hypothesis.

True-False Items: Language, Thinking and Problem Solving

1. Thinking is not a process that we can directly observe.
   (Thinking is a covert process; we infer that thinking has occurred, but we don't directly see thinking. True.)
2. Languages are composed of basic sounds called phonemes.
   (The phoneme is the basic unit of all languages. True.)
3. Phonemes are composed of morphemes.
   (Morphemes consist of combinations of two or more phonemes. False.)

4. The deep structure of a sentence refers to its meaning, whereas the surface structure refers to the actual sentence as sounded.

(Deep structure refers to the ideas conveyed by the sentence and surface structure to the sentence itself. True.)

5. Language learning is principally a matter of associating speech sounds with environmental stimuli.

(This is part of language learning but certainly not the whole picture. Language learning also involves learning sets of grammatical rules which may not be necessarily verbalized by the learner. False.)

6. The linguistic-relativity hypothesis emphasizes that language influences the way we think.

(This hypothesis contends that the structure of languages leads us to conceive the world in particular ways. True.)

7. Persistence of set refers to the fact that humans may tend to apply old rules or principles when they no longer are appropriate.

(The carryover of old rules or habits is called persistence of set. True.)

8. You can have "too much" motivation for efficient problem-solving activity.

(Problem-solving efficiency bears a U-shaped relationship with motivation, indicating that beyond some level an increase in motivation can actually interfere with efficient performance. True.)

9. Stimulus-response theory of thinking regards it basically as a matter of perceptual reorganization.

(Stimulus-response theory of thinking regards it as implicit or covert trial-and-error behavior. Gestalt theory views thinking as perceptual reorganization. False.)

10. Information-processing conceptions of behavior attempt to state the rules of operation (or steps) involved in some process.

(Information-processing conceptions formulate some kind of sequence of rules, usually in the format of a "flow-chart" showing each step in the process. True.)

11. One reason that humans fail to solve problems efficiently is that they fail to understand the problem in the first place.

(This is a common source of difficulty in problem solving. True.)

12. Frustration may be a frequent accompaniment of problem solving; therefore, an important task to be learned is developing adequate ways of responding to frustration.

(A major task is learning how to cope with frustration since it is likely to occur during problem-solving activity. True.)

10

Motor Skills Learning

Skill learning has played a major role in man's history. The development of even elementary forms of society has depended upon man's possession of fundamental skills. For example, man had to acquire the necessary skills for constructing clothing and shelter. Similarly, man learned to construct tools for agriculture, crafts, and warfare. Skills also make possible the enjoyment of many activities. Playing musical instruments, engaging in sports, reading, driving, and dancing are all instances of complex skills from which you may derive pleasure.

With the development of modern technology in the twentieth century, skills that were formerly important have become less so, whereas new skills have become increasingly important. For instance, it is no longer necessary for most of us personally to construct shelter or make clothing. Many crafts formerly produced by individuals are now machine-produced. The rapid development of new devices, coupled with the increased concern with leisure-time activities, has led to a shift in the kinds of skills regarded important. The development of stereo systems, dishwashers, airplanes, automobiles, motorcycles, to mention only a few, provides for a host of new skills to be acquired by the user. With more time for leisure, interest in skill acitvities such as skiing, boating, surfing, scuba diving, and billiards has seen enormous growth in recent years. Old standbys such as golf, tennis, swimming and other athletic activities have also grown in significance for many people.

Another trend in the changes required of human performance is a shift from activities required while standing, or in motion, to more sedentary activities. Many industrial and clerical tasks can be done while the individual is seated. The type of task that has become increasingly important is one that requires a person to keep track of several sources of information and to make appropriate decisions about rapidly changing informational inputs.

Piloting an airplane exhibits these kinds of demands. The pilot must attend to the dials providing him information about speed, altitude, location, other aircraft, and weather. Additional information such as radio messages must be processed. The pilot must keep track of this information and make decisions based on this input. Finally, he must distinguish between effects produced by his manipulation of the controls and effects due to the weather, such as turbulence.

Definition of Motor Skills Learning

Motor skills learning refers to any activity in which the learner must make a sequence of precise motor responses. Motor responses refer to bodily movements. Sometimes the term *perceptual-motor* skills is used to designate the fact that this class of learning requires coordination of input stimuli (perceptual activity) with motor responses. Driving is an excellent example of a perceptual-motor skill because you must coordinate what you "see" with what you "do." Driving requires that you adjust your responses in accordance with a continuously changing input. You must accelerate, slow down, turn, and apply the brakes with respect to an array of environmental stimuli such as a bend in the road, an intersection, stop signs and approaching vehicles.

The terms *motor skills* and *perceptual-motor skills* are used interchangeably in this book. Besides flying and driving, most athletic skills require the coordination of motor behavior with stimulus input. Racquet sports such as tennis, squash, and badminton require that you adjust your motor responses to the speed and anticipated location of the ball. Thus, motor skills learning is frequently called perceptual-motor learning, and motor skills learning refers to the acquisition of a precise sequence of motor responses.

The Study of Motor Skills Learning

Psychologists have used a wide variety of tasks in investigating motor skills learning. Physical education researchers have studied the acquisition of skilled performance in a variety of athletic activities ranging from swimming, gymnastics, to learning to kick a football. Despite the wide range of tasks employed, they can all be classified into basically two types: tasks that consist of specific *discrete* responses and tasks that are *continuous.*

Some motor tasks are composed of discrete responses which are responses separated by intervals of nonresponding. In contrast, other responses are more or less continuous in nature. Kicking a football is an instance of a discrete response; running with a football is essentially continuous (until you stop). Turning the ignition of your car is a discrete response; driving the car is a continuous response (again, until you stop). The distinction between the two is somewhat relative and arbitrary. Nevertheless, you can easily recognize that some responses are discrete, whereas others are essentially continuous.

Both kinds of responses have been studied. A widely used laboratory task is the line drawing task in which the subject must, while blindfolded, learn to draw a line of some arbitrary length. At the end of each trial he is given feedback in the form of being told whether he is "right" or "wrong." Sometimes he is told about the size of his error. Line drawing is an instance of a discrete task.

In contrast, a popular continuous task is tracking. A standard laboratory tracking task is the Rotary Pursuit which consists of a phonograph turntable that turns at some given rate such as 40 or 60 rpm. Set in the disk is a target about the size of a dime, and the subject must try to contact this disk with a metal stylus while the disk rotates. Performance is usually scored in terms of total or percent time on target.

This description of motor tasks is sufficient for an understanding of the two major classes of motor tasks investigated. Let us now turn our attention to some of the principal characteristics of skilled performance.

Characteristics of Motor Skills

There are four fundamental elements of skilled performance. Skilled performance (1) involves a chain of motor responses; (2) it requires coordination of perceptual input with these motor responses; (3) it involves an organized sequence of responses; (4) it depends heavily upon feedback. Let us briefly consider each of these features.

Response Chains

First, any highly developed motor skill represents, at one level, a chain of motor responses. A simple example is tying your shoe. Each response (for example, pulling the shoe strings tight) serves as a stimulus for the next response (for example, crossing the strings) and the sequence consists of a chain of responses. Another example is starting a car. Swimming, diving, running, jumping all involve chains of motor responses that make up the skilled performance.

Perceptual-motor Coordination

We earlier noted that motor skills typically involve the *coordination* of perceptual input with motor responses. This coordination of perception of events with motor activity is readily evident in sports such as tennis, baseball, and basketball and need not be further elaborated.

Response Organization

A third feature of skilled performance is that it involves an organized sequence of responses into response patterns. If we analyze the task of swimming, it can be broken up into a series of subtasks or subroutines. Each of these subtasks can receive particular emphasis by a coach by being taught as a task itself. The arm strokes, proper breathing, and the leg kicks are each subtasks of response chains themselves. Ultimately, these subtasks become organized into an integrated pattern of swimming.

The organization or patterning of such skilled activity involves both temporal and spatial factors. The act of driving is a complex skill involving many subroutines. Consider just one, pressing the accelerator. You must learn where, precisely, to place your foot, when to do so, and the force appropriate for a desired speed. The beginner may fumble in initial efforts in locating the pedal. Moreover, he may press too hard, causing the car to accelerate in a rapid and/or jerking fashion. Ultimately, however, this action becomes smoothly integrated and coordinated with other aspects of driving, such as braking and shifting gears.

Feedback

Finally, motor skills performance is heavily dependent upon *intrinsic feedback. Intrinsic feedback refers to the fact that responses produce stimuli which have consequences for subsequent responses.* When you talk, you hear yourself talking; when you walk, you feel the movement of your legs. The stimuli produced by responses are fed back into the organism in the sense of providing him information about what he is doing.

The only responses that appear to be free from the effects of feedback are those which are so brief in duration that there is insufficient time for the feedback to be processed. For all practical purposes, feedback is extremely important when a response is a few seconds or longer.

The effects of intrinsic feedback can be dramatically illustrated with the playback of delayed speech. A person speaks directly into a microphone and what he says is recorded on tape. His voice is replayed only after a fraction of a second delay into earphones which effectively mask direct airborne sounds. He is then instructed to continue reading some material out loud while the playback of his voice continues. Under this circumstance his performance rapidly deteriorates; he stutters, reads in bursts, talks louder, or faster, and finally grinds to a halt. Although you may be unaware of the importance of feedback when you talk, the powerful effects of a short delay in feedback attests to its significance.

Another illustration of the importance of intrinsic feedback from the muscles is seen in patients with neurological diseases in which certain sensory nerve tracts in the spinal cord have been destroyed. These patients have great difficulty in walking, even though their leg muscles are not damaged, because of the loss of sensory feedback from walking. Only unless they look directly at their feet, and gain a compensatory source of feedback, are they able to walk. Thus, intrinsic feedback is a basic feature of motor skills learning.

Phases of Motor Skill Learning

Although skill learning by humans is largely a continuous process, psychologists distinguish three principal *phases* of motor skill learning. The distinctions among them are not sharp and rigid, because one phase gradually merges into another as learning progresses. The particular classification system described here is one developed by the late Paul Fitts, a distinguished contributor to our understanding of skilled performance. The three phases are: (1) early or *cognitive* phase, (2) *associative* or fixation phase, and (3) final or *autonomous* phase.

Cognitive Phase

During the early or cognitive stage, the learner attempts to understand what it is that is required of him. He attempts to understand the task, to verbalize about the task, and to "intellectualize" the skill in the sense of conceptualizing its components. In turn, a good teacher or coach attempts, during this phase, to describe to the student the elements or components of the task. He instructs the student in what cues are important and how responses should be executed. He avoids, however, burdening the student with excessive detail until the student is capable of processing the information.

For example, the early phase of foreign language learning is characterized by these features. The language teacher, in instructing proper pronunciation of vowels, consonants, dipthongs, and words, first instructs the student on how to make particular sounds. He does this, for example, by telling the student where to place his tongue, and illustrates whether the sound is nasal or guttural. Similarly, a father teaching his son how to catch ball with a glove begins by showing him how to hold the glove, instructing him to keep his arm partly outstretched, to use both hands, and to keep his eye on the ball.

In learning to dance, the instructor first outlines the basic steps, one at a time, and then demonstrates the entire sequence. The learner's task is first that of execution of the basic responses. You may verbalize these responses by saying, for example, "left foot forward" and then "cross over with the right foot." Thus, during this early stage of skill learning, principal effort is devoted toward instructing the learner in the basic components of the task, first by describing the components, and then by requiring the learner to practice each response segment. This first stage is very similar to the *response* learning stage of verbal learning in which discrete responses are made available.

Associative Phase

During the second stage of skills learning, the particular responses learned become associated with particular cues, and the responses become integrated as a highly efficient chain. This stage bears considerable similarity to the associative stage of verbal learning, hence the designation *associative* phase.

The associative phase of motor skills learning can be illustrated by examining the task of typing. In this stage you must learn to touch a particular key in response to a particular letter without looking at the keyboard. Each keyboard response made to a particular letter sound produced by an instructor, or a particular letter in a typing manual, is, in fact, a stimulus-response association that must be learned. The task is one of learning to make a particular response in the presence of a particular stimulus, which characterizes associative learning.

During this stage you also learn to execute a smooth sequence of responses and you learn to respond at a fairly stable rate. Instead of looking at each single letter in your typing manual, the entire word becomes the cue for responding. Indeed, typing instructors tell their students to "think" the entire word rather than look at each letter as typing proficiency increases. The associative stage in typing ranges from when you first learn to associate each keyboard position with a letter stimulus to the stage where you type at a steady rate with errors at a minimum.

In contrast to the associative phase, the first or cognitive stage of learning to type occupies a relatively short time span. During this stage, the learner becomes generally familiar with the requirements of typing, analyzes the skills involved, and verbalizes about what will be learned. While the cognitive phase is relatively brief in a task like typing, it occupies an increasingly important role as the task becomes more complex. For example, in learning to drive or to pilot aircraft, the cognitive phase is much more time-consuming.

Autonomous Phase

The final phase in motor skills learning is the autonomous phase, where performance becomes highly efficient so that it can be executed in more or less automatic fashion. The speed of performance continues to increase because new response patterns become strengthened, not because of simple repetition of the same responses. For example, the fact that a number of girls can now swim faster than did Johnny Weissmuller when he held national records in the 1920s attests to their development of response patterns different from the ones he used. Moreover, there appears to be no evidence for a permanent leveling-off in performance as is found, say, in verbal learning. Motor skills learning appears unique in this respect. Despite continued practice on a specific skill for many years, performance records indicate that speed or efficiency continues to increase even though at a much slower rate. You are witness to this lack of a final plateau in motor skills when you note that athletic records are continually broken. Similarly, industrial production records show that various tasks with a heavy motor skills component continue to show improvement in performance. These improvements in performance are due, however, to new ways of carrying out the tasks, that is, to the development of newer, more efficient response patterns.

During this final stage, performance becomes increasingly immune to sources of interference. A typist continues to type while carrying on a brief conversation; we continue to talk while driving a car; we manipulate the dial on the car radio while driving and watching the road. Thus, we are able to carry out two or more tasks proficiently without serious disruptuon of the principal task.

Factors Which Affect Motor Skills Learning

Like other types of learning, motor skills learning depends upon both characteristics of the task and characteristics of the learner. In this section we shall examine some of the important factors influencing motor skills learning.

Feedback

Feedback is the single most important factor affecting motor skills learning. *Extrinsic feedback* refers to the information that is provided the learner about his performance on a given trial. Extrinsic feedback is often referred to as *knowledge of results*, which emphasize the informational character of feedback. A distinction is made between extrinsic and intrinsic feedback. We saw earlier that intrinsic feedback refers to the response-produced stimuli that result when we make a response, such as the "feel" of the swing of a tennis racquet. Extrinsic feedback, in turn, refers to the information that is provided by another person.

Extrinsic feedback may be in the form of qualitative information, in which the learner is informed that his performance is either correct or incorrect. For example, imagine that your task is to draw a set of lines while blindfolded, the line to be drawn between, say, 3 and 3 1/4 inches. At the end of each trial in drawing the line, you are informed only if your response is correct or incorrect. This is precisely analogous to looking at a discrete temperature gauge on most American cars. You know only if your car is "cold," "normal," or "hot," not how cold or how hot. Similarly, in playing golf, either the putt went in the hole or it didn't.

In contrast, feedback may be in the form of quantitative information. In the line drawing task you may be told how *much* discrepancy there is between your response and the correct response. Similarly, in older models of American cars, the temperature gauge was graded (continuous) so that you could see if your car was, in fact, approaching some point of "heating up." Usually, humans prefer continuous information because it enables them to make more precise judgments about what they should do.

Feedback has two properties. FIRST, FEEDBACK HAS INFORMA-TION VALUE TO THE ORGANISM, ENABLING HIM TO DIRECT HIS PERFORMANCE TOWARD SOME DESIRED OBJECTIVE. SEC-OND, FEEDBACK CAN HAVE REINFORCING PROPERTIES IN THAT IT SERVES TO REWARD PERFORMANCE. Not only does seeing that you made a strike when bowling provide you with information about your performance, but it may also be reinforcing in the sense of strengthening that class of responses produced just prior to the "strike." Unfortunately, it is difficult to separate the informational and reinforcing aspects of feedback; thus, we are not always knowledgeable about their relative roles in affecting performance.

Importance of Feedback

With the above information as background, we can focus on two kinds of questions: (1) Is feedback necessary for acquisition of skilled performance? (2) Does the type of feedback (discrete, qualitative information versus continuous quantitative information) make a difference?

The evidence points overwhelmingly to the importance of feedback as a necessary variable in influencing performance. Where humans have been required to learn motor tasks without feedback, no appreciable evidence of improvement, in the sense of achieving some criterion of learning imposed externally, is found. Humans do, however, become less variable in their performance without external (extrinsic) feedback because they come to adhere more closely to some subjective criterion of performance which they adopt during learning. Thus, in one sense, response changes can occur without *external* feedback.

Intuitively, it is easy to see why feedback is so important for improvement. For example, imagine trying to learn to bowl without knowing the consequences of your actions. Conceive of a situation in which you cannot see what you have hit (if anything), receive no score from an outside observer, hear no noise which might allow some judgment about your performance, and are prevented from even seeing the direction of the bowling ball once you have released it! If you manage to show any improvement in the absence of feed-back, such improvement is likely to be the result of adopting a subjective criterion which corresponds inadvertently with the center of the lane.

With respect to our second question, humans achieve superior performance in motor learning tasks when they are given quantitative information about their performance. Quantitative knowledge about the discrepancy between your performance and some task objective allows you to reduce this discrepancy more effectively than if you are merely told that you are "right" or "wrong."

The effectiveness of quantitative over qualitative feedback can be readily illustrated in several ways. Consider learning to play pool: In one case imagine being informed only if your shots were "good," in the sense of making a pocket, or "bad," in the opposite sense. In this hypothetical situation you are prevented from seeing your shots and know only what you are told. In a second hypothetical situation, imagine being told precisely how far each "miss" is from a pocket. Here, of course, you are given more information about your performance. In this latter situation, your skill at playing pool would develop much more rapidly.

Withdrawal of Feedback and Subjective Reinforcement

Suppose that feedback was immediately withdrawn after it had been given for a number of trials. How would this affect your performance? What is observed is a gradual drop in performance but not to the performance level observed at the beginning of training. More generally, the effect of withdrawal of feedback depends upon the level of ongoing performance. IF LEVEL OF TRAINING IS LOW OR MODERATE, WITHDRAWAL OF FEED-BACK PRODUCES A DETERIORATING EFFECT ON PERFOR-MANCE: AFTER EXTENDED TRAINING, HOWEVER, LITTLE OR NO PERFORMANCE DECREMENT OCCURS. Thus, withdrawal of feedback in humans does *not* act precisely as does withdrawal of reinforcement in instrumental learning of lower animals. This again points to the inadequacy of simply equating feedback with reinforcement, since their effects are not entirely comparable.

The fact that humans can maintain some of their training benefits after withdrawal of feedback has suggested to some psychologists that self-reinforcement may be playing an important role. The basic idea is that after some period of practice in which you receive external feedback, you begin to "internalize" the standards for a correct response and thus are able to inform yourself about the adequacy of a response based on your own standards. This notion of subjective or self-reinforcement should be thought of as a form of internal feedback that is developed over a series of trials with external feedback. It is as if you can learn to discriminate proprioceptive (internal) cues that aid you in defining the correctness of a response.

Many motor tasks are such that you can gradually acquire a "feel" for a good response and thus can distinguish a good from a poor one. For instance, divers generally detect when they have executed a poor dive by the way they "feel" or "sense" body movements before they strike the water. Similarly, experienced golfers and tennis players can frequently judge the quality of their swing or stroke by how it "feels" to them. What they are learning is to judge the pattern and intensity of proprioceptive cues so that they gradually acquire subjective standards as to what "feels" appropriate.

Delay of Feedback

Another feature of feedback concerns the effect of the time delay between the learner's response and informative feedback. This interval is called the *delay of feedback*. Just as in investigations of conceptual learning, delay of feedback exerts virtually no effect on motor skills acquisition. This finding differs, as noted earlier, from results with lower animals, where delay of reward produces a substantial effect on performance.

In contrast, another type of delay known as *postfeedback* delay does exert an effect on performance. Postfeedback delay is the interval between feedback on one trial and the beginning of the next trial. IN GENERAL, INCREASING THE POSTFEEDBACK INTERVAL UP TO SOME POINT BRINGS CORRESPONDING IMPROVEMENT IN PERFORMANCE. Again, just as in conceptual learning, the critical interval is the postfeedback delay, because this appears to be the period in which one processes the information obtained on a particular trial. In effect, as this interval is lengthened you are given more time to "think about" how to execute the next response.

Distribution of Practice

In learning any motor skill, the training conditions can be arranged so that rest intervals are interspersed between trials. In contrast, some tasks can be arranged such that they are continuous, lacking rest intervals during the course of acquisition. *Distributed practice* refers to the introduction of rest intervals throughout the course of acquisition, whereas the term *massed practice* refers to more or less continuous performance.

Distributed practice is an important factor in motor learning and the general rule is that DISTRIBUTED PRACTICE FACILITATES THE ACQUISITION OF MOTOR SKILLS. Most attempts to account for the facilitating effects of distributed practice have assumed the build-up of some fatigue-like or inhibitory process during massed practice. Such theories assume an *inhibition* process that accumulates during acquisition that reduces the tendency to respond. Presumably, during rest intervals this inhibition can weaken or decay, whereas during massed practice opportunity for such inhibition to decay does not occur. Therefore, the increase in inhibition during massed practice produces less rapid learning than occurs during distributed practice. Space limitations allow only a brief discussion of this inhibitory process. (The interested reader may wish to consult a quite detailed discussion of this process, described in the context of a theory of classical conditioning, in Frank Logan's *Fundamentals of Learning and Motivation*, a companion volume in this series).

Stress and Fatigue

As you might expect, <u>both stress and fatigue produce decrements</u> in motor skills performance. Stress has been characteristically defined in several ways. In one case, stress has referred to a state of the organism usually characterized as motivational and or emotional. Thus we sometimes speak of emotional stress of an individual when burdened or faced with unpleasant circumstances.

In a second case, stress refers to the task demands made upon an individual. Thus, if you have to keep track of three events while carrying out some task, you are faced with a greater stress load than if you must keep track of only one event. This second meaning is sometimes called information overload, referring to how much information you must attend to while carrying out a task. For instance, consider driving an automobile alone along a quiet country road as compared with driving on an unfamiliar freeway in a large metropolis at the five o'clock rush hour with a car full of unruly children, one of whom is demanding to go to the bathroom. Clearly, the amount of information impinging upon you is considerably greater in the latter situation.

With either meaning of stress, the relationship of stress and motor performance is similar to that observed in verbal learning and problem solving. AS THE AMOUNT OF STRESS INCREASES, MOTOR SKILLS PERFORMANCE I<u>MPROVES UP TO SOME OPTIMAL POINT</u> BEYOND WHICH INCREASES IN STRESS PRODUCE A REDUCTION IN PERFORMANCE. Thus, the relationship between stress and performance is U-shaped, indicating some optimal level of stress.

Perhaps the notion of optimal stress may sound strange but a moment's reflection on your part will make this principle clear. A little stress alerts you to the demands of a given task and, indeed, facilitates performance. Most of you have experienced the fact that listening to music may help in carrying out a routine repetitive task, such as washing the dishes. On the other hand, as the task becomes more complex, less stress is necessary for optimal performance. THUS, THE GENERAL PRINCIPLE IS THAT LESS STRESS IN THE FORM OF INFORMATIONAL INPUT IS NECESSARY FOR OPTIMAL PERFORMANCE WHEN THE TASK BECOMES MORE COMPLEX. Similar forms of this generalization were noted both with respect to problem solving and verbal learning.

Theories of Motor Learning

Traditionally, theories of motor learning have viewed the process as essentially analogous to, or identical with, instrumental learning. This tradition stems from Thorndike, who viewed motor learning as instrumental in character, dependent upon the classical law of effect. A motor learning task, such as learning to draw a line of a particular length, was viewed as requiring the learner to make a series of discrete motor responses, each being followed by reinforcement in the form of knowledge of results or feedback. As a response approximated the correct or desired response, it achieved reinforcement and was thus strengthened by some amount. In turn, incorrect responses gradually weakened in the course of training because they were not reinforced.

Psychologists have not developed powerful theories of motor learning. As emphasized above, theoretical considerations have treated motor learning as a special case of instrumental learning governed by the principle of reinforcement. Only in the past few years has any serious effort been made to extend theories of motor learning. Most of these recent developments have tended to view motor learning as more than just instrumental learning, emphasizing the *problem-solving* and *cognitive* character of motor learning tasks. One of the better developed of these theories is one proposed by Jack Adams.

Adams assumes that motor learning is best viewed as a problem to be solved, and proposes a theory which contains elements of both S-R and cognitive conceptions of learning. The essential feature of this theory is that it is a *closed-loop* theory, which is a notion borrowed from engineering and servo-mechanism concepts. Before the theory is described, a few comments on closed-loop systems are in order.

The basic idea of any closed-loop system is that responses of a given system feed back into the system, thus making it ultimately self-regulating. A simple example of a closed-loop system involves the thermostat and heating unit found in many homes and buildings. The thermostat is set to some desired temperature. If the actual temperature is below the setting, this discrepancy is detected and the information is given to the heating unit which, in turn, is activated. The room or building is thus heated to the value set by the thermostat. The essential point to note is that a closed-loop system allows for the detection of a discrepancy, called *error*, and responds to this error in an adjusting or self-correcting fashion.

Figure 20 portrays the basic components of a closed-loop feedback system. It contains, first, an *error detector* whose task is to detect the discrepancy between some current state of the system and feedback from the final component of the system. The thermostat in our above discussion is an example of an error detector. The discrepancy or error information goes to the next component, the *controller*, which is some regulating device in the system. The heating unit in the above example is an instance of a controller. Finally, there is a *controlled object*, something to be acted upon, which in this case is the temperature of the room.

The input to the error detector refers simply to some setting of the thermostat, continuing the analogy. The feedback loop goes back to the error detector from the controlled object, informing it of the discrepancy between the output of the controlled object and the setting of the error detector. Thus you can see

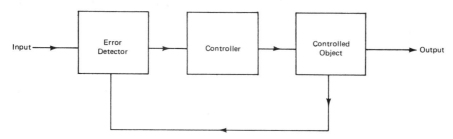

Figure 20. Block diagram of schematic closed-loop system.

that a closed-loop feedback system is dynamic in the sense of responding to error discrepancy and is self-regulating.

The theory outlined by Adams views motor learning as a problem to be solved, where the learner first tries a movement, is then given feedback, tries again on the next trial, and so on, using the information obtained from feedback to gradually acquire the desired response. According to the theory, the learner gradually acquires a *perceptual trace* of the motor movements he makes, where the trace is conceived much like an image. On each trial the learner receives proprioceptive (internal) cues from muscle movements, and attempts to match these cues to the perceptual trace. Here the perceptual trace is viewed as some reference standard which must be acquired itself as a result of gradual experience in detecting feedback. In short, when a response is judged correct, the learner develops a standard for what proprioceptive cues "feel" correct. His memory of these cues, as distinct from those which are associated with incorrect responses, becomes his reference standard. This standard, of course, is not static and changes as it gradually approximates what is necessary for desired behavior.

In addition, the theory proposes a second mechanism, the *memory trace.* The memory trace is an additional memory system whose function is to select and initiate a response on a given trial before the perceptual trace is used. The reasons for using both a perceptual and memory trace are too complex to treat here. The principal point to note is that the learner initiates a given response, after some amount of practice, on the bases of his memory trace and then uses the perceptual trace for his momentary judgment of how far to move.

At present the theory is somewhat informal, with details yet to be developed. Its principal feature is its emphasis on closed-loop assumptions. The more formal relationships between perceptual and memory traces have yet to be fully developed. Its virtue lies in its emphasis upon the importance of feedback and the dynamic, self-regulating character of motor learning. It should be noted that these features are being increasingly incorporated in other theories of learning and are certainly not unique to theories of motor learning.

Some Practical Principles

In this section we shall turn our attention to a brief discussion of some principles that are important in the acquisition of motor skills. Most of these principles are applicable to other categories of learning and have received some emphasis in previous chapters.

1) Understand the Task

At the onset of skills learning your initial objective is to understand what is required. It is good practice to observe the performance of skilled individuals, particularly teachers who can break the skill into its component parts. For instance, competent dancing instructors can show the individual components of a dance sequence as well as the highly integrated series of responses. Here your task is to verbalize about the skill, trying to identify its component parts.

2) Practice on Specific Components

As the task increases in complexity, you should focus your practice on specific components of the task. For example, swimmers may concentrate on one feature such as leg kicks, arm strokes, or breathing during a given training session and later concentrate on coordinating these features. Similarly, in playing pool, you may concentrate on bank shots to the temporary exclusion of other kinds of responses. Finally, in learning to drive a car with a manual transmission, you may focus your efforts on learning to shift gears as a component task before integrating this activity into the total pattern of driving. In general, where motor tasks are simple, they may be directly practiced in their entirety; however, with increasing complexity, motor tasks may more profitably be learned by practicing their component parts.

3) Obtain Feedback

Feedback is the most important factor in achieving skilled performance. Feedback may be both intrinsic and external. Intrinsic feedback refers to cues obtained from your own responses, whereas external feedback refers to information gained from someone else or from other consequences of your behavior. The importance of feedback is that it allows you to evaluate your performance by comparing it against some standard.

4) Practice under Varied Conditions

Stimulus variation was earlier noted as an important factor in transfer. Likewise, practice under varied circumstances facilitates motor performance. Athletic coaches have long observed that basketball players often show some performance decrement when playing in a new or different gymnasium.

Changes in the size of the gym or other features may temporarily influence well-practiced habits. Similarly, swimmers who are familiar with one pool may show some performance deterioration when first swimming in a new pool that is, say, longer. For this reason, varied context in training helps adapt your performance to potential environmental changes.

5/Finally, Practice

Proficiency in skills obviously requires sustained practice. The emphasis is not repetition per se, since one can learn inappropriate responses as well as desirable ones. It is practice in conjunction with understanding the skill objectives, observing skilled performance, and obtaining feedback that is important.

Summary

This chapter has outlined some of the major characteristics of motor skills learning. Despite the automation of many human activities, skill learning was seen as an increasingly important feature of leisure-time and recreational activities.

Motor skills learning refers to any activity which requires the learner to make a series of precise motor responses. Motor skills tasks may consist of either discrete or continuous responses. Although typical laboratory tasks have emphasized line drawing and Pursuit Rotor tracking, a quite wide variety of tasks have been employed in the study of motor learning.

Skilled performance consists of four essential features: (1) a chain of motor responses, (2) perceptual-motor coordination, (3) response organization, and (4) dependency upon feedback. Three phases of skill learning were described: (1) cognitive phase, (2) associative phase, and (3) the autonomous or final stage. These stages were observed to blend into each other rather than being rigidly distinctive.

The most important factor influencing motor skills learning is feedback, sometimes called knowledge of results. Feedback may be either qualitative or quantitative, and may have both informational and reinforcing properties. Feedback appears to be essential for motor skills learning, and quantitative feedback is more effective than qualitative feedback.

The withdrawal of feedback produces its most detrimental effect only with low or moderate levels of training. With extensive training, feedback withdrawal produces virtually no effect, primarily because humans come to depend upon their own subjective reinforcement. The postfeedback interval is the critical period for efficient motor skills learning because humans are able to process feedback information during this period.

Other important variables are distribution of practice, stress and fatigue. An important feature of current theories of motor skills is the adoption of a closed-loop model by which humans are viewed as comparing feedback cues of the moment with some memory of past performance.

Several practical principles for efficient motor skills learning were de- scribed. These emphasized the importance of (1) understanding the task, (2) practicing on specific components, (3) obtaining feedback, (4) practice under varied conditions, and finally (5) practice itself.

True-False Items: Motor Skills Learning

1. Discrete motor responses are responses separated by periods of nonres- ponding.

(Discrete responses are produced for some period followed by a period in which the response does not occur. For example, diving into a pool is a discrete response, whereas swimming 200 meters is a continuous response [until you stop]; jumping the broadjump is a discrete response whereas run- ning a mile is continuous [again, until you stop]. True.)

2. A response chain refers to a sequence of responses in which one response serves as a stimulus for another response.

(A chain of responses consists of a sequence in which each response serves as a stimulus for another response. True.)

3. The way a motor response is practiced is less important than sheer frequency of practice.

(You can practice a response frequently and yet do so incorrect- ly; learning the proper response pattern is an important feature of motor skills learning. False.)

4. The information a swimming coach provides his swimmers about their performance is an instance of intrinsic feedback.

(This is an instance of extrinsic feedback. Intrinsic feedback refers to swimmer's own internal response-produced cues which provide him with information. False.)

5. The first stage of motor skills learning is the cognitive phase.

(It is in this stage that the learner attempts to understand the task. True.)

6. In a swimming race, seeing that you are ahead of all the other swimmers provides you with a source of extrinsic feedback.

(Knowledge that you are in the lead provides you with extrinsic feedback, in the sense of enabling you to compare your momentary perform- ance with that of the other swimmers. True.)

7. Feedback has information value but does not have reinforcing proper- ties.

(Feedback may also have reinforcing properties in that it can serve to strengthen a particular response or class of responses. False.)

for the teacher to give

8. Being given quantitative feedback is more advantageous for motor skills
learning than simply being told that you are "right" or "wrong."

(Quantitative feedback is generally superior to qualitative feedback because it provides you with more information about your performance.
True.)

9. Motor skills learning differs from concept learning in that increasing the
postfeedback delay interval does facilitate concept learning but does not influence motor skills learning.

(Increasing the postfeedback delay interval facilitates both concept and motor skills learning. False.)

10. Listening to the radio is more likely to disrupt performance when
planning and writing a term paper than when reading a magazine.

(As the task becomes more complex, stress in the form of additional input is more likely to be disruptive. In this case we would regard
planning and writing a term paper as more complex behavior than reading
a magazine. True.)

11. Closed-loop theory of motor skills learning emphasizes the manner in
which the learner uses feedback from his movements.

(Closed-loop theory contends that the learner receives proprioceptive cues from muscle movements which he attempts to match with a
perceptual trace or reference standard. True.)

12. If the motor task is fairly complex, it may be desirable to practice on
components of the task at first and then on the entire task subsequently.

(Where the task is complex, practice on specific components at
first is desirable; these components can then be integrated into the entire skill
after each component has been reasonably well-learned. True.)

11 ———————————————————————————

Concluding Remarks

The objective of this book has been to present an elementary but coherent picture of the current state of human learning and cognition. It was written with the conviction that the student can be introduced to these areas of knowledge through a systematic oversimplification so that the essential principles of human learning and cognition are revealed in bold relief. This approach means that many nuances, details, and qualifications are left untouched. Nevertheless, it is the author's belief that the student will gain from having a framework of principles on which details and qualifications may be attached in his subsequent learning. Indeed, without some kind of organizational framework, it would be difficult to integrate new facts and ideas about human learning and cognition.

This book attempts to bridge the gap between the old and new in human learning and cognition. The traditional and well-developed topics of human learning must be integrated with the newly developing topics. The area of human learning and cognition is rapidly changing, so this book should be viewed as an attempt to describe the current state of these areas as distinct from any final description. Thus, in some sense this book must be regarded as a momentary state-of-the-science report rather than as a final picture of these areas.

Despite the attempt at simplification, enabling the student to obtain a reasonably coherent picture of human learning and cognition, an effort has also been made to provide the student with an image of the vitality, controversy, and excitement in these areas. Old views are being revised, new views are still emerging, and mergers of the old and new are in various stages of progress. The psychology of human learning and cognition has begun to come of age, freed from the constraints of a narrow behavioristic psychology of the '40s. Mental imagery, organizational processes, storage and retrieval systems, search processes, and strategies all attest to a growing concern for the fact that humans think. More generally, there is a strong renewed interest in the *cognitive* capacities of the human organism and a willingness of psychologists to grapple with the complex process of human behavior.

In no sense, however, does a cognitive revolution (or renaissance?) imply that older established concepts of human learning must be rejected. Concepts such as generalization, discrimination, mediation, and interference, developed within the framework of a more traditional psychology, are very much alive and useful, and may well be integrated within the framework of the new "cognitive psychology." Indeed, psychologists such as Patrick Suppes have indicated that it is possible to deal with complex cognitive processes in terms of stimulus-response conceptions without resort to more complex theoretical processes. The issue is not, however, a matter of whether stimulus-response or cognitive conceptions of behavior are correct, "true," or more meaningful, but rather which set of conceptions will more efficiently account for the facts of human behavior. These issues, which lie principally in the domain of learning theory, have been largely bypassed in this introductory treatment. Theoretical controversy is to be resolved in terms of how well given theories handle the data of learning and cognition, not in terms of how intuitively appealing they may appear. These issues are left, however, for future study on the part of the student.

What does emerge is a vigorous psychology of human learning and cognition, a psychology that examines a wide range of human capabilities. Psychologists are busy exploring the panorama of activities from human conditioning to problem solving and thinking in an effort to discover regularities and lawfulness in behavior. Moreover, there is an active concern with the applicability of these principles and regularities to problems of everyday life. This enterprise is one of continuous development and evolution and it can be expected to move in new directions, prodded by the stimulus of new research findings and new theoretical conceptions.

Glossary

All-or-none principle: Principle which asserts that verbal associations gain their entire strength in a particular trial or none at all.

Associative stage: In verbal learning the stage in which particular responses become "hooked-up" with particular stimuli, sometimes referred to as the "hook-up" stage.

Attribute: Feature or characteristic of a stimulus. In concept learning attribute refers to some stimulus feature related to the concept.

Backward association: An association formed, as in paired-associate learning, between a response and a stimulus item so that the response item acquires some tendency to elicit the stimulus item.

Behavior modification: An approach to therapy based upon principles of conditioning and learning.

Clustering: One instance of an organizational process. The tendency to order or organize items during recall into some grouping or sequence that differs from the order present during original learning.

Coding: The process by which an item is transformed into some modified or new representation.

Cognition: Class of processes that refer to symbolic, mental, and hence inferred events. Cognition refers to such processes as thinking, problem solving, concept learning, and reasoning, those activities emphasizing the active role of the learner.

Concept: Refers to a class of stimuli or events that share in one or more common characteristics.

Concept learning: Any activity in which a learner must learn to classify or categorize two or more somewhat different events or objects as members of a common class.

Conceptual rule: Rule or principle by which attributes are combined in conceptual tasks.

Contiguity: Condition in which two or more events occur together in time or space.

Conditioning, classical: A procedure in which an initially neutral stimulus, a conditioned stimulus, is paired with an unconditioned stimulus so that the conditioned stimulus comes to elicit a response normally elicited by the unconditioned stimulus.

Conditioning, instrumental: A procedure in which the learning of a response is contingent upon reinforcement; the response is not freely available because discrete-trial procedures are used.

Conditioning, operant: A procedure in which the subject is allowed to respond freely, the rate of occurrence depending upon how reinforcement is scheduled.

Decay theory: A theory of forgetting which contends that forgetting is due to some autonomous decay of memory traces.

Deep structure: Refers to the meaning of a sentence.

Detection: The report of the presence of absence of stimulus contingent upon its presentation.

Discrimination: Perceptual task in which the subject reports the perception of a difference between two stimuli (*See* stimulus discrimination).

Encoding: The process by which material to be learned is placed in some "state" such that its storage is possible.

Extinction: The reduction in the strength of a response following non-reinforcement of the response.

Feedback, extrinsic: Refers to external knowledge of results given to a learner following his response.

Feedback, intrinsic: Refers to the fact that responses made by the organism produce stimuli which are fed back into the organism.

Forgetting: Refers to the amount of material that is inaccessible after some retention interval.

Forward association: An association formed, as in paired-associate learning, between a stimulus and a response item, as evidenced by the tendency of that stimulus to elicit its response mate.

Free learning: Verbal learning task requiring learner to recall the items in any order.

Generalization, response: The tendency to make responses similar to the response learned in the conditioning session.

Generalization, stimulus: The tendency to respond to stimuli similar to the training stimulus employed in conditioning.

Identification: A perceptual task in which the observer makes an identifying (labeling) response appropriate to some stimulus.

Incremental principle: Principle that verbal associations gain associative strength gradually over a series of trials.

Interference theory: A theory of forgetting which contends that events are forgotten because other learning interferes with or prevents these events from being remembered.

Judgment: A perceptual task in which the observer orders or ranks stimuli along some scale.

Learning: A relatively permanent process that is inferred from performance changes due to practice.

Learning to learn: A progressive improvement in the ease with which some new task is learned as a result of practice with a series of related tasks.

Linguistic relativity hypothesis: Hypothesis proposed by Benjamin Whorf contending that the structure of man's language leads one to conceive of the world in particular ways.

Meaningfulness: Scaled property of verbal materials which predicts the ease with which materials are learned. Refers to the number of associations elicited by an item in some standard period of time.

Mediation: Verbal mediation refers to the process by which organisms link stimulus and response terms by way of implicit verbal responses.

Memory, sensory: The brief period in memory in which a stimulus trace persists.

Memory, long-term: A more permanent system of memory in which the information stored has been rehearsed or processed in some fashion so that it remains more accessible.

Memory, short-term: Limited-capacity system of memory in which items must be processed in some way or they drop out of the memory system.

Morphemes: Smallest meaningful unit in a language, consisting of two or more phonemes. (*See* phoneme).

Motor skills learning: Any learning activity in which the learner must make a series of precise motor responses, or learn to coordinate perceptual input with motor responses (sometimes called perceptual-motor learning).

Negative instance: Any instance or example that does not represent the concept in question.

Organizational processes: Those activities engaged in by humans which involve some kind of change or transformation of the verbal materials to be learned.

Paired associate learning: Verbal learning task in which stimulus and response terms become associated.

Partial reinforcement effect: The fact that resistance to extinction is greater following partial rather than continuous reinforcement.

Perception: An inferred process in which changes in performance such as detection, discrimination, recognition, identification, or judgment are produced by changes in stimulus energy conditions.

Perceptual learning: Refers to various changes in perception that are due to or brought about by learning.

Phonemes: Basic unit of language consisting of fundamental vowel and consonant sounds.

Phrase structure: Structural features of a sentence, consisting essentially of a noun and a verb phrase.

Positive instance: Any instance or example that represents the particular concept in question.

Proactive inhibition: The loss in retention of some currently-learned material produced by interference from some previously learned material.

Programmed instruction: Instructional technology in which material to be learned is broken into small steps called frames. Learner must respond to each frame and is given immediate knowledge of results.

Recall: A measure of memory in which you produce the required response(s).

Recognition: A measure of memory in which you select items that are familiar and reject items that are unfamiliar.

Recognition learning: Learning task requiring subject to recognize items.

Reconstructive processes: The fact that humans tend to reconstruct events in memory, altering them to make them more coherent.

Reinforcer, positive: Any event which increases the likelihood of a response when it is presented.

Reinforcer, negative: Any event which increases the likelihood of a response when it is removed.

Reinforcer, secondary: An event that functions as a reward by being associated with primary reinforcing events.

Response bias: Preferences or response tendencies that subjects have prior to entering an experiment, or that they may develop during an experiment.

Response chain: A sequence of motor responses in which one response serves as a stimulus for the next response.

Response competition: The tendency of responses acquired during original and interpolated learning and attached to identical (or similar) stimuli to remain available and compete with each other at the time of recall.

Response differentiation: The process by which a response, or particular aspect of a response such as speed or force, becomes strengthened through differential reinforcement.

Response learning stage: In verbal learning this refers to the stage in paired associate learning in which the responses become recallable or available as units.

Retention: Refers to the amount of material that is still retained after some retention interval.

Retrieval: Process of getting events out of memory storage.

Retrieval cues: Stimuli that humans use to help in retrieving information.

Retroactive inhibition: An event learned during a retention interval can lead to some forgetting of a previously learned event.

Savings: A measure of memory in which you are required to relearn some task.

Schema learning: Learning in which the human acquires some central tendency or average representation of some group of stimuli.

Serial learning: Verbal learning task in which the units are presented in the same order from trial to trial.

Serial position effect: The tendency to make the largest number of errors just beyond the middle of a serial list and fewest at the beginning and end of the serial list.

Similarity: Degree to which materials possess common elements (formal similarity), or are meaningfully or conceptually related.

Similarity, intralist: The degree of similarity among a list of items to be learned.

Spontaneous recovery: The fact that a response may reoccur following some period of time after an extinction session.

Stimulus coding: The process of changing some nominal stimulus into some new "state" or representation.

Stimulus discrimination: The process in verbal learning, of learning to distinguish among the stimulus terms of a list. In conditioning, the process of learning to respond differently to somewhat similar stimuli (*See* Discrimination).

Stimulus identification: The process of coming to treat a given stimulus in a consistent fashion, that is, to regard it in some common way over a series of learning trials.

Stimulus selection: The tendency of humans to select only a part of a nominally-presented stimulus and use it to cue a response.

Storage: Process by which materials are placed in memory and held.

Subjective organization: Tendency of humans to organize verbal materials in accord with some self-developed mode of organization.

Surface structure: Property of a sentence referring to the sentence as it is sounded.

Thinking: Class of covert activities that refer to the manipulation and use of symbols and concepts.

Transfer, crossmodal: Transfer which occurs when learning in one sensory system carries over to another sensory system.

Transfer, general: Transfer effects due to learning-to-learn and warm-up.

Transfer, mechanisms: Principles by which transfer of training occurs. Important mechanisms are generalization and mediation.

Transfer paradigm: A schematic or shorthand description of the task relationships in a transfer study.

Transfer of response learning: Source of positive transfer due to the responses having become available.

Transfer, specific: Transfer effects due to specific features or properties of the task relationships.

Transfer of stimulus discrimination: Source of positive transfer as a result of discrimination among the stimulus terms.

Transfer of training: The influence of prior learning on the learning of some new task.

Unlearning: The loss or weakening or first-list association during the learning of a second-list.

Verbal conditioning: An operant conditioning procedure applied to verbal behavior; a verbal response or response class is selectively reinforced thus strengthening the response.

Verbal discrimination learning: Verbal learning task in which the subject must distinguish between which of a pair of items has been arbitrarily designated as correct.

Verbal learning: Any learning situation in which the task requires the learner to respond to verbal stimulus materials, or to respond with verbal responses.

Warm up: The transitory facilitation in learning some task as the result of prior practice with another task.

Suggested
Readings for Further Study

Adams, J. A. *Human memory*. New York: McGraw-Hill, 1967.

Bilodeau, E. A. (Ed.) *Acquisition of skill*. New York: Academic, 1966.

Bourne, L. E. *Human conceptual behavior*. Boston: Allyn & Bacon, 1966.

Bourne, L. E., Ekstrand, B. R., and Dominowski, R. L. *The psychology of thinking*. Englewood Cliffs, N.J.: Prentice-Hall, 1971.

Bugelski, B. R. *The psychology of learning applied to teaching*. Indianapolis: Bobbs-Merrill, 1964.

Chomsky, N. *Language and mind*. New York: Harcourt, Brace, Jovanovich, 1968.

Deese, J. *Psycholinguistics*. New York: Allyn & Bacon, 1970.

Deese, J., and Hulse, S. H. *The psychology of learning*. New York: McGraw-Hill, 1967.

Dixon, T. R., and Horton, D. L. *Verbal behavior and general behavior theory*. Englewood Cliffs, N. J.: Prentice-Hall, 1968.

Ellis, H. C. *The transfer of learning*. New York: Macmillan, 1965.

Gagné, R. M. *The conditions of learning*. New York: Holt, Rinehart, and Winston, 1971.

Gibson, E. J. *Principles of perceptual learning and development*. New York: Appleton-Century-Crofts, 1969.

Hall, J. F. *Verbal learning and retention*. Philadelphia: Lippincott, 1971.

Jung, J. *Verbal learning*. New York: Holt, Rinehart, and Winston, 1968.

Kintsch, W. *Learning, memory, and conceptual processes*. New York: Wiley, 1970.

Logan, F. A. *Fundamentals of learning and motivation*. Dubuque, Iowa: Brown, 1970.

Marx, M. H. (Ed.) *Learning: Processes*. New York: Macmillan, 1969.

Melton, A. W. (Ed.) *Categories of human learning*. New York: Academic, 1964.

Norman, D. A. *Memory and attention*. New York: Wiley, 1969.

Saltz, E. *The cognitive bases of human learning*. Homewood, Illinois: Dorsey, 1971.

Taber, J. I., Glaser, R., and Schaffer, H. H. *Learning and programmed instruction*. Reading, Mass.: Addison-Wesley, 1965.

Trabasso, T., and Bower, G. H. *Attention in learning*. New York: Wiley, 1968.

Voss, J. (Ed.) *Approaches to thought*. Columbus, O.: Merrill, 1969.

References

Introduction To Human Learning And Cognition

TRENDS IN VERBAL LEARNING
Mandler, G. Verbal learning. In G. Mandler and P. Mussen (Eds.) *New directions in psychology*. 3. New York: Rinehart and Winston, 1967.

TYPES OF HUMAN LEARNING
Melton, A. W. (Ed.) *Categories of human learning*. New York: Wiley, 1964.

REPRESENTATIVE TEXTS
Kintsch, W. *Learning, memory, and conceptual processes*. New York: Wiley, 1970.

Saltz, E. *The cognitive bases of human learning*. Homewood, Ill.: Dorsey, 1971.

PROBLEM AREAS
Dixon, T. R., and Horton, D. L. (Eds.) *Verbal behavior and general behavior theory*. Englewood Cliffs, N. J.: Prentice-Hall, 1968.

APPLICATIONS
Gagné, R. M. *Conditions of learning*. New York: Holt, Rinehart, and Winston, 1971.

Pitts, C. E. *Introduction to educational psychology: An operant conditioning approach*. New York: Crowell, 1971.

Elements of Conditioning

GENERAL
Logan, F. A. *Fundamentals of learning and motivation*. Dubuque, Iowa: Brown, 1970.

Grant, D. A. Classical and operant conditioning. In A. W. Melton (Ed.) *Categories of human learning*. New York: Academic, 1964, pp. 1-31.

D'Amato, M. R. Instrumental conditioning. In M. H. Marx (Ed.) *Learning: Processes*. New York: Macmillan, 1969, pp. 35-118.

Gormezano, I., and Moore, J. W. Classical conditioning. In M. H. Marx (Ed.) *Learning: Processes*. New York: Macmillan, 1969, pp. 121-23.

Kimble, G. A. *Hilgard and Marquis' conditioning and learning*. New York: Appleton-Century-Crofts, 1961.

Keller, F. S. *Learning: Reinforcement theory*. New York: Random House, 1969.

CLASSICAL CONDITIONING (GENERAL)
Pavlov, I. P. *Conditioned reflexes*. London: Oxford, 1927.

217

Prokasy, W. F. (Ed.) *Classical conditioning.* New York: Appleton-Century-Crofts, 1965.

STIMULUS INTENSITY

Grice, G. R., and Hunter, J. J. Stimulus intensity effects depend upon the type of experimental design. *Psychological Review*, 1964, 71: 247-56.

EYELID CONDITIONING

Cerekwicki, L. E., Grant, D. A., and Porter, E. C. The effect of number and relatedness of verbal discriminanda upon differential eyelid conditioning. *Journal of Verbal Learning and Verbal Behavior*, 1968, 7: 847-53.

SEMANTIC CONDITIONING

Maltzman, I. Theoretical conceptions of semantic conditioning and generalization. In T. R. Dixon and D. L. Horton (Eds.) *Verbal behavior and general behavior theory.* Englewood Cliffs, N. J.: Prentice-Hall, 1968, pp. 291-339.

INSTRUMENTAL CONDITIONING (GENERAL)

D'Amato, M. R. Instrumental conditioning. In M. H. Marx (Ed.) *Learning: Processes.* New York: Macmillan, 1969, pp. 35-118.

OPERANT CONDITIONING (GENERAL)

Honig, W. K. (Ed.) *Operant behavior: Areas of research and application. New York: Appleton-Century-Crofts, 1966.*

Reynolds, G. S. *A primer of operant conditioning.* Glenview, Ill.: Scott, Foresman, 1968.

VERBAL CONDITIONING

Greenspoon, J. The reinforcing effect of two spoken sounds on the frequency of two responses. *American Journal of Psychology*, 1955, 68: 409-16.

Kanfer, F. H. Verbal conditioning: A review of its current status. In T. R. Dixon and D. L. Horton (Eds.) *Verbal behavior and general behavior theory.* Englewood Cliffs, N. J.: Prentice-Hall, 1968, pp. 254-90.

RESPONSES AS REINFORCERS

Premack, D. Toward empirical behavior laws. I. Positive reinforcement. *Psychological Review*, 1959, 66: 219-33.

SECONDARY REINFORCEMENT

Egger, M. D., and Miller, N. E. When is a reward reinforcing?: An experimental test of the information hypothesis. *Journal of Comparative and Physiological Psychology*, 1963, 56: 132-37.

EXTINCTION

Williams, C. D. The elimination of tantrum behavior by extinction procedures. *Journal of Abnormal and Social Psychology*, 1959, 59: 269.

PARTIAL REINFORCEMENT

Jenkins, W. O., McFann, H., and Clayton, F. L. A methodological study of extinction following aperiodic and continuous reinforcement. *Journal of Comparative and Physiological Psychology*, 1950, 43: 155-67.

GENERALIZATION (GENERAL)

Mednick, S. A., and Freeman, J. L. Stimulus generalization. *Psychological Bulletin*, 1960, 57: 169-200

SPATIAL GENERALIZATION

Brown, J. S., Bilodeau, E. A., and Baron, M. R. Bidirectional gradients in the strength of a generalized voluntary response to stimuli on a visual-spatial dimension. *Journal of Experimental Psychology*, 1951, 41: 52-61.

DISCRIMINATION

Brown, J. S. Generalization and discrimination. In D. I. Mostofsky (Ed.) *Stimulus generalization.* Stanford: Stanford Press, 1965, pp. 7-23.

DIFFERENTIATION

Herrick, R. M. The successive differentiation of a lever displacement response. *Journal of Experimental Analysis of Behavior*, 1964, 7: 211-15.

CONDITIONING PRINCIPLES, PERSONALITY, AND THERAPY

Krasner, L., and Ullman, L. P. *Research in behavior modification.* New York: Holt, Rinehart, and Winston, 1965.

Kanfer, F. H., and Phillips, J. S. *Learning foundations of behavior therapy.* New York: Wiley, 1970.

Mehrabian, A. *Tactics of social influence.* Englewood Cliffs, N. J.: Prentice-Hall, 1970.

Ullman, L. P., and Krasner, L. (Eds.) *Case studies in behavior modification.* New York: Holt, Rinehart, and Winston, 1965.

INSTRUCTIONAL TECHNOLOGY

Taber, J. I., Glaser, R., and Schaefer, H. H. *Learning and programmed instruction.* Reading, Mass.: Addison-Wesley, 1965.

DeCecco, J. P. (Ed.) *Educational technology.* New York: Holt, Rinehart, and Winston, 1964.

Glaser, R. (Ed.) *Teaching machines and programmed learning*, 2: *Data and directions.* Washington: National Education Association, 1965.

Skinner, B. F. Teaching machines. *Scientific American*, 1961, 205: 90-102.

Pitts, C. E. *Introduction to educational psychology: An operant conditioning approach.* New York: Crowell, 1971.

CHILD DEVELOPMENT AND LEARNING

Bijou, S. W., and Baer, D. M. *Child development: Readings in experimental analysis.* New York: Appleton-Century-Crofts, 1967.

Mussen, P. H., Conger, J. J., and Kagan, J. *Child development and personality.* New York: Harper and Row, 1969, pp. 99-145.

Characteristics of Verbal Learning

SCOPE OF VERBAL LEARNING

Underwood, B. J. The representativeness of rote verbal learning. In A. W. Melton (Ed.) *Categories of human learning.* New York: Academic, 1964, pp. 47-78.

Wickens, D. D. The centrality of verbal learning. In A. W. Melton (Ed.) *Categories of human learning.* New York: Academic, 1964, pp. 79-87.

CONCEPT OF ASSOCIATION

Postman, L. Association and performance in the analysis of verbal learning. In T. R. Dixon and D. L. Horton (Eds.) *Verbal behavior and general behavior theory.* Englewood Cliffs, N. J.: Prentice-Hall, 1968, pp. 550-71.

Kendler, H. H. Some specific reactions to general S-R theory. In T. R. Dixon and D. L. Horton (Eds.) *Verbal behavior and general behavior theory.* Englewood Cliffs, N. J.: Prentice-Hall, 1968, pp. 388-403.

PROBLEMS WITH "ASSOCIATIONISM"

Asch, S. E. The doctrinal tyranny of associationism: Or what is wrong with rote learning. In T. R. Dixon and D. L. Horton (Eds.) *Verbal behavior and general behavior theory.* Englewood Cliffs, N. J.: Prentice-Hall, 1968 pp. 214-28.

SCALING

Archer, E. J. A re-evaluation of the meaningfulness of all possible CVC trigrams. *Psychological Monographs*, 1960, 74 (10, whole no. 497).

Noble, C. E. An analysis of meaning. *Psychological Review*, 1952, 59: 421-30.

SERIAL LEARNING

Young, R. K. Serial learning. In T. R. Dixon and D. L. Horton (Eds.) *Verbal behavior and general behavior theory*. Englewood Cliffs, N.J.: Prentice-Hall, 1968, pp. 122-48.

SERIAL POSITION CURVE

Murdock, B. B., Jr. The serial position effect in free recall. *Journal of Experimental Psychology*, 1962, 64: 482-88.

PAIRED ASSOCIATE LEARNING

Battig, W. F. Paired-associate learning. In T. R. Dixon and D. L. Horton (Eds.) *Verbal behavior and general behavior theory*. Englewood Cliffs, N. J.: Prentice-Hall, 1968, pp. 149-71.

Cofer, C. N., Diamond, F., Olsen, R. A., Stein, J. S., and Walker, H. Comparison of anticipation and recall methods in paired-associate learning. *Journal of Experimental Psychology*, 1967, 75, 545-58.

FREE LEARNING

Tulving, E. Subjective organization and effects of repetition in multi-trial free-recall learning. *Journal of Verbal Learning and Verbal Behavior*, 1966, 5: 193-97.

RECOGNITION LEARNING

Underwood, B. J., and Freund, J. S. Errors in recognition learning and retention. *Journal of Experimental Psychology*, 1968, 78: 55-63.

RECOGNITION AND PAIRED ASSOCIATE LEARNING

Martin, E. Relation between stimulus recognition and paired-associate learning. *Journal of Experimental Psychology*, 1967, 74: 500-5.

VERBAL DISCRIMINATION LEARNING

Underwood, B. J., and Freund, J. S. Relative frequency judgments and verbal discrimination learning. *Journal of Experimental Psychology*, 1970, 83: 279-85.

MEANINGFULNESS

Underwood, B. J., and Schulz, R. W. *Meaningfulness and verbal learning*. Philadelphia: Lippincott, 1960.

Cieutat, V. J., Stockwell, F. E., and Noble, C. E. The interaction of ability and amount of practice with stimulus and response meaningfulness (m, ḿ) in paired-associate learning. *Journal of Experimental Psychology*, 1958, 56: 193-202.

MEANINGFULNESS AND ENCODING

Martin, E. Stimulus meaningfulness and paired-associate transfer: An encoding variability hypothesis. *Psychological Review*, 1968, 75: 421-41.

MENTAL IMAGERY

Paivio, A. Mental imagery in associative learning and memory. *Psychological Review*, 1969, 76: 241-63.

Bower, G. H. Mental imagery and associative learning. In L. Gregg (Ed.) *Cognition in learning and memory*. New York: Wiley, in press.

INTRALIST STIMULUS SIMILARITY

Runquist, W. N. Functions relating intralist stimulus similarity to acquisition performance with a variety of materials. *Journal of Verbal Learning and Verbal Behavior*, 1968, 7: 549-53.

INTRALIST RESPONSE SIMILARITY

Underwood, B. J., Runquist, W. N., and Schulz, R. W. Response learning in paired-associate lists as a function of intralist similarity. *Journal of Experimental Psychology*, 1959, 58: 70-78.

STIMULUS REDUNDANCY

Whitman, J. R., and Garner, W. R. Free recall learning of visual figures as a function of form of internal structure. *Journal of Experimental Psychology*, 1962, 64: 558-64.

Processes in Verbal Learning

TWO-PROCESS THEORIES OF PAIRED-ASSOCIATES

Underwood, B. J., Runquist, W. N., and Schulz, R. W. Response learning in paired-associate lists as a function of intralist stimulus similarity. *Journal of Experimental Psychology*, 1959, 58: 70-78.

Polson, M. C., Restle, F., and Polson, P. G. Association and discrimination in paired-associates learning. *Journal of Experimental Psychology*, 1965, 69: 47-55.

MULTI-PROCESS THEORY OF PAIRED-ASSOCIATES

McGuire, W. J. A multi-process model for paired-associate learning. *Journal of Experimental Psychology*, 1961, 62: 335-47.

STIMULUS DISCRIMINATION

Gibson, E. J. A systematic application of the concepts of generalization and differentiation to verbal learning. *Psychological Review*, 1940, 47: 196-229.

STIMULUS SELECTION

Postman, L., and Greenbloom, R. Conditions of cue selection in the acquisition of paired-associate lists. *Journal of Experimental Psychology*, 1967, 73: 91-100.

STIMULUS SELECTION AND OVERTRAINING

James, C. T., and Greeno, J. G. Stimulus selection at different stages of paired-associate training. *Journal of Experimental Psychology*, 1967, 73: 509-16.

STIMULUS CODING

Underwood, B. J., and Erlebacher, J. S. Studies of coding in verbal learning. *Psychological Monographs*, 1965, 79 (13, whole no. 606).

CONTIGUITY AND ASSOCIATION FORMATION

Spear, N. E., Ekstrand, B. R., and Underwood, B. J. Association by contiguity. *Journal of Experimental Psychology*, 1964, 67: 151-61.

ASSOCIATION FORMATION

Estes, W. K. Learning theory and the new "mental chemistry." *Psychological Review*, 1960, 67: 207-23.

Underwood, B. J., and Keppel, G. One-trial learning? *Journal of Verbal Learning and Verbal Behavior*, 1962, 1: 1-13.

BACKWARD ASSOCIATIONS

Ekstrand, B. Backward (R-S) associations. *Psychological Bulletin*, 1966, 65: 50-64.

ORGANIZATIONAL PROCESSES

Mandler, G. Organization and memory. In K. W. Spence and J. T. Spence (Eds.) *The psychology of learning and motivation: Advances in research and theory*, Vol. I. New York: Academic, 1967, pp. 328-72.

CLUSTERING

Bousfield, W. A., Cohen, B. H., and Whitmarsh, G. A. Associative clustering in the recall of words of different taxonomic frequencies of occurrence. *Psychological Reports*, 1958, 4: 39-44.

Cofer, C. N. On some factors in the organizational characteristics of free recall. *American Psychologist*, 1965, 20: 261-72.

SUBJECTIVE ORGANIZATION

Tulving, E. Subjective organization in free recall of unrelated words. *Psychological Review*, 1962, 69: 344-54.

ORGANIZATION, STORAGE, AND RETRIEVAL

Tulving, E., and Pearlstone, Z. Availability versus accessibility of information in memory for words. *Journal of Verbal Learning and Verbal Behavior*, 1966, 5: 381-91.

CODING (GENERAL)

Miller, G. A. The magical number seven, plus or minus two: Some limits on our capacity for processing information. *Psychological Review*, 1956, 63: 81-96.

RESPONSE CODING

Underwood, B. J., and Keppel, G. Coding processes in verbal learning. *Journal of Verbal Learning and Verbal Behavior*, 1963, 1: 250-57.

MEDIATION

Schulz, R. W., and Lovelace, E. Mediation in verbal paired-associate learning: The role of temporal factors. *Psychonomic Science*, 1964, 1: 95-96.

Jenkins, J. J. Mediated associations: Paradigms and situations. In C. N. Cofer and B. S. Musgrave (Eds.) *Verbal behavior and learning.* New York: McGraw-Hill, 1963, pp. 210-45.

CONNECTED MATERIALS

Deese, J. From the isolated verbal unit to connected discourse. In C. N. Cofer (Ed.) *Verbal learning and verbal behavior.* New York: McGraw-Hill, 1961, pp. 11-38.

Bower, G. H., and Clark, M. C. Narrative stories as mediators for serial learning. *Psychonomic Science*, 1969, 14: 181-82.

INCIDENTAL LEARNING

McLaughlin, B. "Intentional" and "incidental" learning in human subjects: The role of instructions to learn and motivation. *Psychological Bulletin*, 1965, 63: 359-76.

ANXIETY AND LEARNING

Spence, K. W. A theory of emotionally based drive (D) and its relationship to performance in simple learning situations. *American Psychologist*, 1958, 13: 131-41.

Transfer of Training

MEASUREMENT

Murdock, B. B. Jr. Transfer designs and formulas. *Psychological Bulletin*, 1957, 54: 313-26.

Runquist, W. N. Verbal behavior. In J. B. Sidowski (Ed.) *Experimental methods and instrumentation.* New York: McGraw-Hill, 1966, pp. 487-540.

DESIGN PROBLEMS

Twedt, H. M., and Underwood, B. J. Mixed vs. unmixed lists in transfer studies. *Journal of Experimental Psychology*, 1959, 58: 111-16.

PARADIGMS

Postman, L. Differences between unmixed and mixed transfer designs as a function of paradigm. *Journal of Verbal Learning and Verbal Behavior*, 1966, 5: 240-48.

GENERAL

Ellis, H. C. *The transfer of training.* New York: Macmillan, 1965.

Ellis, H. C. *Transfer and retention.* In M. H. Marx (Ed.). *Learning Processes.* New York: Macmillan, 1969, pp. 381-478.

LEARNING TO LEARN

Postman, L., and Schwartz, M. Studies of learning to learn: I. Transfer as a function of method of practice and class of verbal materials. *Journal of Verbal Learning and Verbal Behavior*, 1964, 3: 37-49.

WARM UP

Hamilton, C. E. The relationship between length of interval separating two tasks and performance on the second task. *Journal of Experimental Psychology*, 1950, 40: 613-21.

TRANSFER OF STIMULUS DISCRIMINATION

Ellis, H. C., and Muller, D. G. Transfer in perceptual learning following stimulus predifferentiation. *Journal of Experimental Psychology*, 1964, 68: 388-95.

Underwood, B. J., and Ekstrand, B. R. Differentiation among stimuli as a factor in transfer performance. *Journal of Verbal Learning and Verbal Behavior*, 1968, 7: 172-75.

TRANSFER OF RESPONSE LEARNING

Jung, J. Effects of response meaningfulness (m) on transfer under two different paradigms. *Journal of Experimental Psychology*, 1963, 65: 377-84.

FORWARD AND BACKWARD ASSOCIATIONS

Harcum, E. R. Verbal transfer of overlearned forward and backward associations. *American Journal of Psychology*, 1953, 66: 622-25.

Martin, E. Transfer of verbal paired-associates. *Psychological Review*, 1965, 72: 327-43.

STIMULUS SIMILARITY AND TRANSFER

Bruce, R. W. Conditions of transfer of training. *Journal of Experimental Psychology*, 1933, 16: 343-61.

RESPONSE SIMILARITY AND TRANSFER

Underwood, B. J. Associative transfer in verbal learning as a function of response similarity and degree of first-list learning. *Journal of Experimental Psychology*, 1951, 42: 44-53.

Barnes, J. M., and Underwood, B. J. "Fate" of first-list associations in transfer theory. *Journal of Experimental Psychology*, 1959, 58: 97-105.

TRANSFER PROCESSES

Osgood, C. E. The similarity paradox in human learning: A resolution. *Psychological Review*, 1949, 56: 132-43.

Martin, E. Transfer of verbal paired associates. *Psychological Review*, 1965, 72: 327-43.

TRANSFER AND GENERALIZATION

Underwood, B. J. Associative transfer in verbal learning as a function of response similarity and degree of first-list learning. *Journal of Experimental Psychology*, 1951, 42: 44-55.

TRANSFER AND MEDIATION

Horton, D. L., and Kjeldergaard, P. M. An experimental analysis of associative factors in mediated generalization. *Psychological Monographs*, 1961, 75 (11, whole no. 515).

TRANSFER AND TASK VARIATION

Duncan, C. P. Transfer after training with single versus multiple tasks. *Journal of Experimental Psychology*, 1958, 55: 63-72.

TRANSFER FROM EASY TO DIFFICULT DISCRIMINATION

Lawrence, D. H. The transfer of a discrimination along a continuum. *Journal of Compar-

ative and Physiological Psychology, 1952, 45: 511-16.

DEGREE OF ORIGINAL LEARNING

Postman, L. Transfer of training as a function of experimental paradigm and degree of first-list learning. *Journal of Verbal Learning and Verbal Behavior*, 1962, 1: 109-18.

COGNITIVE VIEW OF TRANSFER

Mandler, G. From association to structure. *Psychological Review*, 1962, 69: 415-27.

ASSOCIATIVE VIEW OF TRANSFER

Jung, J. Comments on Mandler's "From association to structure." *Psychological Review*, 1965, 72: 318-22.

Memory

MEMORY AND LEARNING

Murdock, B. B. Jr. Short-term memory and paired-associate learning. *Journal of Verbal Learning and Verbal Behavior*, 1963, 2: 320-28.

INFORMATION PROCESSING

Broadbent, D. E. Flow of information within the organism. *Journal of Verbal Learning and Verbal Behavior*, 1963, 2: 34-39.

CONCEPT OF ASSOCIATION

Postman, L. Association and performance in the analysis of verbal learning. In T. R. Dixon and D. L. Horton (Eds.) *Verbal behavior and general behavior theory*. Englewood Cliffs, N. J.: Prentice-Hall, 1968, pp. 550-71.

RECALL

Ekstrand, B. R., and Underwood, B. J. Paced versus unpaced recall in free learning. *Journal of Verbal Learning and Verbal Behavior*, 1965, 4: 390-96.

RECOGNITION

Kintsch, W. An experimental comparison of single-stimulus tests and multiple-choice tests of recognition memory. *Journal of Experimental Psychology*, 1968, 76: 1-6.

Murdock, B. B. Jr. An analysis of the recognition process. In C. N. Cofer and B. S. Musgrave (Eds.) *Verbal behavior and learning*. New York: McGraw-Hill, 1963, pp. 10-22.

REPRODUCTIVE MEMORY

Perkins, F. T. Symmetry in visual recall. *American Journal of Psychology*, 1932, 44: 473-90.

COMPARISON OF MEASURES

Bahrick, H. P. The ebb of retention. *Psychological Review*, 1965, 72: 60-73.

RESPONSE BIAS IN RECOGNITION MEMORY

Kintsch, W. Memory and decision aspects of recognition learning. *Psychological Review*, 1967, 74: 496-504.

Egan, J. P. Recognition memory and the operating characteristics. *Tech. Note* No. AFCRC-TN-58-51. Hearing and Communication Laboratory, Indiana University, 1958.

CONTINUOUS RECOGNITION

Shepard, R. N., and Teghtsoonian, M. Retention of information under conditions approaching a steady state. *Journal of Experimental Psychology*, 1961, 62: 302-9.

RECOGNITION AND IMPLICIT ASSOCIATIONS

Underwood, B. J. False recognition produced by implicit associative responses. *Journal of Experimental Psychology*, 1965, 70: 122-29.

SENSORY MEMORY
Sperling, G. A model for visual memory tasks. *Human Factors*, 1963, 5: 19-31.

SHORT-TERM MEMORY
Peterson, L. R., and Peterson, M. J. Short-term retention of individual items. *Journal of Experimental Psychology*, 1959, 58: 193-98.

Melton, A. W. Implications of short-term memory for a general theory of memory. *Journal of Verbal Learning and Verbal Behavior*, 1963, 2: 1-21.

ARGUMENTS FOR A DUAL MEMORY SYSTEM
Glanzer, M., and Cunitz, A. R. Two storage mechanisms in free recall. *Journal of Verbal Learning and Verbal Behavior*, 1966, 5: 351-60.

Waugh, N. C., and Norman, D. A. Primary memory. *Psychological Review*, 1965, 72: 89-104.

ARGUMENTS AGAINST A DUAL MEMORY SYSTEM
Hebb, D. O. Distinctive features of learning in the higher animal. In J. F. Delafresnaye (Ed.) *Brain mechanisms and learning.* New York: Oxford, 1961.

Melton, A. W. Implications of short-term memory for a general theory of memory. *Journal of Verbal Learning and Verbal Behavior*, 1963, 2: 1-21.

REHEARSAL AND SHORT-TERM MEMORY
Bernbach, H. A. The effect of labels in short-term memory for colors with nursery school children. *Psychonomic Science*, 1967, 7: 149-50.

CHUNKING AND MEMORY
Miller, G. A. The magical number seven, plus or minus two: Some limits on our capacity for processing information. *Psychological Review*, 1956, 63: 81-97.

RETRIEVAL CUES
Tulving, E., and Pearlstone, Z. Availability versus accessibility of information in memory for words. *Journal of Verbal Learning and Verbal Behavior*, 1966, 5: 381-91.

DEPENDENCE OF RETRIEVAL UPON STORAGE
Tulving, E., and Osler, S. Effectiveness of retrieval cues in memory for words. *Journal of Experimental Psychology*, 1968, 77: 593-601.

RECONSTRUCTIVE PROCESSES
Brown, R., and McNeil, D. The "tip of the tongue" phenomenon. *Journal of Verbal Learning and Verbal Behavior*, 1966, 5: 325-37.

Carmichael, L., Hogan, H. P., and Walter, A. A. An experimental study of the effect of language on the reproduction of visually perceived forms. *Journal of Experimental Psychology*, 1932, 15: 73-86.

VERBAL LABELS AND MEMORY
Ellis, H. C. Transfer of stimulus predifferentiation to shape recognition and identification learning: Role of properties of verbal labels. *Journal of Experimental Psychology*, 1968, 78: 401-9.

Glanzer, M., and Clark, W. H. Accuracy of perceptual recall: An analysis of organization. *Journal of Verbal Learning and Verbal Behavior*, 1963, 1: 289-99.

STIMULUS MEANING AND MEMORY
Ellis, H. C., Muller, D. G., and Tosti, D. T. Stimulus meaning and complexity as factors in the transfer of stimulus predifferentiation. *Journal of Experimental Psychology*, 1966, 71: 629-33.

Martin, E., and Melton, A. W. Meaningfulness and trigram recognition. *Journal of Verbal Learning and Verbal Behavior*, 1970, 9: 126-35.

RETROACTIVE AND PROACTIVE INHIBITION

Keppel, G. Retroactive and proactive inhibition. In T. R. Dixon and D. L. Horton (Eds.) *Verbal behavior and general behavior theory.* Englewood Cliffs, N. J.: Prentice-Hall, 1968, pp. 172-213.

Underwood, B. J. Interference and forgetting. *Psychological Review*, 1957, 64: 49-60.

INTERFERENCE THEORY

Postman, L., Stark, K., and Fraser, J. Temporal changes in interference. *Journal of Verbal Learning and Verbal Behavior*, 1968, 7: 672-94.

Postman, L., and Stark, K. Role of response availability in transfer and interference. *Journal of Experimental Psychology*, 1969, 79: 168-77.

Barnes, J. M., and Underwood, B. J. "Fate" of first-list associations in transfer theory. *Journal of Experimental Psychology*, 1959, 58: 97-105.

Concept Learning

GENERAL

Bourne, L. E. *Human conceptual behavior.* Boston: Allyn and Bacon, 1966.

Glaser, R. Concept learning and concept teaching. In R. M. Gagné and W. J. Gephart (Eds.) *Learning research and school subjects.* Itasca, Ill.: Peacock, 1968, pp. 1-36.

CONCEPT MATERIALS

Underwood, B. J., and Richardson, J. Some verbal materials for the study of concept formation. *Psychological Bulletin*, 1956, 53: 84-95.

CONCEPT AND PAIRED ASSOCIATE LEARNING

Underwood, B. J., and Richardson, J. Verbal concept learning as a function of instructions and dominance level. *Journal of Experimental Psychology*, 1956, 51: 229-38.

BASIC PROCESSES

Haygood, R. C., and Bourne, L. E. Attribute- and rule-learning aspects of conceptual behavior. *Psychological Review*, 1965, 72: 175-95.

Neisser, U., and Weene, P. Hierarchies in concept attainment. *Journal of Experimental Psychology,* 1962, 64: 644-45.

PARADIGMS

Bourne, L. E., Ekstrand, B. R., and Dominowski, R. L. *The psychology of thinking.* Englewood Cliffs, N. J.: Prentice-Hall, 1971, pp. 189-93.

POSITIVE AND NEGATIVE INSTANCES

Hovland, C. I., and Weiss, W. Transmission of information concerning concepts through positive and negative instances. *Journal of Experimental Psychology*, 1953, 45: 175-82.

Freibergs, V., and Tulving, E. The effect of practice on utilization of information from positive and negative instances in concept identification. *Canadian Journal of Psychology,* 1961, 15: 101-6.

ATTRIBUTES AND POSITIVE INSTANCES

Haygood, R. C., and Devine, J. V. Effects of composition of the positive category on concept learning. *Journal of Experimental Psychology*, 1967, 74: 230-35.

CONCEPTUAL RULES AND INSTANCES

Bourne, L. E. Learning conceptual rules: II. The role of positive and negative instances. *Journal of Experimental Psychology*, 1968, 77: 488-94.

STIMULUS SALIENCE
Suchman, R. G., and Trabasso, T. Color and form preference in young children. *Journal of Experimental Child Psychology*, 1966, 3: 177-87.

STIMULUS REDUNDANCY
Bourne, L. E., and Haygood, R. C. The role of stimulus redundancy in the identification of concepts. *Journal of Experimental Psychology*, 1959, 58: 232-38.

FEEDBACK
Bourne, L. E., and Bunderson, C. V. Effects of delay of informative feedback and length of the postfeedback interval on concept identification. *Journal of Experimental Psychology*, 1963, 65: 1-5.

Bourne, L. E., Guy, D. E., Dodd, D. H., and Justensen, D. R. Concept identification: The effects of varying length and informational components of the intertrial interval. *Journal of Experimental Psychology*, 1965, 69: 624-29.

USE OF CONCEPTUAL RULES
Bourne, L. E. Learning and utilization of conceptual rules. In B. Kleinmuntz (Ed.) *Memory and the structure of concepts*. New York: Wiley, 1967.

MEMORY
Trabasso, T., and Bower, G. H. Memory in concept identification. *Psychonomic Science*, 1964, 1: 133-34.

INTELLIGENCE AND ANXIETY
Denny, J. P. Effects of anxiety and intelligence on concept formation. *Journal of Experimental Psychology*, 1966, 72: 596-602.

S-R THEORY
Bourne, L. E., and Restle, F. Mathematical theory of concept identification. *Psychological Review*, 1959, 66: 278-96.

S-R MEDIATION THEORY
Kendler, H. H., and Kendler, T. S. Vertical and horizontal processes in problem solving. *Psychological Review*, 1962, 69: 1-16.

Kendler, H. H., and Kendler, T. S. Mediation and conceptual behavior. In K. W. Spence and J. T. Spence (Eds.) *The psychology of learning and motivation*, 2. New York: Academic, 1968.

HYPOTHESIS TESTING THEORY
Restle, F. The selection of strategies in cue learning. *Psychological Review*, 1962, 69: 320-43.

Trabasso, T., and Bower, G. H. *Attention in learning*. New York: Wiley, 1968.

INFORMATION PROCESSING
Hunt, E. B. *Concept learning: An information processing problem*. New York: Wiley, 1962.

Perceptual Learning

GENERAL
Epstein, W. *Varieties of perceptual learning*. New York: McGraw-Hill, 1967.

Gibson, E. J. *Principles of perceptual learning and development*. New York: Appleton-Century-Crofts, 1969.

Postman, L. Perception and learning. In S. Koch (Ed.) *Psychology: A study of a science* (Vol. 5). New York: McGraw-Hill, 1963.

Vanderplas, J. M. Perception and learning. In M. H. Marx (Ed.) *Learning: Interactions*. New York: Macmillan, 1970.

Bevan, W. Perceptual learning: An overview. *Journal of General Psychology*, 1961, 64: 69-99.

PERCEPTUAL TASKS
Vanderplas, J. M. Associative processes and task relations in perceptual learning. *Perceptual and Motor Skills*, 1963, 16: 501-9.

Wohlwill, J. F. The definition and analysis of perceptual learning. *Psychological Review*, 1958, 65: 283-95.

Bush, R. R., Galanter, E., and Luce, R. D. Characterization and classification of choice experiments. In R. D. Luce, R. R. Bush, and E. Galanter (Eds.) *Handbook of mathematical psychology*. Vol. 1, New York: Wiley, 1963.

PERPETUAL LEARNING MATERIALS
Attneave, F., and Arnoult, M. D. The quantitative study of shape and pattern perception. *Psychological Bulletin*, 1956, 53: 452-71.

Brown, D. R., and Owen, D. H. The metrics of visual form: Methodological dyspepsia. *Psychological Bulletin*, 1967, 68: 243-59.

Fitts, P. M., Weinstein, M., Rappaport, M., Anderson, N., and Leonard, A. J. Stimulus correlates of visual pattern recognition. *Journal of Experimental Psychology*, 1956, 51: 1-11.

EFFECTS OF PRACTICE ON PERCEPTUAL SKILLS
Gibson, E. J. Improvement in perceptual judgments as a function of controlled practice or training. *Psychological Bulletin*, 1953, 50: 401-31.

Neisser, U., Novick, R., and Lazar, R. Searching for ten targets simultaneously. *Perceptual and Motor Skills*, 1963, 17: 955-61.

Neisser, U. Visual search. *Scientific American*, 1964, 210: 94-101.

REWARD AND PUNISHMENT FACTORS
Epstein, W. *Varieties of perceptual learning.* New York: McGraw-Hill, 1967, chap. 7.

Schafer, R., and Murphy, G. The role of autism in a figure-ground relationship. *Journal of Experimental Psychology*, 1943, 32: 335-43.

Rock, I., and Fleck, F. S. A re-examination of the effect of reward and punishment in figure-ground perception. *Journal of Experimental Psychology*, 1950, 40: 766-76.

ADAPTATION TO TRANSFORMED STIMULATION
Held, R., and Hein, A. Adaptation of disarranged hand-eye coordination contingent upon re-afferent stimulation. *Perceptual and Motor Skills*, 1958, 8: 87-90.

Held, R., and Schlank, M. Motor-sensory feedback and the geometry of visual space. *Science*, 1963, 141: 722-23.

Harris, C. S. Perceptual adaptation to inverted, reversed and displaced vision. *Psychological Review*, 1965, 72: 419-44.

CROSS-MODAL TRANSFER
Holmgren, G. L., Arnoult, M. D., and Manning, W. H. Intermodal transfer in a paired-associates learning task. *Journal of Experimental Psychology*, 1966, 71: 254-59.

Pick, A. D., Pick, H. L., and Thomas, M. L. Cross-modal transfer and improvement of form discrimination. *Journal of Experimental Child Psychology*, 1966, 3: 279-88.

Gaydos, H. F. Intersensory transfer in the discrimination of form. *American Journal of Psychology*, 1956, 69: 107-10.

VERBAL LABELS AND PERCEPTUAL LEARNING
Ellis, H. C., Bessemer, D. W., Devine, J. V., and Trafton, C. L. Recognition of random

tactual shapes following predifferentiation training. *Perceptual and Motor Skills*, 1962, 10: 99-102.

Ellis, H. C., and Muller, D. G. Transfer in perceptual learning following stimulus predifferentiation. *Journal of Experimental Psychology*, 1964, 68: 388-95.

Ellis, H. C. Transfer of stimulus predifferentiation to shape recognition and identification learning: Role of properties of verbal labels. *Journal of Experimental Psychology*, 1968, 78: 401-9.

Katz, P. A. Effect of labels on children's perception and discrimination learning. *Journal of Experimental Psychology*, 1963, 66: 423-28.

VERBAL LABELS AND GENERALIZATION EFFECTS
Malloy, T. E., and Ellis, H. C. Attention and cue-producing responses in response-mediated stimulus generalization. *Journal of Experimental Psychology*, 1970, 83: 191-200.

SCHEMA LEARNING
Attneave, F. Transfer of experience with a class-schema to identification-learning of patterns and shapes. *Journal of Experimental Psychology*, 1957, 54: 81-88.

Evans, S. H. A brief statement of schema theory. *Psychonomic Science*, 1957, 8: 87-88.

Vernon, M. D. The functions of schemata in perceiving. *Psychological Review*, 1955, 62: 180-92.

Oldfield, R. C. Memory mechanisms and the theory of schemata. *British Journal of Psychology*, 1954, 45: 14-23.

THEORETICAL ISSUES
Gibson, J. J., and Gibson, E. J. Perceptual learning: Differentiation or enrichment? *Psychological Review*, 1955, 62: 32-41.

Postman, L. Association theory and perceptual learning. *Psychological Review*, 1955, 62: 438-46.

APPLICATIONS
Gibson, E. J. Perceptual learning in educational situations. In R. M. Gagné and W. J. Gephart (Eds.) *Learning research and school subjects.* Itasca, Ill.: Peacock, 1968.

Language, Thinking, and Problem Solving

LANGUAGE (GENERAL)
Carroll, J. B. *Language and thought.* Englewood Cliffs, N. J.: Prentice-Hall, 1964.

Jakobson, R., and Halle, M. *Fundamentals of language.* The Hague: Mouton, 1956.

Brown, R. W. *Words and things.* Glencoe, Ill.: The Free Press, 1958.

Lenneberg, E. *Biological foundations of language.* New York: Wiley, 1967.

Staats, A. W. *Learning, language, and cognition.* New York: Holt, Rinehart, and Winston, 1968.

PHONEMES AND MORPHEMES
Bourne, L. E., Ekstrand, B. R., and Dominowski, R. L. *The psychology of thinking.* Englewood Cliffs, N. J.: Prentice-Hall, 1971, pp. 308-14.

Miller, G. A., and Nicely, P. E. An analysis of perceptual confusions among some English consonants. *Journal of the Acoustical Society of America*, 1955, 27: 338-52.

PHRASE STRUCTURE
Fodor, J., and Bever, T. The psychological reality of linguistic segments. *Journal of Verbal*

Learning and Verbal Behavior, 1965, 4: 135-39.

Garrett, M., Bever, T., and Fodor, J. The active use of grammar in speech perception. *Perception and Psychophysics*, 1966, 1: 30-32.

Johnson, N. F. Linguistic models and functional units of language behavior. In S. Rosenberg (Ed.), *Directions in psycholinguistics.* New York: Macmillan, 1965.

SURFACE AND DEEP STRUCTURE

Mehler, J., and Carey, R. Role of surface and base structure in the perception of sentences. *Journal of Verbal Learning and Verbal Behavior,* 1967, 6: 335-38.

TRANSFORMATIONAL GRAMMAR

Chomsky, N. *Syntactic structures.* The Hague: Mouton, 1957.

Chomsky, N. *Aspects of the theory of syntax.* Cambridge, Mass.: M.I.T., 1965.

LANGUAGE DEVELOPMENT

Ervin-Tripp, S. Language development. In L. W. Hoffman and M. L. Hoffman (Eds.) *Review of Child Development Research,* 2. New York: Russell Sage Foundation, 1966.

Brown, R. W., and Fraser, C. The acquisition of syntax. In C. N. Cofer and B. S. Musgrave (Eds.) *Verbal behavior and learning.* New York: McGraw-Hill, 1963.

LANGUAGE AND THOUGHT

Ranken, H. B. Language and thinking: Positive and negative effects of naming. *Science,* 1963, 141: 48-50.

Glucksberg, S., and Weisberg, R. W. Verbal behavior and problem solving: Some effects of labeling in a functional fixedness problem. *Journal of Experimental Psychology*, 1966, 71: 659-64.

LINGUISTIC RELATIVITY HYPOTHESIS

Whorf, B. L. *Language, thought, and reality.* Cambridge Press, and New York: Wiley, 1956. (Ed. J. B. Caroll).

LANGUAGE AND PERCEPTUAL RECALL

Glanzer, M., and Clark, W. H. Accuracy of perceptual recall: An analysis of organization. *Journal of Verbal Learning and Verbal Behavior*, 1962, 1: 288-99.

LANGUAGE AND PERCEPTUAL RECOGNITION

Ellis, H. C., Bessemer, D. W., Devine, J. V., and Trafton, C. L. Recognition of random tactual shapes following predifferentiation training. *Perceptual and Motor Skills,* 1962, 10: 99-102.

Ellis, H. C., and Muller, D. G. Transfer in perceptual learning following stimulus predifferentiation. *Journal of Experimental Psychology*, 1964, 68: 388-95.

THINKING AND PROBLEM SOLVING (GENERAL)

Dominowski, R. L. Problem solving and concept attainment. In M. H. Marx (Ed.) *Learning: Interactions.* New York: Macmillan, 1970, pp. 107-91.

Kleinmuntz, B. (Ed.) Problem solving: *Research method, and theory.* New York: Wiley, 1966.

Bourne, L. E., Ekstrand, B. R., and Dominowski, R. L. *The psychology of thinking.* Englewood Cliffs, N. J.: Prentice-Hall, 1971.

Bruner, J. S., Goodnow, J. J., and Austin, G. A. *A study of thinking.* New York: Wiley, 1966.

Duncan, C. P. Thinking: *Current experimental studies.* Philadelphia: Lippincott, 1967.

McGuigan, F. J. *Thinking: Studies of covert language processes.* New York: Appleton-Century-Crofts, 1963.

PERSISTENCE OF SET

Luchins, A. S. Mechanization of problem solving: The effect of Einstellung. *Psychological Monographs*, 1942, 54 (6, whole no. 248).

Adamson, R. E. Functional fixedness as related to problem solving: A repetition of three experiments. *Journal of Experimental Psychology*, 1952, 44: 288-91.

PROBLEM SOLVING AND TRANSFER

Schulz, R.- W. Problem solving behavior and transfer. *Harvard Educational Review*, 1960, 30: 61-77.

ANXIETY AND PROBLEM SOLVING

Russell, D. G., and Sarason, I. G. Test anxiety, sex, and experimental conditions in relation to anagram solution. *Journal of Personality and Social Psychology*, 1965, 1: 493-96.

MOTIVATION AND PROBLEM SOLVING

Svedfeld, S., Glucksberg, S., and Vernon, J. Sensory deprivation as a drive operation: Effect upon problem solving. *Journal of Experimental Psychology*, 1967, 75: 166-69.

S-R THEORY

Maltzman, I. Thinking: From a behavioristic point of view. *Psychological Review*, 1955, 66: 367-86.

GESTALT THEORY

Kohler, W. *The mentality of apes.* New York: Harcourt, Brace, 1925.

INFORMATION PROCESSING

Miller, G. A., Galanter, E., and Pribram, K. *Plans and the structure of behavior.* New York: Holt, Rinehart, and Winston, 1960.

Simon, H. A., and Kotovsky, K. Human acquisition of concepts for sequential patterns. *Psychological Review*, 1963, 70: 534-46.

Motor Skills Learning

GENERAL

Adams, J. A. Motor behavior. In M. H. Marx (Ed.) *Learning: Processes.* New York: Macmillan, 1969, pp. 481-507.

Bilodeau, E. A. (Ed.) *Acquisition of skill.* New York: Academic, 1966.

Fitts, P. M. Perceptual-motor skill learning. In A. W. Melton (Ed.) *Categories of human learning.* New York: Academic, 1964, pp. 243-85.

Fitts, P. M., and Posner, M. I. *Human performance.* Belmont, Cal.: Brooks-Cole, 1967.

HISTORY

Irion, A. L. A brief history of research on the acquisition of skill. In E. A. Bilodeau (Ed.) *Acquisition of skill.* New York: Academic, 1966, pp. 1-46.

RESPONSE CHAINS

Gagné, R. M. *The conditions of learning.* New York: Holt, Rinehart, and Winston, 1965, chap. 4, especially pp. 87-92.

RESPONSE ORGANIZATION

Vince, M. A. The part played by intellectual processes in a sensory-motor performance. *Quarterly Journal of Experimental Psychology*, 1953, 5: 75-86.

FEEDBACK (GENERAL)

Gould, J. D. Differential visual feedback of component motions. *Journal of Experimental*

Psychology, 1965, 69: 263-68.

PHASES OF SKILL LEARNING

Fitts, P. M. Perceptual-motor skill learning. In A. W. Melton (Ed.) *Categories of human learning*. New York: Academic, 1964, pp. 243-85.

Fitts, P. M., and Posner, M. I. *Human performance*. Belmont, Cal.: Brooks-Cole, 1967, chap. 2.

INTRINSIC FEEDBACK

Smith, K. U., and Smith, W. M. *Perception and motion*. Philadelphia: Saunders, 1962.

EXTRINSIC FEEDBACK

Elwell, J. L., and Grindley, G. C. The effect of knowledge of results on learning and performance. I: A coordinated movement of the two hands. *British Journal of Psychology*, 1938, 29: 39-53.

QUANTITATIVE AND QUALITATIVE FEEDBACK

Trowbridge, M. H., and Cason, H. An experimental study of Thorndike's theory of learning. *Journal of General Psychology*, 1932, 7: 245-60.

WITHDRAWAL OF FEEDBACK

Bilodeau, E. A., Bilodeau, I. McD., and Schmusky, D. A. Some effects of introducing and withdrawing knowledge of results early and late in practice. *Journal of Experimental Psychology*, 1959, 58: 142-44.

DELAY OF FEEDBACK

Bilodeau, E. A., and Ryan, F. J. A test for interaction of delay of knowledge of results and two types of interpolated activity. *Journal of Experimental Psychology*, 1960, 59: 414-19.

DISTRIBUTION OF PRACTICE

Kimble, G. A., and Bilodeau, E. A. Work and rest as variables in cyclical motor learning. *Journal of Experimental Psychology*, 1949, 39: 150-57.

INFORMATIONAL STRESS

Miller, J. G. Adjusting to overloads of information. In D. McK. Rioch and E. A. Weinstein (Eds.) *Disorders of communication*. Research Publications, Association for Research in Nervous and Mental Disorders, 1964, 42: 87-100.

MOTOR LEARNING THEORY

Adams, J. A. A closed-loop theory of motor skills learning. *Journal of Motor Learning*, in press.

Index

Abstractness, 145
Acquisition, 18-20
Adams, J. A., 202, 215, 231, 232
Adamson, R. E., 231
All-or-none principle, 69
Anagram problems, 182-183
Anderson, N., 228
Anxiety and learning, 75-76
Archer, E. J., 36, 220
Arnoult, M. D., 228
Asch, S. E., 219
Association, concept of, 111
Association formation, 68-69
Associationism, 35, 110-112
Association probability theory, 51
Associative learning, 63
Attention, 65-66
Attneave, F., 228, 229
Attributes, 142-143
Austin, G. A., 230
Ausubel, D., 131

Backward association, 69
Baer, D. M., 219
Bahrick, H. P., 224
Barnes, J. M., 129, 223, 226
Baron, M. R., 218
Battig, W. F., 220
Behavior modification. See therapy.
Bernbach, H. A., 225
Bessemer, D. W., 228, 230
Bevan, W., 227
Bever, T., 229
Bigram, 36

Bijou, S. W., 219
Bilodeau, E. A., 215, 218, 231, 232
Bilodeau, I. McD., 232
Bourne, L. E., 215, 226, 227, 229
Bousfield, W. A., 221
Bower, G. H., 150, 215, 220, 222, 227
British associationists, 35
Broadbent, D. E., 111, 224
Brown, D. R., 228
Brown, J. S., 218, 219
Brown, R. W., 225, 229, 230
Bruce, R. W., 223
Bruner, J. S., 230
Bugelski, B. R., 215
Bunderson, C. V., 227
Burtt, H., 116
Bush, R. R., 228

Carey, R., 230
Carmichael, L., 225
Carroll, J. B., 229
Cason, H., 231
Cerekwicki, L. E., 218
Chomsky, N., 175, 215, 230
Cieutat, V. J., 220
Clark, M. C., 222
Clark, W. H., 225, 230
Clayton, F. L., 218
Closed loop theory, 201-203
Clustering, 43-44, 71
Coding, 42, 72-73
    response, 72
    stimulus, 72-73
Cofer, C. N., 220, 222

233

Cognition, 3, 5, 209
Cohen, B. H., 221
Component analysis, 42-43, 62
Concept, defined, 138
Concept learning, defined, 137-139
Concept learning, theories of:
  S-R association theory, 148-149
  S-R mediational theory, 149-150
  hypothesis-testing theories, 150
Conceptual peg hypothesis, 55
Conceptual rules, 142, 143, 146-147
  affirmational, 147
  biconditional, 147
  conditional, 147
  conjunctive, 147
Concreteness, 145
Conditioning Procedures:
  comparisons, 13-15
  classical, 8-10, 18-19
  instrumental, 11-12
  operant, 10-11, 19
  verbal, 12-13
Conger, J. J., 219
Conservation principle, 130
Contingencies of reinforcement, 13,
  15-16, 131
Counter-conditioning, 27
Covert responses, 171, 178
Cross-modal transfer, 164
Cunitz, A. R., 225
CVCs. See nonsense syllables

D'Amato, M. R., 217
Daniel, T. C., 220
Decay theory, 123
DeCecco, J. P., 219
Deep structure, 175
Deese, J., 215, 222
Denny, J. P., 227
Detection, 160
Devine, J. V., 226, 228, 230
Diamond, F., 220
Differentiation, response, 25-26
Directionality of associations, 69-70
Discrimination (perceptual), 160
Discrimination, stimulus, 23-25, 63-64,
  140-141
Distribution of practice, 200
Dixon, T. R., 215, 217, 218, 219, 224,
  225
Dodd, D. H., 227
Dominowski, R. L., 215, 226, 229, 230
Duncan, C. P., 223, 230

Ebbinghaus, H., 35, 111
Echoic responses, 176
Egan, J. P., 224
Egger, M. D., 218
Ekstrand, B. R., 215, 221, 223, 224, 226,
  229
Ellis, H. C., 165, 215, 220, 223, 225, 228,
  229, 230
Elwell, J. L., 231
Encoding, 42, 109
Epstein, W., 227, 228
Erlebacher, J. S., 221
Ervin-Tripp, S., 230
Estes, W. K., 221
Evans, S. H., 166, 229
Extinction, 20-22

Familiarity, 54
Feedback, 145-146, 194-195, 197-200
Fitts, P. M., 195, 228, 231
Fleck, F. S., 228
Fodor, J., 229
Forced-choice recognition, 114
Forgetting, 109
Forward association, 69
Fraser, C., 230
Fraser, J., 226
Free learning, 43-44, 57
Freeman, J. L., 218
Freiberg, V., 226
Frequency, 54
Freund, J. S., 220
Functional fixedness, 181-182
Functional stimulus. See stimulus

Gagné, R. M., 215, 217, 229, 231
Galanter, E., 228, 231
Garner, W. R., 221
Garrett, M., 229
Gaydos, H. F., 228
Generalization, 22-23, 140-141
  stimulus, 22-23
  response, 23
Generalized response competition, 130
General transfer, 84, 89-91
  learning to learn, 89-90
  warm up, 90-91
Gephart, W. J., 229
Gibson, E. J., 167, 168, 215, 221, 227,
  228, 229
Gibson, J. J., 164, 229
Glanzer, M., 225, 230
Glazer, R., 215, 219, 226
Glucksberg, S., 230, 231

Goodnow, J. J., 230
Gormezano, I., 217
Gould, J. D., 231
Grant, D. A., 217, 218
Greenbloom, R., 221
Greeno, J. G., 221
Greenspoon, J., 218
Grice, G. R., 218
Grindley, G. C., 231
Guy, D. E., 227

Halle, M., 229
Hall, J. F., 215
Hamilton, C. E., 223
Harcum, E. R., 223
Harris, C. S., 228
Haygood, R. C., 226
Hebb, D. O., 225
Hein, A., 228
Held, R., 164, 228
Herrick, R. M., 219
Hogan, H. P., 225
Holmgren, G. L., 228
Honig, W. K., 218
Horton, D. L., 215, 217, 218, 219, 223,
    224, 225
Hovland, C. I., 63, 226
Hull, C., 16, 185
Hulse, S. H., 215
Hunt, E. B., 227
Hunter, J. J., 218

Identification, 160
Identifying response, 53
Imagery. See mental imagery
Incidental learning, 74-75
Incremental view, 69
Information processing:
    and memory, 110-112
    and problem solving, 186-187
Interference paradox, 52
Interference theory, 123, 128-130
Intralist similarity, 56-57
Irion, A. L., 231
Irrelevant attributes, 144-145

Jakobson, R., 173, 229
James, C. T., 221
Jenkins, J. J., 222
Jenkins, W. O., 218
Johnson, N. F., 229
Judgment, 161
Jung, J., 215, 223, 224
Justensen, D. R., 227

Kagan, J., 219
Kanfer, F. H., 218, 219
Katz, P. A., 229
Keller, F. S., 217
Kendler, H. H., 219, 227
Kendler, T. S., 227
Keppel, G., 221, 222, 225
Kimble, G. A., 217, 232
Kintsch, W., 215, 217, 224
Kjeldergaard, P. M., 223
Kleinmuntz, B., 227, 230
Kohler, W., 185, 231
Kotovsky, K., 187, 231
Krasner, L., 219
Kurtz, K., 63

Language, 172-178
Language and thought, 177-178
Language development, 175-177
Lawrence, D. H., 223
Laws of association:
    contiguity, 34
    frequency, 34
Lazar, R., 228
Learning:
    concept, 136-155
    defined, 4, 157-158
    free, 43-44
    motor skills, 191-209
    paired-associate, 39-41
    perceptual, 156-170
    recognition, 44-47
    serial, 37-38
    verbal, 33-79
    verbal discrimination, 47-48
Learning to learn, 89-90
Lenneberg, E., 229
Leonard, A. J., 228
Linguistic-relativity hypothesis, 178
Logan, F. A., 8, 103, 200, 215, 217
Long-term memory, 119-120
Lovelace, E., 222
Luce, R. D., 228
Luchins, A. S., 230

McFann, H., 218
McGuigan, F. J., 230
McGuire, W. J., 221
McLaughlin, B., 222
McNeil, D., 225
Malloy, T. E., 229
Maltzman, I., 218, 231
Mandler, G., 52, 217, 221, 224

Manning, W. H., 228
Martin, E., 220, 223, 225
Marx, M. H., 215, 222, 231
Meaningfulness, 45-54
   defined, 36
   response meaningfulness, 50, 52-53
   stimulus meaningfulness, 50, 52-53
Mediation, 73
Mednick, S. A., 218
Mehler, J., 230
Mehrabian, A., 219
Melton, A. W., 215, 217, 219, 225
Memory storage, 117-120
   long-term, 119-120
   short-term, 118-119
   sensory, 117-118
Memory trace, 203
Mental imagery, 54-56
Miller, G. A., 222, 225, 229, 231
Miller, J. G., 231
Miller, N. E., 218
Moore, J. W., 217
Morpheme, 173, 174
Motor skill phases:
   associative, 196
   autonomous, 196-197
   cognitive, 195
Motor skills learning, 171-209
Muller, D. G., 223, 225, 228, 230
Murdock, B. B., 222, 224
Murphy, G., 228
Mussen, P. H., 219

Negative instances, 143-144
Neisser, U., 226, 228
Nicely, P. E., 229
Noble, C. E., 36, 220
Nominal stimulus. See stimulus
Nonsense syllables, 36
Norman, D. A., 215, 225
Novick, R., 228

Oldfield, R. C., 229
Olsen, R. A., 220
Organizational processes, 43-44, 70-73
   clustering, 71-72
   coding, 72-73
   mediation, 73
Original learning, degree of, 103-104,
   127
Osgood, C. E., 223
Osler, S., 225
Owen, D. H., 228

Paired-associate learning, 39-41
Paivio, A., 55, 220
Pavlov, I. P., 8, 9, 217
Pearlstone, Z., 222, 225
Perception, 65-66, 158-159
Perceptual adaptation, 163
Perceptual defense, 163
Perceptual learning, 156-170
Perceptual-motor coordination, 193
Perceptual trace, 203
Perkins, F. T., 224
Persistence of set, 180-181
Peterson, L. R., 119, 225
Peterson, M. J., 119, 225
Phillips, J. S., 219
Phoneme, 172, 173
Phrase structure, 174
Piaget, J., 172
Pick, A. D., 228
Pick, H. L., 228
Pitts, C. E., 217, 219
Polson, M. C., 221
Polson, P. G., 221
Porter, E. C., 218
Positive instances, 143-144
Posner, M., 166, 231
Postman, L., 129, 219, 221, 222, 223,
   224, 225, 227, 229
Premack, D., 17, 218
Premack principle, 17-18
Pribram, K., 231
Proactive inhibition, 126-128
Problem-solving, 178-183
Programmed instruction, 28
Prokasy, W. F., 218
Pronunciability, 54

Ranken, H. B., 230
Rappaport, M., 228
Recall: 112-113
   aided recall, 112
   free recall, 112
Reception paradigm, 141-142
Recognition learning:
   forced-choice, 47
   multiple-item procedure, 46
   single-item procedure, 46
Recognition (memory), 113-114, 160
Reconstructive memory, 122
Redundant attribute, 144-145
Reinforcement:
   negative, 16
   partial, 21

positive, 16
responses as, 17
secondary, 17
Relevant attributes, 144-145
Response:
  bias, 114-115, 163
  chains, 193
  competition, 128
  integration, 42
  learning, 63
  organization, 193
  produced stimuli, 197
Restle, F., 150, 221, 227
Retention, 109
Retrieval, 109, 120-122, 133
Retrieval cues, 121-122
Retroactive inhibition, 124-126, 126-128
Reynolds, G. S., 218
Richardson, J., 226
Rock, I., 228
Rote learning, 35
Runquist, W. N., 220, 221, 222
Russell, D. G., 231
Ryan, F. J. A., 232

Saltz, E., 215, 217
Sarason, I. G., 231
Savings, 116
Schaefer, H. H., 215
Schema learning, 166
Schlank, M., 228
Schmusky, D. A., 232
Schulz, R. W., 52, 63, 220, 221, 222, 231
Schwartz, M., 223
Selection paradigm, 142
Sensory memory, 117-118
Sequential dependencies, 74
Serial learning, 37-39
Serial position curve, 38-39
Shafer, R., 228
Shepard, R. N., 224
Short-term memory, 118-119
Signal detectability, theory of, 115
Similarity:
  between-tasks, 94-100
  common elements, 95
  conceptual, 57
  dimensions, 95-96
  formal, 57
  intralist, 56-57
  learned, 97
  meaningful, 57
Simon, H. A., 187, 231

Skinner, B. F., 11, 28
Smith, K. U., 231
Smith, W. M., 231
Spear, N., 68, 221
Specific transfer, 91-94
Spence, K. W., 222
Sperling, G., 224
Spontaneous recovery, 22, 129
Staats, A. W., 229
Stark, K., 226
Stein, J. S., 220
Stimulus:
  compound, 65
  conditioned, 8-9
  elements, 65
  functional, 64
  nominal, 64
  unconditioned, 8-9
Stimulus coding, 66-67
Stimulus discrimination, 23-25, 63-64, 140-141
Stimulus identification, 67
Stimulus salience, 145
Stimulus selection, 64-66
Stockwell, F. E., 220
Storage, 109, 117-120
Stress, 201
Subjective organization, 44, 71
Successive approximations, 11
Suchman, R. G., 226
Suppes, P., 209
Surface structure, 175
Svedfeld, S., 231

Taber, J. I., 215, 219
Teghtsoonian, M., 224
Therapy, 27-28
Thinking, 178-179
Thomas, M. L., 228
Thorndike, E., 111
Tosti, D. T., 225
Trabasso, T., 215, 226, 227
Trafton, C. L., 228, 230
Transfer and similarity: 94-100
  response similarity, 99-100
  stimulus similarity, 96-98
Transfer effects:
  negative, 82
  positive, 81
  zero, 82
Transfer mechanisms:
  generalization, 100-101
  mediation, 101-102

Transfer paradigms, 85-88
Transformational rules, 175
Trigram, 36
Trowbridge, M. H., 232
Tulving, E., 44, 220, 222, 225, 226
Twedt, H. M., 222
Two-stage theory (of paired associate
    learning), 63

Ullman, L. P., 219
Underwood, B. J., 52, 63, 129, 219, 220,
    223, 224, 226
Unitization, 51-52
Unlearning, 129

Vanderplas, J. M., 227, 228
Variability:
    reinforcement, 21
    response, 22
    stimulus, 21-22
Verbal discrimination learning, 47-48
Verbal labeling, 164-166
Verbal learning:
    defined, 34

factors influencing, 48-59
procedures, 36-48
processes, 43-43, 62-76
Vernon, J., 231
Vernon, M. D., 229
Vince, M. A., 231
Voss, J. F., 215

Walker, H., 220
Walter, A. A., 225
Warm up, 90-91
Waugh, N. C., 225
Weene, P., 226
Weinstein, M., 228
Weisberg, R. W., 230
Weiss, W., 226
Whitman, J. R., 221
Whitmarsh, G. A., 221
Whorf, B., 178, 230
Wickens, D. D., 219
Williams, C. D., 218
Wohlwill, J. F., 228

Young, R. K., 220